Entrepreneurship and Community Economic Development

Entrepreneurship and Community Economic Development

MONICA C. DIOCHON

McGill-Queen's University Press
Montreal & Kingston · London · Ithaca

ISBN 0-7735-2510-6 (cloth)
ISBN 0-7735-2540-8 (paper)

Legal deposit first quarter 2003
Bibliothèque nationale du Québec

Printed in Canada on acid-free paper.

This book has been published with the help of a generous subvention from the Canadian Institute for Research on Regional Development.

McGill-Queen's University Press acknowledges the support of the Canada Council for the Arts for our publishing program. We also acknowledge the financial support of the Government of Canada through the Book Publishing Industry Development Program (BPIDP) for our publishing activities.

Canadian Cataloguing in Publication Data

Diochon, Monica C.
Entrepreneurship and community economic development/ Monica C. Diochon.
Includes bibliographical references and index.
ISBN 0-7735-2510-6 (bnd)
ISBN 0-7735-2540-8 (pbk)
1. Community development. 2. Entrepreneurship. 3. Community development – Canada – Case studies. I. Title.
HC79.E44D56 2003 338.9 C2002-903356-X

Typeset in Sabon 10/12
by Caractéra inc., Quebec City

For my parents

Contents

Tables and Figures

TABLES

FIGURES

Foreword

Community-based development is now believed by many both within and outside government to be the most promising approach to promoting economic growth in Canada's smaller and more remote regions. It is not at all clear what gave rise to this view.

It was in the spring of 1998 that I first heard about the economic success of Isle Madame in Nova Scotia. Without putting too fine a point on it, the view in Ottawa was that past federal regional development efforts in Atlantic Canada had failed and that the focus in future should be on promoting community economic development. For ideas on how to do this, one could do a great deal worse than to look at the Isle Madame experience. To highlight this last point, John Manley, then federal industry minister, visited Isle Madame to get a first-hand look, and when he returned, he too spoke in glowing terms about its success. The implications for federal regional development policy, I thought, were both obvious and important. I could not help but suspect that the enthusiasm surrounding community economic development was, in fact, an excuse for governments to shift their responsibility to local people and leave them to get on with the job for their communities.

The literature on community economic development is still in its early days. Some of it lacks a practical side and has left the professionals bewildered as to how to apply its approaches and prescriptions, let alone understand them. There is also a kind of missionary zeal to much of the literature. It seems to say that if only the right people could see the light, our smaller communities would be well on the road to economic development.

Monica Diochon has done students and practitioners of regional economic development a great service. Her book sheds light on a timely topic. It is scholarship at its best: accessible, thorough, and creative. She not only provides a workable theoretic framework; she also has the capacity to zero in on the key issues, bring them to life, and tease out important lessons. It should be required reading for all those wishing to better understand community economic development, the nature of rural entrepreneurship, and how communities could be better organized to promote economic development.

DONALD J. SAVOIE
Clément-Cormier Chair in Economic Development
Université de Moncton

Acknowledgments

This book owes a great deal to Donald Savoie of The Canadian Institute for Research on Regional Development (CIRRD) at the Université de Moncton, who encouraged me to pursue publication of this work on entrepreneurship in community economic development. I thank him most sincerely for his support and his efforts on my behalf. Published through funding provided by the CIRRD, this book attests to the key role the Institute plays in promoting research related to regional development issues. I am grateful for this advocacy.

I would also like to thank two anonymous reviewers of an earlier draft. It is clear they spent many hours reading the manuscript to determine how it could be improved. Their comments and suggestions were very helpful. I benefited a great deal as well from the editorial advice of Joan Harcourt of McGill-Queen's University Press and the careful eye and sharp pencil of Olga Domján.

Most importantly, I wish to acknowledge the numerous people in the communities of Eastern Guysborough County and Isle Madame who willingly made time to share their experiences with me. On a personal level, I especially want to thank my family for their unconditional encouragement and support.

I began this work with a very ambitious goal: establishing a conceptual basis for developing more effective Community Economic Development policy and practice. In this regard, I owe much gratitude to Allan Gibb of the University of Durham Business School. In supervising my doctoral work, his tenacious intellectual challenge was invaluable in helping to shape my ideas and argument. It now remains for the reader to determine the extent to which that goal has been accomplished.

Abbreviations

ACOA	Atlantic Canada Opportunities Agency
ADA	Area Development Agency
BDC	Business Development Centre
CED	Community Economic Development
CEIC	Canada Employment and Immigration Corporation
CES	Community Employment Strategy
CF	Community Futures
CWADC	Canso Waterfront and Area Development Corporation
DEVCO	Cape Breton Development Corporation
DFO	Department of Fisheries and Oceans
DIMA	Development Isle Madame Association
DNR	Department of Natural Resources
DREE	Department of Regional Economic Expansion
DRIE	Department of Regional Industrial Expansion
ECBC	Enterprise Cape Breton Corporation
EGCDA	Eastern Guysborough County Development Association
EI	Employment Insurance
ERA	Economic Renewal Agency
ERC	Employment Resource Counsellor
GCBDC	Guysborough County Business Development Centre
GCRDA	Guysborough County Regional Development Authority
HRD/HRDC	Human Resources Development Canada
IAS	Industrial Adjustment Services
LED	Local Economic Development
LEDA	Local Economic Development Assistance

RDA Regional Development Authority
RDIA Regional Development Incentives Act
SHRDC Strait-Highlands Regional Development Commission
TAGS The Atlantic Groundfish Strategy Program
UI Unemployment Insurance

Entrepreneurship and Community Economic Development

1 Introduction

Over the past two decades, community-based development activity has been gaining momentum as a way of dealing with economic and social problems associated with global economic restructuring. Having virtually abandoned the traditional, centrally devised, regional economic development policies and initiatives, government policymakers throughout industrialized nations increasingly favour community-based development approaches.

In Canada, government began abdicating its interventionist role during the 1980s by increasing the level of community involvement in policy and program development. During this time, social safety nets such as income transfers and "make-work" projects continued to play a strategic role in government response to economic disparity and poverty. By the 1990s, however, rising deficits and lower rates of economic growth were diminishing the resources allocated to the social safety nets as well as to other programs conventionally used in dealing with economic and social problems. Yet demands on programs were increasing as socioeconomic restructuring not only affected greater numbers of people but put the survival of entire communities at risk.

With conventional regional development policies and programs viewed as ineffective, both the federal and provincial levels of government in Canada perceived a need for more inclusive development approaches capable of integrating economic and social objectives. Community Economic Development (CED), which assumes that a community's problems are best understood and solved endogenously, began to capture the interest of policymakers. Policy statements heralded CED as the panacea for both economic and social problems, and asserted, moreover, that effectiveness in stimulating development within the context of the clichéd "global economy" would require entrepreneurship and innovation. However, with responsibility for economic and social development now delegated to communities, government has yet to formulate a comprehensive CED policy. Indeed, the basis for establishing policy is not altogether clear.

What is most puzzling is that, on the one hand, policymakers, practitioners, and academics are endorsing CED as a means of addressing economic and/or social adversity while, on the other hand, they are concluding that communities that fail to demonstrate entrepreneurship in their efforts to deal with the negative effects of socioeconomic restructuring lack development potential. Having worked in various communities, I have found no evidence indicating a lack of development potential. Indeed, within the field of entrepreneurship, it has been shown that every individual has some degree of entrepreneurial potential. This being the case, would not every community likewise have development potential? My experience in entrepreneurship education and community-based small business development indicates that entrepreneurship can be acquired if individuals are given the opportunity.

The claim that some communities lack development potential suggests that the nature of the relationship among entrepreneurship, innovation, and economic development is not well understood. Given that communities with the greatest reliance on social safety nets have typically been judged to be lacking in these three capabilities, a key research question concerns why some communities are entrepreneurial in addressing their problems while others are not. Determining the potential of endogenous approaches to deal successfully with problems or opportunities arguably depends upon a better understanding of the role of entrepreneurship in the development process. The latter is, in turn, fundamental to understanding whether and how community-based development can be effective in addressing existing disparities. Given the lack of scholarly attention paid to these issues, research in this area has both academic and practical importance. Establishing a basis for policy facilitating community-based economic development would therefore also assist economically disadvantaged communities.

OUTLINE OF THIS RESEARCH

The aim of this book is to contribute to the understanding of community-based development by dealing specifically with the role of entrepreneurship in the development process. I begin in chapter 2 by tracing the emergence of local Community Economic Development as an issue within conventional regional development theory and policy. Exploring the shift away from "top-down" exogenous theory and policy, I focus on the background to the perception that government policy intervention was ineffective. Foremost among the challenges to the conventional interpretation and analysis of development was the emergence of territorially diffused development in some regions of Europe. By assessing the three main schools of economic thought underpinning policy – neoclassical, Keynesian, and development pole – we can determine the extent to which that perception is justified. Failure to incorporate a host of non-economic factors influencing the development process is one of the chief shortcomings of frameworks rooted in these traditions. Moreover, the lack of systematic policy evaluation makes accurate assessment of effectiveness and the refutation of criticism difficult. A key criticism that I consider is the role of exogenous policy in creating dependency and thereby inhibiting entrepreneurship.

Amidst waning confidence in traditional economic theory and policy, a new development paradigm began to emerge. Endogenous development represents a different understanding of the development process – one acknowledging the influence of local factors. It prompted economists to reappraise the role of "space" in the development process. However, the lack of agreement on the essentials of endogenous influence has posed difficulties in clearly demarcating exogenous and endogenous development. To this end, the salient characteristics of development are dichotomized, with a proclivity for one end determining classification.

The terms "local" and "development" are core conceptual building blocks within the endogenous paradigm. However, because of the definitional imprecision and debates surrounding these terms, an appropriate basis for interpreting and influencing development "locally" is lacking. This problem can be overcome. By considering the implications of existing definitions, we can identify the relevant issues. A critical examination of endogenous theory indicates that models tend to emphasize one or two aspects of the development process. This tendency limits their explanatory value as they are unable to incorporate the interactive effect of local economic and sociocultural forces on different forms of productive organization and disparate innovative capacities. Although research has established the effect of non-economic factors on innovation within small firms, they have been ignored by policy initiatives aimed at achieving local development by encouraging entrepreneurship, innovation, or the formation of new firms. The absence of a rationale for policy and of an adequate assessment of its effectiveness is an important void to be filled. The first step is to understand the development process. As a basis for doing so, the chapter concludes by drawing on knowledge and practice to synthesize the range of economic, demographic, and sociocultural factors affecting the development process.

Chapter 3 sets the context for the ensuing discussion with a more focused background look at the issues surrounding the exogenous/endogenous development debate in Canada. A brief sketch of the Canadian economy and its disparities features Atlantic Canada as the most disadvantaged region. Subregionally, disparities in income and employment are even more pronounced, particularly between urban and rural settings. Nova Scotia, the province where growth-centre policies were pursued most vigorously, has the greatest imbalance in economic growth between its urban core and the rest of the province. While the province has tried to remedy this situation, its efforts are questioned for failing to take into account the diverse socioeconomic circumstances of rural Nova Scotians.

A federal system makes Canada's approach to regional development more complex. However, the issues associated with top-down policy efforts were no different from those experienced in other industrialized nations. Tracing the federal and provincial governments' abandonment of exogenous theory and policy, chapter 3 examines the emergence of a stronger local emphasis to deal with persisting regional economic disparities and stagnation, particularly in rural disadvantaged areas. To promote endogenous growth in the small business sector, policy-makers adopted Community Economic Development as a strategy for creating a business environment that encourages entrepreneurship and responsiveness to market conditions. While government has increasingly been allocating responsibility for development to communities, it has done so without understanding why or how CED can be more effective than the strategies of the past in addressing disparities.

Chapter 4 has the twofold aim of determining the appropriateness of CED for addressing the problems faced by rural disadvantaged communities and for identifying the factors essential to a better conceptual understanding of what constitutes an effective process. A review of the literature uncovers a mêlée over the precise definition of the approach, its objectives, its practice, its success, and consequently its potential. Tracing the evolution of CED, the chapter clarifies the impasse by uncovering two distinct development philosophies, one socially oriented, the other economically oriented. The chapter deals with the conceptual deficiencies of both perspectives and discusses the issues that both facilitate and constrain a more holistic explanation of community-based development. In identifying the various factors purported to characterize the development process, my analysis indicates that, although entrepreneurship and innovation are afforded a key role in the development process, the relationship between them has yet to be addressed. To this end, the two terms are defined in a way that is clear and meaningful within the Community Economic Development context. Finally, the chapter differentiates the understanding of community-based development espoused in this book from that of economists or sociologists by proposing the term Community Enterprise Emergence.

Chapter 5 develops a conceptual framework to address the question of how to facilitate entrepreneurship and innovation when they are not emerging autonomously. It begins by establishing a meso-level analytic focus as a means of understanding the factors that make a community more entrepreneurial. This is an important discussion, as there is currently a gap between the micro and macro levels of analysis in the literature. Examined next are the disciplinary challenges in finding a framework capable of incorporating the various antecedent conditions, actors, tasks, structures, and outcomes associated with the development process.

In establishing the criteria that a model needs to meet, it becomes evident that few frameworks are available. Since an understanding of the entrepreneurial process is essentially a behaviour issue, I examine the potential of frameworks offering holistic explanations of complex patterns of behaviour. My assessment considers the appropriateness of these models for understanding behaviour and effectiveness in a community context. The Congruence Model of Organizational Assessment is ultimately selected as a basic organizing framework. It provides a holistic conceptual framework for understanding the Community Economic Development process and its effect on entrepreneurship, innovation, and economic development within communities.

The Community Enterprise Emergence (CEE) model draws on the literature to specify the variables making up the four main process components: task, individual, organizational arrangements, and informal organization. While the primary focus is on process, also considered is how the inputs (or context) affect process and how the process affects the nature of the outcomes (effectiveness). The model is a means of exploring how entrepreneurship and innovation are fostered, and how they affect Community Economic Development outcomes.

Chapter 6 provides a rationale for adopting a qualitative methodology, and explains how this methodology influences the research design. To test the framework, I use three interdependent research design considerations: choosing a research strategy, linking the data to the initial questions of the study, and establishing the quality of the design. Case study is determined to be the most appropriate research strategy for studying Community Enterprise Emergence. The five components of a case study research design are therefore examined: the key question(s), the propositions or hypotheses, the unit(s) of analysis, the logic linking the data to the propositions or hypotheses, and the criteria for interpreting the findings.

The question of how communities can effectively influence development establishes the community as the main unit of analysis. The main hypothesis is that an entrepreneurial pattern of congruence will be required for strategic effectiveness in responding to changed circumstances. I note that the theoretical framework facilitates data collection and guides data analysis and interpretation; it is the logic linking data and hypotheses. The use of two cases – Eastern Guysborough County and Isle Madame – makes it possible to test the model's theoretical replication (i.e., whether contrasting results are produced for predictable reasons).

The analysis of evidence is one of the least developed and most challenging aspects of case study. The general analytic strategy is to follow the hypotheses that led to the case study. Using the technique of pattern-matching, the empirically based pattern is compared with the one proposed. Since there is no precise way of setting the criteria for determining a match, decision rules were developed for interpreting the data.

Chapter 7 presents the analysis and results of the empirical work. A within-case analysis compares the empirical pattern to the one proposed in the framework. The results of this analysis are then used to determine the extent of support for the exploratory hypotheses, as well as the effect of entrepreneurship on a community's effectiveness in achieving the desired goals. The chapter concludes with a cross-case analysis of the framework's analytic generalization, essentially addressing the question of whether the findings make sense beyond a specific case.

Overall, the findings provide considerable support for the fundamental proposition that a community's effectiveness in influencing economic development is dependent upon the extent to which the process it adopts fosters entrepreneurship. Entrepreneurship needs a strategic focus if it is to build a community's capacity to achieve its goal(s). For a community to succeed in adapting to changing circumstances, the process must obtain the broad-based involvement of those affected by these circumstances, which enables people to learn and practise entrepreneurship. The nature of the development activities undertaken plays a major role in this regard: when they are diversified in scope and time frame, they provide more opportunities for involvement. Producing tangible results in a short time frame encourages others to participate. In discussing the interactive, yet relative, influence of other aspects of the development process on effectiveness, I note the role of community-based authority and accountability, business experience, and a shared vision of goals and outcomes. This comprehensive examination of the factors identified as important in the literature raises questions concerning the appropriateness of studying factors in isolation. Clearly, the results challenge the significance of several factors.

Since the aim of this book is to develop a better understanding of community-based development, it is fitting to conclude by considering the extent to which this objective has been accomplished. Chapter 8 begins by discussing how the findings relate to the existing knowledge base. In particular, it is relevant to reflect on the conceptual framework, given the lack of analytical frameworks in the Community Economic Development literature. Finally, in light of the conclusions, recommendations are provided for future research, practical uses for the framework, and policy development.

2 The Theory and Practice of Endogenous Development: Roots and Challenges

Since the mid-1980s there has been a substantial shift in approaches to regional development, away from exogenously weighted models carrying with them cultures and values associated with top-down policy intervention, toward the new paradigm of a more locally focused "bottom-up" endogenous approach. It involves a fundamental reappraisal of the development process, along with a wider conceptual debate about the certainties, nature, and purpose of development. Impetus for this shift has been provided by the fact that regional disparities in both Europe and North America have endured and, in some cases, become more pronounced (Cappellin and Molle 1988, 1) amidst policy attempts to alleviate them.

While economic explanations of regional differences formed the basis of spatial development policy after World War II, since the mid-1970s there has been a reappraisal of the role of space in the development process. As various social science disciplinary perspectives were brought to bear on the debate, considerable ambiguity emerged within the regional development literature (Bingham and Mier 1993, ix), with a proliferation of ill-defined terminology.

With support for a bottom-up local focus gaining momentum, certain fundamental issues still remain to be resolved. What constitutes endogenous development as opposed to exogenous development? How can the meaning of key terms be established? Who are the participants in the process, and how might their roles influence the process and its outcomes in the movement from exogenous to endogenous development? How may the nature of the process/outcome itself be contingent upon the nature of the problem and location? (For example, do urban and rural development problems differ fundamentally in nature?) How will success be measured? Finally, which major components of this bottom-up process need to be explored in greater detail?

THE CONTEXT FOR THE SHIFT FROM EXOGENOUS TO ENDOGENOUS DEVELOPMENT APPROACHES

Following World War II and until the 1970s, the economic development of regions within industrialized nations relied upon the expansion of urban-based large-scale industries and central government policies (Stöhr 1990, 1; Garofoli 1992b, 4). This approach, known as *exogenous development*, assumes that regional development is primarily prompted by economic factors external (exogenous) to the region in question, such as export markets and outside investment (Nelson 1993, 31; Garofoli 1992b, 2). Large-scale businesses are viewed as the dominant creator of wealth and jobs, while the role of the public sector is to devise redistributive policy measures that will increase regional equity in income and employment. Within this perspective, "territory" or space is largely considered a passive element in the development process.

Based on a development pole model, the diffusion of development from above was aided by government policies seeking to address the underdevelopment of rural areas in Europe and North America by enticing manufacturing facilities to locate in those regions. For the most part, these were branch plant facilities that in practice often involved low-skill assembly-line production (Howland 1993, 66–8; Stöhr 1990, 1).

In the mid-1970s, the pace of economic development slowed in all industrialized countries. A shift in policy focus gradually became evident as governments grappled with this situation: from top-down exogenous policy rooted in traditional economic frameworks to a bottom-up endogenous approach. *Endogenous development* gives prominence to territory, seen as the parameter within which local (endogenous) economic and sociocultural factors interact to influence the development process. The small business sector is considered to play a pivotal role in wealth and job generation. Because each region is assumed to have some manœuvring room to influence economic development, the role of the public sector is to encourage regions to design measures that will fashion development patterns in keeping with the regional milieu. This shift in approach involves significant changes in the means used to stimulate growth (for example, decentralization of decision-making).

Several factors contributed to the policy shift. First, governments have generally had less money to spend on efforts to stimulate the economy (Glasson 1992, 516; Cappellin and Molle 1988, 6; Stöhr 1990, 22). A search for more cost-effective alternatives has been the result.

Second, countries in the industrialized world have been facing a much more uncertain environment. Global socioeconomic restructuring has rendered unilateral government action, particularly in the United States and Western Europe, less capable of producing predictable economic outcomes (Bennett and McCoshan 1993, 10), whether on a national or a regional level.

Third, the global nature of product and service markets, technology, and competition has increased business demands for flexibility, quality, cost-effectiveness, and timeliness. To respond effectively to environmental conditions, many large organizations have altered their competitive strategies, resulting in structural adaptations characterized by downsizing, decentralization, subcontracting, and outsourcing. Among large industrial firms undergoing restructuring, we now see greater disaggregation of the various phases of the production process, smaller production units, a reduced labour force, and a transfer of job-related authority and responsibility from managers to workers (Miles and Snow 1991, 591; Pequeur and Silva 1992, 17). Overall, the changes in strategy and structure have resulted in an increase in both the number and the interdependence of stakeholders.

Today, partnerships or cooperative relations among small firms and between small firms and large corporations are on the increase. A socioeconomic environment affording a more prominent role to small and medium-sized enterprises (SMEs) and a large business sector that is becoming less labour-intensive and less willing to locate in disadvantaged areas (Cappellin and Molle 1988, 6) together pose a major challenge to regional development strategies biased toward the relocation and expansion of large businesses.

The fourth factor is the growing perception that traditional policies have not produced the results expected of them (Cappellin 1992, 2; Kockel 1992, 101; Hansen 1989, 289; Vazquez-Barquero 1992a, 31). However, the dearth of evaluation studies set against concrete objectives leaves the effectiveness and efficiency of traditional development theory and policy largely speculative.

The fifth, and perhaps the biggest, challenge to existing policy and its economics-based theoretical frameworks has come from the industrial development in some European regions. Its pattern has shifted from spatial concentration to territorial diffusion; from a crucial role played by large firms to a greater role for small firms. While the global socioeconomic reality presents a novel context, these "autonomous development" experiences suggest that spatial differences in institutional, social, cultural, and political factors *within* nations and regions interact to influence the nature and scope of economic development (Stöhr 1990, 24; Garofoli 1992b, 4).

Piore and Sabel (1984) are not alone (Glasson 1992, 508; Garofoli 1992b, 2) in arguing that environmental complexity and uncertainty enhance the potential of SMEs in regional economic growth. Indeed, much of the innovative capacity in meeting changing demands in the global economy has been attributed to the flexibility and responsiveness of smaller business units (Pequeur and Silva 1992, 17).

Innovation and entrepreneurship have assumed a strategic role in the global economy. Although fostering them is said to be a goal of emerging regional policy objectives (Pecqueur and Silva 1992, 19; Cappellin 1992, 4; Glasson 1992, 525), there is no theoretical framework to explain or justify this aim. Without a framework, it becomes impossible to demonstrate any link between development and innovation or entrepreneurship or to explore the influence of a particular theoretical perspective on empirical indicators (Rose 1982, 34–6). Furthermore, the problem is compounded by the fact that these concepts are often given a great deal of attention in the regional development literature, yet are rarely defined or differentiated. For example, Gibb (1987, 3) and others (Bygrave 1989, 14) are quick to point out that entrepreneurship is a concept whose meaning lacks academic consensus or clarification. Indeed, the salience afforded it in endogenously-based development approaches is difficult to defend.

THE CHALLENGES TO EXOGENOUS THEORY AND PRACTICE

The challenge to the more traditional regional economic development approaches arose from two main sources: autonomous development experiences, which existing economic theory could not easily explain, and the perceived inability of centrally initiated government policy intervention to produce the expected results. The latter has made an understanding of the development process increasingly important to politicians and policymakers, who face public pressure for both job creation and fiscal accountability.

Challenges to Regional Economic Theory

Regional economics sees the national economy as ensuing from the contributions of interdependent regions (Armstrong and Taylor 1985, 1, 139; Anderson 1988, 2–3; Bennett and McCoshan 1993, 9). It attempts to describe and understand the distinctive regional characteristics that affect economic performance.

Regional growth models attempt to show how income and employment are spatially determined. They are deemed useful if they contribute to knowledge of how regional economies function, or if they can be used as a planning tool (Armstrong and Taylor 1985, 25). These models rest on arguments concerning comparative advantage, specialization, interregional factor flows, and eventual diversification (Weaver 1984, 145–6).

The economic base model, one of the first attempts to model differences (Nelson 1993, 28), tests the proposition that regional income and employment depend heavily on a base sector that sells its output to buyers in other regions. Economic growth is assumed to result from exogenous demand for regional resources (Weaver 1984, 79). Armstrong and Taylor (1985, 25) criticized this model for being pragmatic and having no basis in economic theory. While their criticism may be questioned, the significance of the model may not, as it provides one foundation for regional science.

Although many theoretical frameworks have been used to identify and interpret regional differences, these theories and the associated policies echo the three main schools of economic thought mentioned earlier: neoclassical models, which stress supply-side influences on growth; Keynesian models, which stress the importance of demand in the growth process; and development pole models, which stress the self-perpetuating nature of the growth process (Armstrong and Taylor 1985, 81; Cappellin and Molle 1988, 5).

NEOCLASSICAL TRADITION

Neoclassical theory assumes that regional development occurs when stimulated by exogenous forces such as export markets, investment from outside, and migration (Nelson 1993, 31; Bovaird 1992, 344). If the economy is allowed to operate without interference, market forces will establish an equilibrium, thereby eliminating regional disparities (Howland 1993, 68–9). The model posits that, in disadvantaged regions, capital flows into low-wage regions and labour flows out, until returns and wages are equalized (Borts and Stein, 1964).

On the assumption that production methods and economic structures are fixed, a local labour force has three alternatives in circumstances of declining demand: emigration, unemployment, or lower wages. Implicit in this model is the notion that regional labour demand is determined exogenously and is therefore unaffected by the local labour force's behaviour, size, or constitution (Coffey and Polese 1985, 87).

In both the United States (Howland 1993, 68–9) and Europe (Cappellin and Molle 1988, 5), there are those who regard neoclassical growth theory as irrelevant for rural economies and less developed regions because the self-correcting mechanisms that are predicted to reverse decline in investment are considered weak in these areas. Myrdal's (1957, 13–23) theory of cumulative causation supports this contention. Basically, it argues that market forces, rather than being self-correcting in regions of disparity, perpetuate the prevailing economic trajectory. Disinvestment leads to unemployment, which often weakens a community's sense of place and stimulates the out-migration of skilled workers (Bolton 1992). Indeed, emigration is said to deplete both markets and human resources, decreasing the attractiveness of less developed regions for investment. Other factors that make a region less attractive for investment include restrictive lending practices (reflecting the financial community's risk assessment) and a shrinking tax base, which often leads to a decline in the level of infrastructure provided.

The neoclassical model has been criticized for failing to address long-term economic growth, as well as any accompanying demographic, cultural, structural, or sociological changes. For example, Coffey and Polese (1985) found that those who emigrate tend to possess greater levels of capital, education, and initiative. The implication for long-term growth is that interregional migration might increase regional economic disparities. Inferring that regional productive capacities are largely embodied in people, these authors argue that policies should be directed toward supply side initiatives, which will keep people in a region, raise their skill and knowledge level, and encourage local entrepreneurship.

KEYNESIAN TRADITION

Keynesian economists, recognizing that a capitalist system fluctuates between growth and decline, postulate that market forces alone will not alleviate regional disparity. The unemployment experienced in less developed regions is considered a direct consequence of a fall in the demand for goods and services, which lowers the demand for labour. Government intervention, often in the form of public sector spending, is therefore advocated to stimulate employment, particularly in severely affected areas.

The Keynesian approach to development has come under criticism in both Europe and North America. It ignores the spatial origins of investment as regards the creation of linkage effects. Intra-firm flows and subcontracting, which are often influenced from head offices outside a region, may or may not be endogenous. Linkages are generally much lower for investments originating outside the area. Additionally, large firms located in peripheral areas have not contributed as much as expected to the self-sustainable growth of these areas. The costs of resources have far exceeded the benefits achieved, while the attraction of large plants has in some instances negatively affected existing small businesses: for example, through the effect on the labour market (Molle and Cappellin 1988, 6; Coffey and Polese 1985, 87).

DEVELOPMENT POLE/GROWTH CENTRES TRADITION

Development poles (also known as "growth poles" or "growth centres") and diffusion of development from above constituted the predominant theoretical paradigm influencing growth strategies of the 1950s and early 1960s. The contributions of Hirshmann, Perroux, and Myrdal (Weaver 1984, 83–4) were instrumental in guiding a strategy that sought to stimulate regional economic growth through induced urban-industrialization. Generally, these models argue that growth is self-perpetuating, and – while the process involves the concentration of economic activity in different places, at different times, and in different intensities – it can be artificially stimulated through the establishment of a large industry (Matthews 1983, 43; Savoie 1992, 6). Establishing conditions within selected centres will encourage economic expansion: agglomeration and scale economies, infrastructure and service availability, linkage patterns, and so on. Essentially, development pole theory posits that locations where growth is deliberately pursued will become self-sustaining.

According to Weaver (1984, 84) the growth centre strategy has the ability to bridge the gap between theories of unequal development and the idea of inducing regional growth through the integration of unevenly developed areas. It accomplishes this end by stimulating a depressed region's growth via focused expenditure of public money in a growth centre, which, in turn, develops a comparative advantage in export activities. The resulting growth is assumed to spread throughout the region to integrate the whole area into the national economy by developing interregional linkages with other areas (Weaver 1984, 89; Hansen 1989, 286). However, this assumption has been challenged by the emergence of "dual economies" characterized by "cores" more economically, politically, and socially developed than their "peripheries" (Welhofer 1989, 342; Macdonald 1988, 13).

Challenges to Regional Development Policy

By the 1970s, with little evidence that economic disparities had been reduced, criticism of regional development policies mounted in France, Britain, Canada, and the United States (Weaver 1984, 146; Cappellin and Molle 1988, 7; Stöhr 1990, 40). In Britain, for example, there were three major criticisms. The first was that capital investment subsidies to specific areas were wasted because the investment would have occurred anyway. Second, assistance concentrated on the manufacturing sector even though manufacturing employment had been in decline since the mid-1960s, while the service sector's potential contribution to employment was ignored. The third criticism was that regional assistance relied too heavily on encouraging outside firms to locate new plants in assisted areas and did not sufficiently promote endogenous growth.

Governments were largely unable to respond to the criticism. In Canada, policymakers often introduced new policy without assessing prior initiatives to determine whether it was justified (Savoie 1992, 208). Without evaluation, there was no basis for discerning *what* happened, or *why*. According to Stöhr (1990, 22), the lack of assessment perpetuated the belief that local and regional development initiatives were unfeasible.

Even where evaluation was conducted, the conclusions are open to question. Success was often determined according to the cost-effectiveness of job creation (Bovaird 1992, 361; Foley 1992, 563). For example, an initiative that spent $50,000 in creating seventy-five jobs would be considered more cost-effective and therefore "better" than one spending the same amount on thirty jobs, because it had a lower cost per job. However, a mere count of jobs created emphasizes outputs, not effect. Without information regarding the type of jobs created, their duration, and whether the people getting them are unemployed or from a disadvantaged group, it is difficult to measure the effect of an initiative. Applying the same performance criteria to all initiatives, irrespective of differences in development contexts, mandates, or objectives (Foley 1992, 563), also leads to questionable conclusions.

Since policy objectives are often vague, multiple, and lacking prioritization, their evaluation is problematic. Broad, vague objectives may be set deliberately, to hedge against unforeseen circumstances that could affect goal achievement. Indeed, the practical demands of monitoring are avoided for the most part by adopting objectives of this nature. As Savoie (1992, 239) suggests, the political cost of specifying and prioritizing policy objectives may be a contributing factor. Nonetheless, the problems associated with setting and evaluating policy objectives cannot be dealt with retroactively. It is therefore impossible to infer absolutely that exogenous, top-down policy based on traditional economic frameworks is ineffective.

UNANTICIPATED CONSEQUENCES

Stöhr (1990, 36) and Robertson (1987, 59) suggest that one outcome of policy that was neither anticipated nor desired was the development of dependency. As industrialized nations focused on large-scale enterprise to contribute to economic growth, more people came to rely on having work supplied to them.

In the rural areas of Europe and North America especially, people became dependent on government policy to stimulate economic growth and employment. Many rural communities in the United States whose economic base became dominated by a single routine assembly or production industry (Blakely 1989, 34; Howland 1993, 64) increasingly saw decisions affecting their economic health being made in centralized urban locations. They became extremely vulnerable to relocation or restructuring decisions.

There is considerable consensus that the use of capital incentives, transfer payments, and public sector employment has contributed to the creation of dependency (Frank 1969; Courchene 1978, 156; Caporaso and Zare 1981, 48; Stöhr 1990, 36; Cappellin 1992, 2). Some neoclassical economists maintain, furthermore, that government intervention actually contributes to disparity by interfering with self-correcting market mechanisms. Courchene (1978, 1980) contends that, in Canada, federal transfer payments make the poorer provinces dependent on federal assistance and less likely to address fundamental problems or opportunities.[1] While he suggests changes to induce migration and other "natural" economic adjustments, he gives no consideration to non-economic factors or the consequences of a "pure" market economy.

Others consider dependency a consequence of domination by "developed" regions over "underdeveloped" regions, as capital and resources are siphoned from one region by others (Ghai 1990, 99). The failure of local initiatives is attributed to the inability of local leaders to control the economic forces that make their region dependent (Matthews 1983, 76; Galtung 1981, 175). While this argument may be refuted, it does suggest that an understanding of development (or its lack) requires consideration of non-economic factors, particularly social process and organization.

An increase in dependency indicates a decrease in the autonomy of people in disadvantaged areas (Stöhr 1990, 40–1), for the antithesis of dependency is autonomy. If, as Galtung (1981, 177) argues, entrepreneurship is the cornerstone of self-reliance and autonomy, then government policy measures that reduce autonomy may also contribute to a decreasing level of entrepreneurship (Stöhr 1990, 44). Excessive reliance on large business investments to fill gaps in regional economies will arguably prevent development of local entrepreneurial skills (Keating 1989, 308). Given the emphasis on entrepreneurship and innovation in the current socioeconomic reality, a major challenge for policy is to increase entrepreneurship, thereby increasing autonomy and decreasing dependency.

Finally, while many disadvantaged regions continue to depend upon outside help to stimulate development (Pecqueur and Silva 1992, 28; Stöhr 1990, 1), the opportunities to use traditional measures are waning.

Conclusion

The reduction of disparities in employment has been the dominant regional policy objective of industrialized nations since World War II (Weaver 1984, 108; Nelson 1993, 28). Theoretical perspectives, from which the ends and means of policy are derived, embody a set of values and beliefs.

Exogenous theory implies that people need stewardship – that the "best" decisions are made on the basis of economic considerations by specialists in centralized locations who can influence the key change factors external to the local and regional economic and social system. The sanctioning of decision-making by external actors insinuates that internal regional stakeholders are less capable of influencing the development process.

Autonomous development experiences indicate a very different set of underlying values. In part, growth is achieved through endogenous initiative and self-reliance, not by dependence on exogenously made decisions. This suggests that, as circumstances change, a different set of values might be required for development efforts to be effective.

EXOGENOUS AND ENDOGENOUS DEVELOPMENT: PARADIGMATIC DEMARCATION

Walter Stöhr introduced the term "bottom-up development" in the early 1980s. Since then, challenges to the implicit assumptions of established development theory and policy have mounted. As a different understanding of the development process emerged – one acknowledging the influence of local factors – a new development paradigm arose (Garofoli 1992b, 4). Multidisciplinary in nature, it reflects a different view of what should be studied and how research should be done.

Within the endogenous paradigm, the major factors affecting local development potential are assumed to be relatively fixed: for example, the endogenous skill base or institutional structures (Cappellin 1992, 3). Rather than taking a deterministic stance, the paradigm posits that localities *can* influence the development process by using their own resources to seize opportunities (Stöhr 1990, 26). In acknowledging the dynamic and circumstantial nature of influence, it recognizes that the process may not be linear (Garofoli 1992b, 6).

Table 1
Characteristics of Exogenous and Endogenous Development Approaches

Characteristics	*Exogenous Development ←→*	*Endogenous Development*
Source and nature of development impetus	Factors external to the local or regional economic and social system largely determine development, requiring mobility of capital and labour.	Critical change factors are seen as inherent in the local or regional economic and social system.
Structures	Bureaucratic top-down organizational structure as basis for production and support of economic activity	Flexible organizational structures of local production and support
Key values underlying initiatives	Dependency on large-scale enterprise and central government policies for initiative and control of development	Endogenous entrepreneurship and innovation are key success factors for competitive advantage in global economy.
Strategy for development	Pursuit of growth through urban-based large-scale enterprise based on standardization and capital-intensiveness	Small firms key to development, with emphasis on specialization and skill; tendency toward de-urbanization
Decision-making	Top-down decision-making initiated outside the local area by a limited number of professionals and/or others in centralized locations	Broad-based local participation, decision-making; use, development, and control of local resources
Goals	Primary goal: reduction of disparity	Primary goal: growth

Some endogenous theorists explicitly acknowledge the interactive influence of both exogenous and endogenous factors on patterns of development (Pecqueur and Silva 1992, 18; Johannisson 1990, 67). For example, external conditions may be "catalysts" of the development process. Others, who focus exclusively on identifying endogenous factors, have been criticized for ignoring the effect of broader environmental influences on the process.

While the literature shows some consistency in the general characteristization of endogenous development, there is little agreement as to what constitutes the essence of endogenous influence. For example, Stöhr (1990, 32–3) does not consider it necessary for the initiative to originate within the local area, while Coffey and Polese (1985, 86) do. Indeed, the demarcation between exogenous and endogenous development is not altogether clear.

Rather than debating the definitive characteristics of endogenous development, I have decided to conceptualize development according to a continuum. When the salient characteristics associated with exogenous or endogenous development are dichotomized, a predisposition toward one approach forms the basis of classification. This method recognizes that any attempt to establish a dichotomy is arbitrary and tends to involve an overlap of issues. Bearing this in mind, the demarcation summarized in Table 1 has been based on the source and nature of development impetus, the structure(s) facilitating business growth and development, the key values underlying initiatives, the strategy for development, decision-making, and goals.

Scholars tend to delimit the process by focusing on one or two key characteristics. Such a conceptualization does little to capture the complexity of the various economic and sociocultural factors influencing that process. In fact, it is difficult to justify the position that endogenous development overcomes the "weakness" of exogenous approaches, which use mainly economic factors to explain development, without explicitly addressing the interrelationships between economic and sociocultural factors or incorporating them into frameworks.

As we gain more knowledge about the non-economic factors that influence development, a major task will be to incorporate them into emerging development models, so that economic performance of regions can be better understood and influenced.

ISSUES AND IMPLICATIONS OF A LOCAL FOCUS

Since the 1980s, the emphasis on Local Economic Development (LED) has increased within the regional development literature. Confusion has resulted, as LED has been associated with both exogenous and endogenous development. For example, centrally initiated exogenous micro-area policy initiatives intended to deal with problems of geographically concentrated unemployment and low family incomes have been discussed under the auspices of LED. So have initiatives derived from within a local area.

Compounding the confusion is the lack of definitional precision for the fundamental unit of analysis: the local level. For example, Stöhr (1992, 206) and others (Coffey 1991; Polese 1993; Pecqueur 1989) use the terms "local" and "regional" synonymously. According to Blakely (1989, 15), either term refers to "a geographic area composed of a group of local government authorities that generally share a common economic base, and are close enough together to allow residents to commute between them for employment, recreation, or retail shopping." However, if "region" refers to anything smaller than a nation state (Armstrong and Taylor 1985, 4) and "local" is defined as anything smaller than a region (Bovaird 1992, 343), then the failure to differentiate between the two is problematic.

Coffey and Polese (1985, 86) contend that interdependence is required in order to exploit development opportunities. Johannisson (1990, 61) introduces a psychological and subjective dimension into the notion of interdependence by using the term "local" to denote "a certain territory that an individual identifies with." Arguably, the spatial context of a region is too broad for interdependence to develop, as people there do not necessarily share activities and interests. Consider a region such as the North of England. Not only does it have multiple economic bases but its residents typically do not commute very far for employment or other purposes. Therefore, it is unlikely that people from York would have a common purpose with people from Newcastle in pursuing development opportunities.

Since variations in development are often greater *within* regions than *between* regions (Armstrong and Taylor 1985, 142–5), the territorial basis for analysing the interactive influence of economic and sociocultural factors needs to be the subregional or "meso-level" between the enterprise and the market (Stöhr 1990, 43; Cappellin and Molle 1988, 7). It is at this level that the interdependence requisite to capitalizing strategically on development opportunities occurs (Vazquez-Barquero 1992a, 31).

The suggestion that differences in outcome could be influenced by endogenous process was first made by Stöhr in 1981. He argues that development can be local in origin, in application, or both (Stöhr 1990, 32–3). Further, he sees it necessary to consider

> four aspects of local development: the origin of the initiative, of the resource inputs and the control mechanisms, and the destination of the benefits ... Ideally, a majority of these factors should be predominantly local ... It seems particularly important that benefits and control should be predominantly local, as under these conditions external resources and initiative can, at least temporarily, be harnessed in the local interest until these factors can also be mobilised internally to a higher degree. A further important factor is that the benefits should be distributed broadly within the locality.

However, when the key unit of analysis is not defined, determining how localized these factors are or assessing the scope of benefit/control presents a quandary. At issue, once again, is the need for an operational definition, which will be further dealt with in chapter 4.

THE CONCEPTUAL DEBATE ABOUT THE UNDERSTANDING OF DEVELOPMENT

The economic growth achieved in Southern European and other areas through local systems of small firms indicates that development can be achieved in a variety of ways (Vazquez-Barquero 1992a, 36; Pecqueur and Silva 1992, 19). Not only does it challenge the assumption that development is exogenously determined, but it also diminishes confidence in conventional interpretation and analysis of development (Garofoli 1992c, 49; Pecqueur and Silva 1992, 17).

Economists define development in terms of wealth creation. This involves both growth – increases in primary economic indicators (income, employment, and production) – and improvements in the structure of the economy – for instance, the industry mix. Consequently, the relationship between economic growth and development is inextricable.

Within regional economics, the focus is on explaining and influencing regional disparities in income and employment. Traditionally, these disparities are measured by using income and employment indicators (Nelson 1993, 27; Macdonald 1989, 14). The two most common indicators of regional income are regional gross domestic product (regional GDP) and regional disposable income (regional DI), per capita. GDP is frequently used by politicians as a measure of the "success and progress of an economy, the value it has generated, and the human happiness or welfare derived from it" (Anderson 1991, 19).

One of the main criticisms of these measures of "welfare" centres on their inability to measure all the benefits (or costs) of economic development (O'Neill 1990, 8). In addition to the income received during a particular period, people derive benefit from what they already own. Moreover, in ignoring non-monetary output, GDP does not accurately measure total production of goods and services. In the absence of consideration of income distribution or the perceived adequacy of income, aggregate measures of welfare can be misleading. For example, while a region may experience growth – such as a rise in per capita income – it does not necessarily follow that the additional income has become more evenly distributed, or that the issue of need or circumstance is being addressed (Anderson 1991, 24; Matthews 1983, 45). Although objective assessment might conclude that the economic well-being of two areas is comparable, on the basis of per capita income levels, it is possible that residents of a predominantly rural area might consider the adequacy of income more favourably than residents of a more urban area.

Economists assume that social disparities result from economic disparities. Consequently, success in addressing the former is measured according to improvements in income and employment. Yet improvements in "objective" social indicators have been achieved despite the persistence of economic disparities (Matthews 1983, 33–4). In Canada over the past twenty-five years, regional differences in the acquisition of basic household necessities such as a telephone, a refrigerator, and indoor bathroom facilities have been eliminated (Savoie 1992, 234). Likewise, there is little regional difference in many quality-of-life factors such as education, health, and other public services. Since income measures do not reflect these conditions, a twofold question arises. What indicators are appropriate in measuring regional differences, and are there other aspects of development that warrant consideration?

Reinterpreting Development

Social scientists, many of whom adhere to the endogenous paradigm, challenge the conventional meaning of development by placing much more emphasis on non-economic welfare. Frequently, a multi-sectoral and multi-dimensional definition that includes but is not limited to economic development is preferred (Perry 1987, 127; Korten 1990, 67; Verge 1992, 2; Nelson 1993, 28). Poostchi (in Gerace 1990, 153) sees development as a pattern of economic, social, and political change. Similarly, Christenson and Robinson (1990, 11) argue that development is a locally initiated social action process for changing the economic, social, cultural, and/or environmental situation. For Bryant and Preston (1987a in Coppack 1990, 80), this change "results in an improvement in the quality of life of the population, under conditions of their own choosing."

These definitions are noteworthy in that the process emphasis is on change as opposed to growth. Moreover, their inclusion of non-economic factors challenges the universality of the assumption that people seek, above all else, to maximize income (Sitwell and Seifried 1984, 26). Improving the quality of life in an area may involve choices that do not have this result. In fact, when people face the choice between staying where they are or moving elsewhere to take a job providing greater income, many, particularly in rural areas, choose to stay where they are (Sitwell and Seifried 1984, 90; Matthews 1983, 66). It is possible that the decision to stay may be based on the perception that this choice *is* maximizing "human happiness or welfare." For example, in rural areas there are often significant benefits to be derived from the informal economy and the social structure: being able to draw on family and friends for assistance or being able to afford a house because it was built through their help. Consideration of these non-economic factors raises questions not only about people making decisions on the basis of maximizing income, but also about the ability of conventional indicators to measure "human happiness or welfare."

Finally, the emphasis placed on the role of human volition in the process is a major departure from traditional economic definitions, which assume that development is deterministic. If people become participating stakeholders, they become "development makers" rather than "development takers." It is their values that inform judgments about economic and material well-being. An assessment of quality of life by outsiders may differ significantly from that determined endogenously (Matthews 1983, 31).

If people's perception of an economic situation and how it *should* be departs markedly from that of conventional interventionists (Webster 1990, 38–9), outside intervention may be met with resistance. Resistance arises when the social and cultural fabric of a community is threatened. This reaction underscores the interactive role of economic, social, and cultural conditions in shaping development. Moreover, it implies that the interpretation of development and its attainment will vary on a local basis. If the stakeholders affected by a local economic crisis participate in generating a response, they will judge the situation according to their own values and will perceive the crisis according to the shared meaning of well-being in the area. This in turn suggests that development goals and strategies to achieve these goals will vary among local areas.

A reinterpretation of development raises the issue of how well-being will be measured. The use of social and environmental indicators, such as infant mortality rates, divorce rates, or pollution levels, has been suggested by Anderson (1991, 49) and Matthews (1983, 20). While alternative indicators may provide "objective" measures of non-economic welfare (and, indeed, of economic welfare), will these aspects of non-economic welfare be important in different locales? For instance, while pollution levels may be a valid indicator of environmental sustainability, if residents of an area do not define development in environmental terms, then it may be difficult to defend using this "objective" non-economic indicator. It may, therefore, be important to reconsider the role of stakeholders' subjective judgments when defining development objectives and measuring results.

Implications of the Debate for Regional Economics

Regional disparities in employment have changed little since the 1960s in industrialized countries such as Canada (Economic Council of Canada 1990) and the United Kingdom (Armstrong and Taylor 1985, 142). In the latter, relative unemployment rates have exhibited a stable geographical pattern, enduring over time and economic conditions. The regions of high unemployment (such as Wales, the Northwest, and the North) all contain subregions with unemployment rates below the national averages. Similar findings in the United States (Blakely 1989, 18) suggest that regional policy measures will need to be sensitive to circumstances if they are to become more effective in reducing disparities. To use an analogy, if two people are sick and seek medical treatment, one for cancer, another for diabetes, chemotherapy will not be effective in both cases. Likewise, if unemployment results from differing economic circumstances, then the ability of indiscriminate measures to provide effective "treatment" is open to question.

While a new development paradigm is emerging, its assumptions are based largely on the processes and structures characterizing a limited number of autonomous development experiences. It is yet to be established how the non-economic factors and subjective perceptions affecting the development process might effectively be mobilized to influence development in declining or stagnating communities. Conceptualization of the relationship between economic and sociocultural factors warrants further consideration.

ENDOGENOUS THEORY, POLICY, AND KEY FACTORS IN DEVELOPMENT

Models within the endogenous paradigm share the assumption that differences in production, consumption, and non-economic activities have become important in explaining economic and social change (Bovaird 1992, 346). However, since there is no consensus in defining, describing, and classifying theoretical frameworks,[2] I will attempt here to categorize the models according to two major groupings: productive restructuring models, which analyse regional dynamics through a functional approach; and spatial development models, which analyse regional dynamics in relation to territory (Garofoli 1992b, 8).

Productive restructuring models are considered endogenous, yet they seek to explain local economic change in terms of response to macroeconomic shifts at the industry sector level. Some scholars seek to identify the main sociocultural environment that characterizes various industries; others attempt to explain the influence of organizational and institutional capacity on the restructuring process.[3]

Although productive restructuring models acknowledge the strategic role of the SME sector and local agglomeration economies, they largely ignore the wider range of factors affecting Local Economic Development.[4] Fothergill and Gudgin (Bovaird 1992, 345) point out this shortcoming by demonstrating that industrial structure factors cannot explain significant changes in local employment. In late-developing countries (Vazquez-Barquero 1992d, 384; Garofoli 1992, 7), functional explanations fare no better in conveying an understanding of the local industrialization of non-metropolitan areas. Indeed, a functional approach, though accepting that industrial structure may vary over space, does not see space as an important variable in economic change. These models therefore offer no explanation as to why areas of similar size, resources, and industrial structure experience different economic outcomes (Weiwel, Teitz et al. 1993, 81).

Spatial development models[5] are said to have the analytical potential for explaining local development experiences because they can incorporate productive restructuring dynamics (Garofoli 1992b, 7; Vazquez-Barquero 1992a, 35). Territory represents the place where economic, sociocultural, and political relationships interact to determine forms of business organization as well as product and process innovative capacities. Development is seen to be facilitated by face-to-face decision-making opportunities and a shared sense of identity.

The emphasis placed by spatial development models on a particular aspect of the process limits their explanatory value. For example, factors such as endogenous control or stakeholder participation (Garofoli 1992b, 4; Pecqueur and Silva 1992, 18) have been found to be key to the process. However, these factors by themselves cannot explain the economic development of particular locales (Nelson 1993, 51). Therefore, while scholars in the endogenous tradition generally agree that economic and sociocultural forces interact to determine different forms of production organization and different innovative capacities, for the most part these models do not provide a comprehensive description or explanation of this interaction.

The Relationship Between Theory and Policy

In response to the challenges of the global socioeconomic reality – particularly since the mid-1970s – a variety of local development and employment initiatives have been supported in Europe and North America. These policy initiatives have largely lacked a rationale for their effectiveness. Indeed, in the case of high-tech development experiences in the United States, it was concluded that some policy measures were adopted because they were "in vogue" (Goldstein and Luger 1993, 148), or because there was a political need to appear to be doing something (Feller 1988; Anton 1989).

It may be possible to justify some programs according to productive restructuring models: for example, saying that the training is needed to equip people with skills required by the global marketplace. However, there is little evidence to indicate that consideration is given to the factors – non-economic as well as economic – that interact uniquely in each locale and impact on the program in question.

Recognizing the long-term impact of new ventures on employment growth and economic development (Mason and Harrison 1990), policymakers sought to encourage the formation of new firms, especially in economically disadvantaged rural areas (Vazquez-Barquero 1992a, 38). The fact that many new ventures are small has probably contributed to the increased level of policy focus received by the SME sector. Some local development initiatives attempted to solve infrastructure problems: for example, trying to make incubator facilities available for new businesses. Others sought to stimulate the inception of firms by providing advisory, technical, and financial assistance. Still others focused on training initiatives to improve skill levels or managerial capacity.

Research confirms the effect of non-economic factors, such as networks, on innovation within SMEs (Stöhr 1990, 43). How can initiatives that ignore these factors effectively achieve the policy objective of influencing entrepreneurship, innovation, or the formation of new firms?

Another policy-related issue is how the various initiatives within a local community affect development. Although Stöhr (1990, 49) argues that local synergy is a key success factor in local business development, no studies have assessed the interactive contribution(s) of separate initiatives to the development process. Where local initiatives are evaluated, there is little evidence that the problems related to the evaluation of exogenous policy initiatives have been addressed. In the absence of reliable, valid evaluation, it cannot be proven that locally focused development initiatives are more appropriate interventions for stimulating economic development than their exogenous predecessors.

Shaping the Development Experience: Key Factors

A lack of systematic research (Vazquez-Barquero 1992a, 37) makes it somewhat difficult to gain a comprehensive perspective on the nature and extent of development occurring locally, as well as the factors, structures, and processes that influence it. Although theory and policy have limitations, insight can be gained by synthesizing the range of factors identified by both knowledge and practical experience as instrumental in various endogenous development circumstances.

ECONOMIC INFLUENCES

The small business sector is one of the fastest growing segments of the economy, responsible for the majority of net employment creation (Birch 1979; Cannon 1991, 15; Bennett and McCoshan 1993, 94). In both the United States and Europe, the inception and expansion of firms accounts for more employment growth than their regional mobility (Cappellin 1983). Moreover, the creation of new firms is associated with the structural change of an economy (Vazquez-Barquero 1992a, 34). This association can be traced to the eminent economist Joseph Schumpeter, who defined economic development as "the carrying out of new combinations" (i.e., innovation). Schumpeter saw new firms as key drivers of the wealth creation process. By combining resources in new ways, they disrupted the general equilibrium of the market to produce changes in the economic system. A high rate of formation of new firms increases the diversification of a local economy, providing greater flexibility for coping with the uncertainty and complexity of both local and global socioeconomic change (Glasson 1992, 508). How does the economic structure of an area influence the rate and volume of small business start-up and growth?

Economic Structure: Influences on the Small Business Sector

Generally, the rate of new venture creation is lower in areas where large enterprises engaged in mass production form the economic base (Stöhr 1990, 8). In traditional industrial districts, the labour force's orientation toward paid employment and the barriers to entry created by the capital intensiveness of certain industrial sectors are seen as factors contributing to this situation (Garofoli 1992c, 56). Low-skill assembly line manufacturing firms usually provide little opportunity for the development of managerial, professional, or technical competencies associated with the background of new venture founders (Mason 1991, 82; Gould and Keeble 1984; Whittington 1984). Indeed, Fothergill and Gudgin (1982) find that many founders of new firms previously worked in small firms or small divisions of large companies.

As low-skill work moves to Third World countries, the economies of industrialized nations see a growth in small firms specializing in non-standardized products (Howland 1993, 66–7). The ability to capitalize on this opportunity depends on the availability of a skilled work force. In single-industry communities engaged in routine assembly, the local work force is not likely to have the skills required for specialization.

Implications of Spatial Variations in New Venture Creation
In the United States, spatial variations in employment creation by new firms are greater than spatial variations in job losses through closures (Birch 1979, 4; Wever 1985). This finding suggests that attention should be focused on stimulating the creation of new jobs rather than on diverting resources to the protection of jobs in declining industries. However, Macey's research (Armstrong and Taylor 1985, 136–7) on regions of the United Kingdom indicates that policymakers should not ignore regional disparities in closures and contractions if they are concerned with net employment change. Thus, although the small business sector makes a significant contribution to employment, marked spatial differences exist in development opportunities and constraints. Furthermore, these differences are influenced by the occupational and industry structure. All things being equal, areas whose net employment change is significantly affected by closures and contractions will face a greater challenge in stimulating the small business sector.

DEGREE OF URBANIZATION: EFFECT ON NEW VENTURE CREATION
In Western Europe, research indicates (Mason 1991, 76–7) that large metropolitan areas have the highest rates and volumes of manufacturing and service-oriented new ventures, while "underindustrialized" rural areas have high rates but lower volumes of small-scale industrial ventures. The lowest rates and volumes of new venture creation are in older urban industrialized regions typified by branch plants attracted by regional industrial policy initiatives of the 1960s and 1970s and by declining industries dependent upon large-scale production.

Regional differences in the industry mix are not significant in spatial variations in the rate of formation of new firms in the United Kingdom (Mason 1991, 81) or in regional differences in the unemployment rate (Armstrong and Taylor 1985, 149). In Western Europe, rates of regional new venture formation vary according to whether the setting is urban or rural, and have been found to distinguish areas of high employment growth from those of slow growth or decline (Mason 1991, 100). However, these patterns are not universal. For example, Birch (1987) reports that in the United States the formation of new firms is more of an urban phenomenon.

Rural Areas: Distinct Development Needs and Opportunities
The economies of rural areas have been in decline in both Canada and the developed countries of Europe. The ability of these areas to respond to socioeconomic restructuring and stimulate growth differs substantively from that of urban areas (Mason 1991, 76). This difference has

implications for theory and policy. In addition, both opportunities and threats influencing development often vary substantially between rural and urban areas (Bennett and McCoshan 1993, 224).

The problems facing rural areas are twofold. First, labour requirements in the major resource sectors – fishing, farming, and forestry – are declining as a result of technological advancement. Second, the rural routine manufacturing base is shrinking (Troughton 1990, 24). Evidence suggests that small communities dependent on staple exports have trouble adapting to market conditions (Anderson 1988, 5). Because of their smaller size and lack of diversity, rural economies based on single industry routine manufacturing are more vulnerable than urban areas when facing plant closures, downsizing, or relocation (Blakely 1989, 34; Howland 1993, 65).

Magnifying the severity of the problems are the sparse population and geographic isolation of many rural areas. These attributes often result in a lack of access to transportation networks, service structures (O Cinneide 1992, 77; Pecqueur and Silva 1992, 28; Bennett and McCoshan 1993, 274), information, and capital. A long tradition of out-migration further compounds the problems.

Neither private enterprise nor centrally initiated local development policy has proven effective in dealing with the problems facing structurally weak economies (Stöhr 1990, 44; Garofoli 1992b, 2). Many peripheral rural areas – for instance, in parts of Southern Italy, Portugal, and Canada – have stagnated, exhibiting an absence of any new forms of development and a continued dependence on outside assistance (Economic Council of Canada 1990, ix; Pecqueur and Silva 1992, 28). However, there has been little analysis or explanation of the persistent stagnation or decline of peripheral areas (Latella 1992, 61). The analysis of development in rural areas – for example, in Canada (Coppack, Beesley et al. 1990) – tends to focus on those communities lying within urban fields. Because of their relatively close geographic proximity to the city, they have greater access to resources and opportunities than the more peripheral rural communities located outside the urban field.

The trend toward specialization in non-standardized products puts rural areas with a primary resource or single industry base at a disadvantage, since the people lack the requisite skills to pursue new venture opportunities. Furthermore, rural areas in the United States and Canada have historically attracted manufacturing facilities that are tied tightly to suppliers and customers located in distant centralized urban locations (Howland 1993, 67). As a result, the opportunity for the growth of local "spin-off" businesses – supplying raw materials or distributing products – is minimal.

Studies of local environments have attempted to identify factors supporting higher rates of venture formation and expansion. Bruno and Tyebjee (1982, 288–306) provide the following list of factors:

- financial institutions supportive of the small business sector
- experienced entrepreneurs
- a technically skilled and/or professional labour force
- accessible suppliers and markets
- favourable government policies
- proximity of universities
- availability of land and facilities
- access to transportation
- a receptive population
- availability of supporting services and information
- attractive living conditions
- a social climate favouring individualism

People living in areas with these characteristics are more likely to have access to the resources needed to start a new business successfully and to perceive such a venture to be a "credible and relatively low-risk action with relatively high rewards" (Mason 1991, 99). Indeed, these facts would indicate that urban areas are more likely to nurture a supportive development environment for small business. However, given that people in rural areas have a stronger sense of place (Howland 1993, 71) and community, with many wanting to remain where they are despite a lack of employment, and that people are more likely to start businesses where they live (McMullan and Long 1990, 443), can these factors be capitalized on in building an economic development strategy for rural areas?

In summary, rural areas, particularly more peripheral ones, generally have fewer resources to draw upon in the form of infrastructure, human resource skills, and capital resources. This has been the experience in the Gaeltacht areas of Ireland (O Cinneide 1992, 79) and other European areas (Stöhr 1990). The economy of rural towns is usually based on one of the following: agribusiness, family farming, resource extraction, manufacturing, tourism, retirement, government employment, or government transfers (Howland 1993, 61). Though on an individual level rural communities are rather uncomplicated, collectively they are quite diverse. Each community will have a unique capacity for dealing with development. While rural areas face different problems than urban areas, more research is required for a fuller understanding of the needs and interests of people within the former, as well as for determining their notion of development. Given that stakeholder participation is a key characteristic of the endogenous development approach, the local interpretation of development is important as "deciding whether, when, and how to intervene in a process is predicated upon how the process is understood to operate" (Holupka and Shlay 1993, 175).

SOCIOCULTURAL FACTORS

In studies of the new regional development patterns in Southern Europe, aspects of the local sociocultural environment have emerged as key influences on the capacity of small firms and small towns to play a heightened role in the development process. A culture of entrepreneurship and innovation, the formation of partnerships, and participative decison-making and control are among the most formidable of these factors.

Entrepreneurship and Innovation

Pellegria (1989, 9) contends that the prosperity of communities can be differentiated according to their ability to instill a "certain culture of innovation and enterprise" that ultimately leads to the creation and growth of small firms. "Local entrepreneurial qualities have been decisive for ... local development ... Small firms adjust more readily to changes in the economic environment, and a favourable regional environment has enabled them to keep their production costs in check" (Molle and Cappellin 1988, 6). Similarly, Vazquez-Barquero (1992b, 110) and Garofoli (1992c, 51) argue that development is influenced by a recognition of local initiative and entrepreneurial capacity as positive social values. While such a stance avoids explaining all development in economic terms, it has not been empirically established that the prosperity of different communities hinges upon an entrepreneurial culture.

The role of entrepreneurial culture in contributing to spatial variations in new venture creation is not well understood, largely because of the difficulty of testing the relationship and interpreting results (Mason 1991, 88). Nevertheless, Jones and Clark (1976) suggest that the collective psychological attitude (i.e., optimistic or pessimistic) of a community influences the level of entrepreneurial activity there. O'Neill (1993, 8) and others (Dykeman 1990; Luther 1990, 35; Amdam 1992, 38) argue that "collective entrepreneurship" is what differentiates community-based economic development from other forms of development in achieving job creation and community economic revitalization. Yet despite overwhelming assertions, it has not been validated empirically that entrepreneurship, in one form or another, is key to the development process.

The issue may have been ignored because entrepreneurship is an internal force embedded in the culture of the community and cannot be measured directly. Instead it is inferred from individual behaviour. Indeed, while various scholars explicitly argue that entrepreneurial capacity and innovative factors are essential to development, the meaning and interrelationship of entrepreneurship and innovation are largely indeterminate. If entrepreneurship and innovation *are* key factors in the development process, then they must be defined and conceptualized in order that development may be better understood and influenced.

Partnerships

One significant aspect of the local development process in small towns or non-urban areas of Southern Europe is the synergy achieved by the strategic use of strong interrelationships among local firms (Garofoli 1992c, 51). Cooperation is facilitated by social structures supportive of local interaction. The sharing of goals and expectations by the various independent small businesses expedites the dispersion of innovation throughout the local system of firms. Collective partnerships between endogenous stakeholders and united relations in dealing with external stakeholders (such as suppliers) provide the means by which technological innovation is successfully exploited in the development process (Pecqueur and Silva 1992, 22).

The nature of local industrialization in Southern Europe has facilitated both formal and informal cooperation in the diffusion of innovation, largely because of shared common goals and relatively equal resources. Is it reasonable for scholars to conclude that cooperative relations among local stakeholders are required for effective response to market challenges? In other development domains, stakeholders' interests, objectives, and resources are more diverse. This diversity poses challenges in the absence of definitive mechanisms for facilitating partnerships, formal or informal. Indeed, coordination of action is often thwarted by a lack of established channels for easing the process (Vazquez-Barquero 1992d, 394). The opportunity to use partnerships effectively in other development arenas is not well understood.

Participation in Decision-making and Control

The importance of participation to the success of the development process is pointed out by Dykeman (1990) and Luther (1990, 35). O Cinneide's (1992, 79) research in the Gaeltacht areas of Ireland indicates that, when local development agencies initiate local development *for* the community, the intervention does not serve to stem migration or foster entrepreneurship. This suggests that although local control is necessary it may not be sufficient to achieve the results expected.

Development initiatives originating within the community may not necessarily involve those community stakeholders directly affected by the opportunity or threat (Ghai 1990, 82). Assuming that need or circumstance will influence stakeholders' definition of development, and that those with the largest stake will be directly affected by a crisis, it would be important to learn more about the level and nature of their participation.

FACILITATING THE DEVELOPMENT PROCESS: STRUCTURES

The success of local development has been attributed to the flexibility and speed of the adaptation of firms to changing economic conditions (Vazquez-Barquero 1992a, 36). The informal organizational structures characteristic of the small business sector facilitate high levels of lateral communication and decentralized decision-making. Thus, these structures encourage innovation and timely response to problems and opportunities, in contrast to the bureaucratic structures typical of public sector and large business organizations, which have the opposite effect.

A shift from the organizational to the community level in the structural capacity to adapt to changing economic conditions raises several issues. A community, unlike a private or public sector organization, has no prescribed structure for coordinating and controlling local development action among stakeholders. When economic crisis permeates a community, numerous stakeholders, with differing objectives and regulating structures, are affected. If the majority of stakeholders dealing with the crisis have traditionally operated within bureaucratic structures, they are likely to have a negative influence on the ability of the community to mount a timely and effective response.

Increased stakeholder involvement in local development goes hand in hand with increased information and communication requirements. How decision-making is coordinated in the absence of a formal structure, as well as by whom (Garofoli 1992c, 51), requires further study.

CONCLUSION

Research has identified a range of factors affecting the success of an endogenous development approach. However, there is no theoretical basis for claiming that broad-based community action can be more effective than interventionist action in stimulating the development of disadvantaged areas. Since much of the criticism of regional policy centres on the continued disparity of disadvantaged areas, the real challenge lies in better understanding and stimulating the growth of peripheral areas. Indeed, the situation facing many local communities in various countries is vastly different from that facing the Southern European communities from which many assumptions and conclusions are drawn. An understanding of the interrelationship between the contributing factors in development is needed.

While crisis conditions may provide the greatest impetus for action (Johannisson 1990, 63), it is not well understood how the economic or sociocultural structure of rural communities influences the mobilization process. Social structures are both the medium and the outcome of individual actions, which simultaneously enable and constrain (Burrows 1991, 4; Kunkel 1971, 151–4). Social relationships condition behaviour patterns by reinforcing those activities judged desirable. Clearly, if different behaviour patterns are needed for development, it is important to understand more fully the role of the development process in facilitating them.

Territorial nuances will manifest different development capacities. For example, while researchers argue that some rural areas lack entrepreneurial capacity (Stöhr 1990, 6), this assertion has not been verified. In fact, validation becomes problematic when the key concept is not defined. Furthermore, the fact that entrepreneurship is not found in an initiative does not necessarily mean there is no entrepreneurial capacity in the community.

⁂

This chapter has identified a number of definitional issues that need clarification before either theoretical or policy development at the local level can be enhanced. This achieved, there remains a need for a theoretical endogenous framework sensitive to the differences within regions and capable of explaining more precisely what a bottom-up development process is and how it can be more effective in influencing economic development than approaches used in the past.

3 The Exogenous/Endogenous Development Debate in Canada

Like many countries, Canada is characterized by unbalanced economic growth. The dominant approach to Canadian economic geography is the heartland-hinterland model of spatial activity (Anderson 1988, 3–8). Within this model the country is often viewed as a hinterland in the world economic system, with most export income entering the Canadian economy as a result of hinterland sales of raw materials, primary manufactures, and agricultural goods to the United States and other foreign markets. The heartland, in turn, is heavily dependent on domestic hinterland expenditures.

The nation itself is comprised of an industrial heartland extending from Windsor to Quebec City in central Canada and a hinterland consisting of the rest of the country. Regional specialization based on resource endowments characterizes the spatial structure of the economy. Exploitable resources attract capital and labour to hinterland locations, resulting in the export of staple commodities on which most of Canada's merchandise earnings in international markets depends (Anderson 1988, 2).

The Canadian economy has traditionally been examined on a regional basis. Ontario and Quebec are primarily considered the heartland; the Atlantic region (consisting of Newfoundland, Nova Scotia, New Brunswick, and Prince Edward Island) is the east-coast hinterland; the western interior provinces of Manitoba, Saskatchewan, and Alberta comprise the prairie hinterland. British Columbia and the northern region of the country – Yukon, the Northwest Territories, and Nunavut – are treated separately (Anderson 1988, 11).

THE NATURE OF REGIONAL DISPARITIES

Until the mid-1950s, Canadian economic policy was concerned primarily with growth. Subsequently, concern shifted to addressing regional disparities (Savoie 1992, 25). One expression of this shift was a greater focus on the Atlantic region. Indeed, the Atlantic provinces are commonly referred to as the "have-not" provinces, with the country's lowest wages, employment rates, per capita incomes, labour force participation rates, and immigration rates (Anderson 1988, 14; Stevenson 1996).

The traditional indicators of economic well-being have been per capita income and unemployment rates. Canadians living in the north and in the extreme eastern end of the country experience lower per capita incomes and greater unemployment than those living elsewhere in the nation (Macdonald 1988, 13). Ontario and British Columbia have enjoyed higher than average per capita personal incomes for over half a century. During the same period, the prairie region has had slightly less than average per capita incomes, with income fluctuations reflecting changes in its agricultural and energy sectors. Per capita income in Quebec has been about 90 per cent of the Canadian average; in the Atlantic region, it has varied from 65 to 80 per cent (Anderson 1988, 56; Stevenson 1996, 15).

When a distinction is made between per capita income and *earned* income per capita, the figure for Atlantic Canada is reduced to 70 per cent of the national average. (Un)employment insurance[1] benefits alone accounted for 20 per cent of total wages and benefits in the region in 1988 (Savoie 1992). Through the late 1980s and early 1990s, federal government transfers to individuals accounted for 30 per cent of personal income in the region. Generally, although income levels have increased, the underlying problem of unemployment remains.

A large share of the disparities in average wages among regions is attributed to differences in labour quality, as measured by educational attainments, skill levels, age, and the male/female composition of the regional labour force. With productivity at 85 per cent of the Canadian average and a lower share of the working-age population employed (85 per cent of the national average), Atlantic Canada's per capita GDP growth lags behind that of the rest of the country by 29 per cent.

A dependency on natural resources characterizes many areas of highest unemployment. The Economic Council of Canada (1990, 2) considers much of the country's unemployment problem to be one of small, remote communities whose resource base is depleted or facing declining prices. A high unemployment rate is usually the primary indicator of disparity between a region or province and other areas. Yet it does not take into account either labour force participation rates or discouraged workers (those who drop out of the labour force when unemployment rates are high and return when they fall to a lower level).

During the 1980s, the job creation rate in Atlantic Canada kept pace with that across the country, but the gap between the jobless rate in the region and the rest of the nation widened. Historically, a much smaller proportion of working-age people had entered the work force than in the country as a whole. This phenomenon has been attributed to the lack of available jobs and to the fact that half of Atlantic Canadians live in rural areas, where two-income families have been less common. However, in this decade the participation rate rose twice as fast as in the rest of the country, largely as a result of an increased female participation rate (ACOA 1991, 7–8).

Contributing to the under-utilization of the work force in Atlantic Canada are high levels of involuntary part-time work and seasonal employment (Anderson 1988, 72). According to *Profile of the Labour Force in Atlantic Canada* (Canadian Labour Market and Productivity Centre 1990), 37 per cent of part-time workers in Atlantic Canada would prefer full-time employment, compared to 21 per cent in the country at large.

Seasonal employment is concentrated in the fisheries, tourism, and agriculture sectors and in summer jobs for students. Since the income of workers is subsidized through employment insurance benefits in the off-season, it is easier for employers to attract seasonal workers (ACOA 1991, 10). The effect of EI on the pursuit of other personal income options, such as launching a small business, remains unclear because of a lack of research. Conceivably, forfeiting a guaranteed annual income for the financial uncertainty of business ownership presents a risk that many are unable or unwilling to bear.

Examining income and employment levels on a subregional basis reveals even greater disparities between the economic well-being of Atlantic Canadians and their compatriots. For example, in Nova Scotia some counties have an average per capita income that is less than 71 per cent of the provincial average; in other counties, this income figure is 118 per cent of the provincial average (Savoie 1992, 193–4). Indeed, some communities report unemployment rates of 50 per cent (Economic Council of Canada 1990, 1).

Subregional disparities between urban and rural settings also appear. The urban structure of a region is seen as a key determinant of earned per capita income, participation rates in the labour force, and overall economic growth. Atlantic Canada is characterized by a few core urban areas amidst a largely rural structure. Concentration of economic activity in the major urban centres has created regional economic dualism. Using regional income per capita, index of employment, index of transfer payments, and net migration, Macdonald (1988, 14–18) confirms the intra-regional imbalances found by other researchers (Burke and Ireland 1976; Macdonald 1979; Coffey, Macdonald et al. 1983; Murrell and Rector 1987). In Nova Scotia, for example, the Halifax metropolitan area has shown improvement, while the remaining parts of the province are considerably worse off.

Employment growth in Atlantic Canada, as in other parts of the industrialized world, has been considerably faster in the service sector than in the goods-producing sectors. Since the manufacturing sector is relatively small and primarily supplies regional markets, the opportunity for economic development outside the urban cores is narrowing. The Atlantic region imports manufactured goods from all other Canadian regions except the prairies. Its major exports are fish products, wood pulp, electricity, newsprint, and petroleum and coal products. Just over half of its industrial output is shipped outside the region, with 25 per cent going to other Canadian regions and 30 per cent going to American and European markets. The closure of the Atlantic groundfish industry, combined with an uncertain future for many of the other resource-based industries, has placed many communities in crisis.

Nova Scotia, the province of Atlantic Canada that was most aggressive in pursuing growth centre policies, has the strongest imbalance in economic growth between its urban core (the greater Halifax-Dartmouth metropolitan area) and the rest of the province. This core, which includes five counties, encompasses over half of the province's population and has an average income over 20 per cent higher than that of the other thirteen counties (Nova Scotia Department of Economic Development 1993, 8). As the province's "best and brightest" migrate to the urban core or to other parts of the country, a severe strain is placed upon the tax base. The results include a decline in services or higher taxes, both of which make it increasingly difficult to attract business to an area (Macdonald 1988, 21–2).

Although the province recognizes the dilemma, there is no indication that attention is paid to the diverse socioeconomic circumstances of Nova Scotians when policy and programs are devised to address the situation in the thirteen counties. While many communities facing economic crisis are resource-based single-industry towns or villages, each has unique capacities that have been shaped by the interaction of individual, sociocultural, and economic factors. The differences between rural areas therefore need to be considered.

Despite government intervention, inequality in per capita income and in employment opportunity has increased (Polese 1993, 9–10). Though policies have contributed to the improvement of income levels in the Atlantic region, they have been unsuccessful in addressing the problems of productivity, job creation, and unemployment. Rural areas are particularly problematic in that they often lack the diversity needed to withstand a corporate employer's decision to restructure, close, or relocate. In the case of Nova Scotia, Macdonald (1988, 22) suggests more direct interventions outside the urban core. But can economic development programs be more appropriately and effectively pursued at a subregional level? Can development best be achieved *for* the community or *by* the community?

THE CANADIAN APPROACH TO REGIONAL ECONOMIC DEVELOPMENT

The federal government has been involved in regional economic development since the early 1900s. The fact that explicit responsibility for addressing regional disparities is not constitutionally assigned has not diminished the federal government's role in this field. Provincial governments, too, are key players in economic development. Federal involvement was defined on the basis of spending power, while provincial involvement stems from jurisdiction over natural resources, land use, and human resource determinants (Savoie 1992, 14).

The Canadian federal system results in a redistributive mechanism more complex than in a country managed solely by a central government. Spending is conducted and financed by both the central government and a set of provincial and local governments. It is driven by the desire for equity and by political interests, with economic efficiency a secondary consideration (Anderson 1988, 222). Although the provincial and federal governments share responsibility for economic development, very little systematic coordination of effort has taken place (O'Neill 1990, 35). Many federal and provincial programs have overlapped in responsibilities and objectives. While the need for cooperation between the two levels of government is acknowledged, its achievement is complicated by competition for visibility and status with respect to activity (Savoie 1992, 15–17). The federal government has been particularly prone to problems with visibility because it often funds or cost-shares programs delivered provincially. Very few people are aware of federal involvement when a program is provincially delivered.

Porter (1991) contends that political action to protect employment is the main cause of Canada's alleged decline in industrial competitiveness. He is of the opinion that market protection and paternalistic government policies have contributed to low productivity, high unit labour costs, chronic unemployment, lagging investment in training and technology, and lack of support for investment in the economy. It is difficult to separate the influence of political interests and the desire for social equity on the Canadian approach to regional development; the two are intertwined.

The stated objective of equalization is to raise the fiscal capabilities of low-income provinces to a national standard, so that their residents have access to a level of provincially-provided goods and services comparable to that standard. Equalization is achieved through revenue transfers, which constitute the largest single form of transfers from the federal to the provincial governments (Anderson 1988, 234–5).

The Atlantic region, with 40 per cent of its provincial expenditures financed by equalization payments, is often described as transfer-dependent. Indeed, it has been argued that government policies inhibit migration through transfer payments and unemployment insurance (Coffey and Polese 1985, 87; Courchene 1984) and exacerbate disparities. "The relative geographical immobility of the labour force in Canada has allowed regional disparities to emerge and persist as long-run structural phenomena" (Anderson 1988, 117).

While regional economists agree that no single theory explains regional disparities, there is no consensus on an appropriate theoretical approach to the situation (Savoie 1986, 5). As regional disparities are considered to result from the operations of the market, government attempted to influence demand through transfer payments of both a provincial and an individual nature. In addition, development pole models had a pervasive influence on Canadian policy and programs, characterized by capital incentive grants and investment in infrastructure (Savoie 1992, 6–7).

THE RISE AND FALL OF TRADITIONAL REGIONAL DEVELOPMENT POLICY AND PROGRAMS

Originally, federal policies for economically underdeveloped areas consisted of transportation subsidies to designated industries and ad hoc grants to poorer provinces to balance budgets. In 1957, equalization grants were established to deal with provincial revenue deficiencies (O'Neill 1993, 9). However, it was not until the early 1960s that the federal government began developing policies explicitly to address regional disparities (Savoie 1986, 21).

In shifting its emphasis away from promoting national economic growth, policy aimed primarily to bring employment to slow-growth regions (Savoie 1986, 118). A variety of region-specific initiatives was the result (Savoie 1986, 3; Anderson 1988, 251). For example, the Atlantic Development Board, a research and planning body, was formed in 1962. In 1963 it began administering a regional development fund that invested in infrastructure such as highways and utilities. Also in 1963, the Area Development Agency was created to provide capital investment subsidies for new or expanding manufacturing facilities that would locate in areas of high unemployment.

As the number of policies and programs increased, many had differing objectives and overlapping responsibility. In response to the resulting criticism, the federal government created the Department of Regional Economic Expansion (DREE) in 1969. With full responsibility for policy and program development for economically disadvantaged regions, DREE developed two major programs. The Special Areas program, using a growth centre approach, aimed to enhance prospects for future development in twenty-three designated areas through infrastructure expenditures. However, the strategy exacerbated the disparities between rural areas and their urban cores. The other program, the Regional Development Incentives Act (RDIA), provided location incentive grants for new firms to set up in the Atlantic Provinces, most of Quebec, or Northern Ontario. It came under attack for claiming that *all* jobs associated with RDIA grants were jobs that would not otherwise have appeared in the region. Indeed, focusing on the number of jobs associated with subsidized projects ignores crowding-out effects and reduced out-migration from lagging regions. Springate (1973), who interviewed grant recipients, concludes that the grants were not necessary for attracting recipients to designated areas or were larger than the minimum size required to attract them.

Over time, DREE made numerous changes to the nature and structure of its policies and programs. Its mandate to address economically disadvantaged regions was significantly diluted when it made programs accessible in all provinces. In 1982, DREE was combined with the Department of Industry, Trade and Commerce to form the new Department of Regional Industrial Expansion (DRIE). Under DRIE, new programs were established to provide special incentives to Atlantic Canada. In general, these federal departments were criticized because of the difficulty in determining whether the regional development programs selected were effective tools for increasing employment in lagging regions (Anderson 1988, 254). Woodward (1974) argues that the effect of subsidies on job creation is difficult to detect, and that subsidies provide grant recipients with an incentive to substitute capital for labour.

While the primary focus of regional development is on relatively large geographic areas, many regional economic development initiatives have had a local focus. For example, the Cape Breton Development Corporation (DEVCO) was established in 1967 as a joint effort between the federal and provincial governments. This crown corporation's mandate was to provide a new economic base for industrial Cape Breton. Evidence (Macdonald, 1988) that economic well-being in Cape Breton is far below that in the Halifax metropolitan area directly challenged the corporation's ability to fulfill its mandate. A second example was the incentives provided by the federal Area Development Agency (ADA) to industries that located in designated areas of high unemployment and slow growth. The grants were conditional upon the creation of new employment in these places. However, the ADA program was criticized for assisting the wrong type of community – slow growth and low potential – for focusing exclusively on manufacturing, and for ignoring the uniqueness of the designated areas. Invariably, efforts to stimulate development in local areas were initiated for the people, not by the people.

Many tools have been tried in order to foster economic development, including tax rebates, tax incentives, low-cost loans, non-repayable loans, various subsidies, infrastructure expenditure, and capital reallocation programs (moving jobs to people by using investment location inducements [O'Neill 1993, 9–13]). Indeed, the emphasis on attracting large plants to a region suggests a belief that the region's problems could be solved only from the outside. Over the years, people increasingly came to rely on government to save existing jobs or to create new ones to replace those lost.

Despite considerable spending on regional economic development, little is known about the success of policy. In fact, it has been criticized for supporting higher levels of consumption and service than could be sustained by the economic output of the region. According to Savoie (1992, 3), "There is probably no other field of government expenditure in which so much public money is committed but so little known about the success of the policy. There exist very few objective research studies on regional development efforts in Canada."

In the face of persistent regional economic disparities and stagnation, top-down policies fell into disrepute, creating an awareness that new approaches would need to be considered. Starting in the 1980s, policymakers increasingly focused on encouraging endogenous growth in the small business sector (ACOA 1991, 1–2). A *Consultation Paper on Small Business* (Government of Canada 1985, 3) states that "the government recognizes the fundamental need to promote and improve the small business sector ... Canadians must begin a process of change toward a new business environment that encourages entrepreneurship and facilitates adaptation to changing market realities."

According to the Economic Council of Canada (1990, 18), "people who live in the small and more remote communities that are stagnating face three options – chronic dependency, migration or development."

However, the window of opportunity for the first two options is quickly closing as the future availability of transfer payments is becoming more uncertain and migration is becoming more difficult as job opportunities shrink nationwide. If communities are to survive and thrive, development may be the only option. The challenge is to overcome the status quo mentality and to break the cycle of dependency. Increasingly, governments are responding to this challenge by designing programs requiring community involvement.

THE EVOLUTION OF ENDOGENOUS ECONOMIC DEVELOPMENT INITIATIVES

An early federal initiative for enhancing community involvement was the 1974 job creation package known as the Community Employment Strategy. When it ended in 1979, several community development corporations were formed under the Local Economic Development Assistance (LEDA) program, whereby community organizations were given financial assistance to develop new business activity and create employment opportunities. These were perhaps the first federally funded organizations with a clear small business focus in conjunction with a community focus. In 1986, LEDAs were replaced by the Community Futures (CF) program, which was specifically designed to address development problems in communities. Targeted at non-metropolitan communities experiencing high unemployment, economic decline, plant closures, and/or massive layoffs, the program required representation from both the public and the private sector. The chosen representatives would then be responsible for deciding which program options the community would pursue. However, the success of Community Futures, like that of the programs before it, is debatable because of inadequate or inappropriate evaluation.

Another federal initiative, involving the restructuring of regional development agencies and programs, resulted in the creation of three regional agencies: the Atlantic Canada Opportunities Agency (ACOA), the Western Diversification Office (WDO), and Federal Economic Development for Northern Ontario (FEDN). In addition to local administration and authority, the agencies were given a mandate to develop programs and initiatives responsive to regional needs, to exercise flexibility in the types of business assistance and the scope of programs offered, and to connect with other stakeholders in the region. Additionally, local representation on decision-making boards was to provide greater sensitivity to each region's unique needs. However, since economic disparities are more pronounced at the subregional level, the appropriateness of a regional orientation for agencies and programs attempting to address economic disparities locally has been questioned.

While expressing interest in Community Economic Development as a mainstream development approach, the federal government acknowledges a number of unresolved issues. They include how best to allocate funding, how the three levels of government would coordinate resources, how effective interaction would be promoted among community and government stakeholders, and how evaluation criteria would be effectively established (Economic Council of Canada 1990, 17–18).

Provincial CED policy and program efforts began in the early 1990s. Circumstance played a major role. For example, in Newfoundland, the economic and fiscal situation was deteriorating, especially in rural areas (Government of Newfoundland and Labrador 1992). During the public consultation process, people expressed the belief that dependency on transfer payments, particularly unemployment insurance, was stripping them of self-worth and dignity, was a disincentive to work, and generally was counterproductive to social and economic development. In acknowledging that the status quo contributed to the problem and was no longer an option for the province, the resulting government economic development plan recognized the need for fundamental changes in many social and economic areas.

In Nova Scotia, too, "the only certainty is that the status quo is no longer an option" (Voluntary Planning 1991, 17). Because of changes in the global economy and in federal-provincial funding formulas, the province was becoming more dependent economically. Fostering an entrepreneurial culture and developing a policy to facilitate CED are two strategies developed in response.

The Nova Scotia government considers CED a three-way partnership involving community groups, all levels of government, and the business sector (Voluntary Planning 1991, 47). It sees its role as one of support rather than intervention. Practitioners have taken a similar stance. For example, Verge (1992) argues that government support must gain the participation of Nova Scotians in the process. Yet the question of how to form, coordinate, and manage the necessary relationships has not been clearly delineated or addressed.

In assuming responsibility for developing Nova Scotia's CED policy, the Department of Economic Development and Tourism has defined CED as "a process that aims to improve the long-term economic viability of geographic sub-areas of the province. It involves managing economic change to effectively meet an area's needs and objectives through emphasis on self-help, participation, partnership and control ... [C]ommunity economic development is achieved when new economic activity, usually business activity, begins in an area" (Nova Scotia Department of Economic Development 1993, 2).

In 1993, the Department began establishing twelve Regional Development Authorities (RDAs) with a mandate to stimulate and coordinate CED. However, there was no clear indication of how they would accomplish this goal. One of the service areas encompasses four sparsely populated counties comprised of communities with widely differing economic bases and, consequently, very disparate economic needs and objectives. It is difficult to understand how a RDA could assist such an area.

On the positive side, there is both willingness and commitment to increase the capacity for change, to strengthen the participation of all stakeholders in the process, and to improve integration and cooperation between the federal and provincial governments. Yet despite monetary backing and support in principle for CED, little is known about the process. Until both CED itself and related issues are more fully understood, determining its effectiveness in addressing disparity, particularly in the rural parts of Atlantic Canada, will be elusive.

CONCLUSION

For decades, Atlantic Canada has been one of the most economically disadvantaged regions of Canada. However, the nature and significance of subregional differences in economic well-being have only recently begun to receive attention. While Nova Scotia, for example, is attempting to stimulate CED in subregions of the province, little rationale has been provided for establishing the geographic boundaries of these areas or, for that matter, for adopting this particular endogenous approach.

It is important to define the space within which economic and non-economic factors interact to influence the development process. It is also important to define other key concepts in order to develop a theoretical framework for understanding endogenous development. Moreover, in light of the economic, demographic, sociocultural, and organizational factors inherent in diverse endogenous development circumstances, it is necessary to determine whether – and if so, how – CED can be used to respond effectively to the problems facing rural natural resource-based single-industry communities, particularly in the region of Canada that has historically presented the greatest economic development challenge.

4 Community Economic Development: The Community as a Development Actor

The term Community Economic Development[1] originated in the United States during the 1960s (Fontan 1993, 12). It has been used increasingly over the past decade to describe an endogenous development approach that uses locally based collective action for mobilizing community resources to improve well-being and increase self-sufficiency (Perry 1987, 73; Blakely 1989; Ketilson, Fulton et al. 1992, 3; Brodhead 1993; Swack and Mason 1993).

The interest CED is attracting both in Canada and elsewhere points up the impasse in establishing a precise definition of the approach, its objectives, its practice, as well as its success and therefore its potential (Lamontagne 1993, 1; MacNeil and Williams 1994, 4). Although Fontan (1993, 13–15) laments the absence of research, this lack alone does not account for the confusion. Others (New Economy Development Group Inc. 1992, 20; Polese 1993, 5) have attributed the interpretational debates to an absence of commonly accepted terminology. While this deficiency is also problematic, as this chapter will show, much of the controversy stems from the fact that two discrete spheres of activity, underpinned by different development philosophies, have emerged within CED. The result has been confusion in both understanding and resolving problems. Indeed, there is a lack of consensus *within* the two camps as much as *between* them.

It is difficult to discover a reason for the growing support for CED when there is no conceptual framework to explain how or why it would be any more effective than earlier exogenous approaches. This chapter focuses on identifying and analysing the gaps in an enumeration of the key elements of CED, with a particular emphasis on defining it. The chapter begins with a historical overview tracing the emergence of distinct fields of development activity.

ORIGINS AND EVOLUTION

With beginnings ascribed to the cooperative movement, community-based development has been widely acknowledged since the 1930s in Europe and North America as a process that seeks to stimulate development from within a community by pursuing economic or social ends – although the emphasis has traditionally been on the latter (Lotz 1991, 1). Until recently, within the United States and Canada, the term "Community Development" was used to describe this process.

The trailblazers of Community Economic Development were social reform proponents, whose understanding of development was very different from that of economists. From a Marxist perspective (or a variation thereof, such as dependency theory), disparity was seen to result from social as much as economic processes (Matthews 1983, 51; Mifflen 1977, 78). In Canada, the Antigonish Movement of the early 1900s was one of the first recognized efforts to deal with the economic problems of rural residents through a process of self-help. Since that time, the process has been used world-wide, in both industrialized and Third World countries, to help traditionally disadvantaged groups gain certain economic and social ends.

The Antigonish Movement, sponsored by the clergy and adult educators, was "a practical program of social reform based on the principle of self-education and action by the people themselves, organized in community groups" (Mifflen 1977, 78). As a social movement, it embodied three essential characteristics: collective behaviour, commitment to cultural change, and a degree of organization. While central to the reform process, education was not a goal in itself. Rather, its function was providing a means for people to overcome exploitation through cultural change. Education involved having people form small groups to study their problems, prioritize the areas of concern, and determine solutions. On the basis of this learning, collective action was used in addressing the problems. As the main tool for human development (primary goal), education afforded people the opportunity to develop to their full potential economically, politically, socially, culturally, and spiritually (intermediate goals) through cultural change (that is, change related to a way of life learned and passed on by one member of society to another). The economic aspect was seen as the main intermediate goal, because economic institutions were perceived as exerting the greatest influence on the entire cultural pattern. The cooperative technique, which provides members with ownership and control of their economic institutions, was adopted because ownership was considered an effective method of redistributing income and preventing economic exploitation. However, economic ends were pursued solely as a steppingstone in building human capacity.

Community Economic Development first gained currency as an alternative to traditional top-down development strategies when it was used in the United States during the 1960s in dealing with problems associated with urban poverty (Fontan 1993, 12; MacNeil and Williams 1994, 1; Perry 1987, 3). As social movements did, community development organizations championed social reform and self-help to advance the opportunities for groups marginalized by the market system or existing development approaches (Lotz 1990, 2; Ketilson, Fulton et al. 1992, 32; OECD 1993, 28). CED organizations in the United States were oriented toward improving housing or health care, largely because of an absence of government activity in these fields (APEC 1994, 10). The fact that many of the early interventions had an economic focus, such as job creation or equal opportunity hiring for blacks, may have contributed to the shift in the name of the approach from Community Development to Community Economic Development.

In Canada, the growth of CED organizations gained momentum in the late 1960s, as the federal government initiated activities on behalf of local communities, to deal with the economic disparities of particular areas. However, it was not until the 1970s that the economic development initiatives of government began to include community involvement. The 1970s marked a period of increased growth in the government programs available to deal with problems in economically depressed areas. Various projects were launched with the aid of government funding, some by CED organizations intent upon helping traditionally disadvantaged people help themselves in combatting poverty, unemployment, or inadequate services (MacNeil and Williams 1994, 1), others by government agencies focused on generating jobs in economically distressed areas through the collaborative efforts of local public, private, and voluntary sector representatives. So it was that two distinct fields of community-based activity emerged. While the latter initiatives were referred to as Local Economic Development, today both fields of activity are known as Community Economic Development.

For CED organizations, the current climate differs from the past in two significant respects. During the 1960s and early 1970s, the economic growth experienced in industrialized countries made it possible to access both financing and operating money from a variety of government programs and departments. Today, governments have significantly reduced both the number of programs and the financial resources available. The constraints upon CED organizations can be considerable, since few, if any, of them are financially self-supporting. In response, they have become more involved in income-generating ventures to diversify their revenue base. Furthermore, economic pressures to address the problems of the disadvantaged have occasioned public and private collaboration in bringing an economic perspective to bear on issues traditionally dealt with from a social perspective (National Council for Urban Economic Development 1993, 85).

Although the effects of restructuring blur the division between social and economic problems, there is no evidence of a concomitant merger among government agencies or policy stakeholders who deal with these matters. Indeed, two distinct groups now exist: those with a social development mandate (New Economy Development Group Inc. 1992, 3) such as the federal Department of Human Resources Development, and those with an economic development mandate, such as Nova Scotia's Department of Economic Development and Tourism. Those in the former group see CED as an approach that can achieve social development by pursuing both social and economic objectives (National Welfare Grants 1991; New Economy Development Group Inc. 1992, 3). However, those in the latter group show no interest in using CED to attain social objectives in the pursuit of economic development.

Both the federal and the provincial levels of government consider CED a mainstream policy option for social as well as economic development. Yet in their search for comprehensive approaches, governments have ostensibly ignored the challenges inherent in reconciling incompatible mandates. Because of ideological differences, economic and social aims are not necessarily complementary. Integrating them runs the risk of political conflict if economic and social development policymakers are compelled to compete for scarce resources. Much energy can be expended in focusing on internal resource needs, overshadowing the needs of the market. While claims of success add impetus for adopting CED as a development strategy, a lack of consistency in evaluation makes its effectiveness debatable. When there is no basis for ranking social and economic aims, judging effectiveness is difficult.

UNDERSTANDING THE IMPASSE

In this section we explore the two distinct development philosophies and the resultant issues of consensus and difference in order to gain a better understanding of the present impasse.

Two Development Philosophies

An understanding of the chief aim of the process is what divides CED into two streams of activity. One stream, hitherto referred to as the economic development perspective, sees CED as a strategy for addressing economic disparities in employment and income within geographically defined areas. The second stream, the social development perspective, views it as a strategy for combatting the problems of marginalized social groups (Fontan 1993, 9).

Defining development as an economic growth process (Polese 1993, 5), the economic development perspective holds a particular philosophy of how development can be encouraged. The achievement of social goals is predicated upon economic success. For example, it is believed that community action should concentrate on reducing unemployment, since this will help alleviate the undesirable social problems produced by unemployment, such as crime and poor health (Economic Council of Canada 1990, 4). Indeed, O'Neill (1993, 7) argues that wealth and employment creation are primary goals while social goals are at best intermediate objectives. Economic development proponents believe that economic disparity can be reduced if the growth process involves endogenous collective action aimed at stimulating business activity and/or employment. According to Blakely (1989, 15), "The principal goal of local economic development is to develop local employment opportunity in sectors that improve the community using existing human, natural, and institutional resources."

With the alleviation of poverty as their raison d'être, social development proponents interpret development as an individual growth process. Economic factors create a situation of social exclusion[2] wherein the traditionally disadvantaged lack control of the economic resources needed for individual development (National Council for Urban Economic Development 1993, 86; Ninacs 1993, 19; Swack and Mason 1993, 2). The situation is exacerbated by the negative effect of economic restructuring. Social development is seen as seldom occurring without a corresponding improvement in economic conditions, whereas pursuing economic development can negatively affect social development (Brodhead 1993, 19).

While social development proponents claim that both social and economic objectives are pursued in attempts to influence development, Douglas (1989) asserts that social goals transcend economic ones. Indeed, the initiatives pursued support his assertion. For example, when business ventures are established, they typically adopt unconventional organizational forms such as cooperatives or community enterprises (Fontan 1993, 8; Joyal 1994, 14), which incorporate collective decision-making seen as contributing to social development. Furthermore, these ventures tend to give precedence to collectively agreed-upon social and ethical objectives – for example, an individual's need for meaningful employment – and to seek viability rather than profitability (Ketilson,

Fulton et al. 1992, 35). The achievement of economic objectives is seen as enhancing the capacity of the poor to become more self-sufficient (Ninacs 1993, 19). This viewpoint undoubtedly explains why blending social and economic objectives has created considerable difficulty and tension (Brodhead 1993, 20).

Economic development proponents see collective action as providing a vehicle through which the institutional base identifies problems and develops solutions that create innovation and entrepreneurship, more and better jobs, increased wealth and incomes, and greater opportunities for personal fulfilment (Blakely 1989, 73; OECD 1993; Economic Council of Canada 1990, 18). With the major factors affecting local development potential considered to be relatively fixed and underdeveloped, development solutions depend upon building the capacity of a community's human resources to exploit the potential of underutilized natural and institutional resources (Blakely 1989, 67; O'Neill 1993, 8; Economic Council of Canada 1990, 3). Attempts to increase income and/or employment have aimed at supporting small business development and skill development. For example, some initiatives provide financial capital to local businesses; others provide training to improve the effectiveness or productivity of the local labour force. The attention to human capacity-building implicitly affirms the interrelation of economic and sociocultural factors within the process. However, there is no theoretical foundation underpinning practice (Blakely 1989, 60).

An Economic Council of Canada report (1990, 3) borrows from community development organizations to outline the key characteristics of the process: local initiative; broad-based participation; partnerships among the public, private, and voluntary sectors; local leadership; entrepreneurship and innovation; individual and collective skill development; and local institutions with the authority and responsibility for decision-making and resource control.

Social development proponents regard collective action as enabling individuals who lack the resources needed to improve their well-being independently to achieve this end mutually. In the words of Bill Ninacs (1993, 19), "CED's leitmotif of economic empowerment is a direct result of its overall objective of social inclusion." Ketilson, Fulton et al. (1992, 34) and Fontan (1993, 29) contend that advocacy is essential when CED does not emerge spontaneously. This role is best filled by independent community-based groups and agencies who can gain broad-based participation and establish partnerships with public and private stakeholders from within and outside the community.

Social change is an integral aspect of the process. The goal is to afford marginalized individuals access to greater wealth and participation in the decisions affecting them (Fontan 1993, 6–16; Ninacs 1993, 19). This aim is accomplished through a planning process that provides the community with the skills, attitudes, and resources needed to improve self-sufficiency. The resulting activities broadly encompass four diverse areas of intervention: land use planning, employment, private or collective business development, and private or collective investment.

It is clear that adherents of each philosophy have very distinct ways of thinking about development, the means of influencing it, and why it should be influenced in that way. Our further exploration of the two perspectives considers whether they are appropriate within the current development environment.

ISSUES OF CONSENSUS

Proponents of the two streams of activity are in agreement on a number of issues: the impetus for Community Economic Development, the essentials making the process effective, the nature and functions of the required structure, and the importance of focusing initiatives on capacity-building.

Both perspectives share the assumption that *crisis* provides the stimulus for people to engage in CED, particularly economic crisis, which jeopardizes the subsistence of community members (Economic Council of Canada 1990, 7; Broadhead 1993, 20). However, because its orientation is long-term, Brethour (1994, 34) asserts that conditions of extreme crisis constrain the opportunity to use CED successfully, since they require immediate short-term solutions.

On the assumption that development can be influenced from the bottom up, both perspectives reject the view that the global village supersedes the community's influence on behaviour (Curran and Blackburn 1994, 20–2). Indeed, the global village argument fails to explain why communities with similar economic structures and resources exhibit different levels of development.

Proponents of CED argue that effectively building a community's self-reliance requires the active involvement of community members. Having the greatest understanding of the problems it faces, the community is in the best position to develop solutions. A shared sense of identity, produced by the interaction of economic and sociocultural factors within a spatial area, creates a common purpose in mobilizing local resources in response to economic problems. Strategic planning with a long-term focus reflecting the nature of development is the means by which communities use their knowledge and resources to plan and manage their own destiny (Blakely 1989, 68; Brethour 1994, 34). Local leadership is vital to the successful initiation and management of the process, with national government and exogenous stakeholders allocated an indirect role. Public funds are also deemed necessary to support CED initiatives (Joyal 1994, 15).

Directing and motivating behaviour toward greater self-reliance requires a formal structure. Coordinating the process calls for a democratically controlled community-based institution, with representation from the public, private, and voluntary sectors (Blakely 1989, 252; Fontan 1993, 29). Its function tends to be defined in terms of planning, consultation, and/or facilitation of intervention activity. Among its main activities is the formation of partnerships among community stakeholders, as well as between the community and outside institutions. These partnerships play a key role in eliminating duplication of effort (O'Neill 1990, 32) and competition (New Economy Development Group Inc. 1992, 13) by synergistically mobilizing resources to achieve objectives. Other activities include fostering broad-based participation (O'Neill and Bryant et al. 1993, 16), exerting local control over resources (Ketilson, Fulton et al. 1992, 4), creating and maintaining networks (Polese 1993, 15), and, in some instances, operating enterprises (Blakely 1989, 78).

While diverse, initiatives are aimed at developing a community's capacity to mobilize underutilized human, physical, and financial resources to achieve the objectives laid out in the strategic planning process. Fundamental to capacity-building is the creation of an entrepreneurial culture (Blakely 1989, 268; APEC 1994, 8). Indeed, entrepreneurship, innovation, and business development all have a role in enhancing a community's capacity for self-reliance.

Overall, both perspectives assume that development can be influenced *in* the community, *by* the community, making people pivotal to its success. Although there is broad agreement about the nature of the process and its attributes, the activities associated with each philosophical orientation demonstrate that the meaning and emphasis of the essentials of the approach differ.

ISSUES OF DIFFERENCE

The philosophical divergence in CED appears in these issues: the definition of community, the main participants in the process, the role of empowerment and resource control, the nature of the requisite initiatives, and the understanding of self-help As noted earlier, lack of agreement and clarity within the discrete fields of practice on some of these matters compounds the confusion surrounding CED.

Adherents of the economic development perspective typically define community on the basis of administrative boundaries (O'Neill 1993, 4). The terms "local" and "regional" are used interchangeably in demarcating a "community" within which a sense of identity is instrumental in mobilizing stakeholders to take collective action to increase the area's economic self-sufficiency.

Social development proponents define community in terms of a marginalized social (e.g., single-parent families) or cultural (e.g., an ethnic minority) group sharing a geographic locality and a sense of identity (Perry 1987, 60; MacLeod 1986, 56). While the word "community" is used arbitrarily to denote a specific area, a specific group, or both (Fontan 1993, 9), the notion of marginalization is invariably central to the definition. Indeed, this perspective's understanding of "community" always involves a particular group *and* a particular locale. For example, if "community" denotes a marginalized social or cultural group, this group requires a shared locality to facilitate joint action. Similarly, if "community" is used to denote a geographic area, demographics is employed to identify those in it who are socially excluded.

Because economic development advocates allocate responsibility for identifying problems and formulating solutions to the local institutional base, the process is understood to be one of collectively influencing action rather than one of influencing collective action. Social development advocates do not afford the local institutional sector the lead role. Nonetheless, its stakeholders are expected to become actively involved in the coordinating organization as members of the board of directors, alongside members of the community. Because self-help is understood to be a collective process in which a marginalized community participates, delegation of responsibility for studying problems and finding solutions is encouraged (Fontan 1993, 8). The process is seen as one of influencing collective action rather than one of collectively influencing action – in direct contrast to the view of the economic development perspective.

Economic development proponents see empowerment and resource control as inherent in the process (O'Neill 1993, 7), while social development proponents see them as desired ends (Fontan 1993, 7–8). To re-integrate the most disadvantaged into the mainstream of both the economy and society, initiatives focus on fostering individual and collective empowerment and control and the utilization of local resources within the community.

Economic development solutions, primarily focused on generating employment, involve two types of initiatives: those intended to establish or develop private enterprises, and those aimed at improving individual skill levels (Lewis 1993, 1; Joyal 1994, 13). On the other hand, social development solutions primarily focus on reducing social exclusion. Indeed, while the stated aims of initiatives vary, the most common ones are local control over resources and institutions (Swack and Mason 1993, 3), social solidarity, and individual and collective empowerment (Fontan 1993, 7). The initiatives themselves often involve direct intervention, with the CED organizations engaging in activities from running daycare centres to loaning funds.

There have been attempts to embrace both social and economic approaches within broad categories. For example, using a practitioner's perspective, Lewis (1993, 3–4) classifies initiatives along four lines: the growth equity model, which focuses on building the economic base through a direct ownership stake in business creation and expansion; the loan and technical assistance model, which emphasizes financial, technical, and training assistance to local business; the employment development model, which focuses on enhancing local human resources; and the planning and advisory services model, which addresses the provision of specialized services to a specific group.

Finally, with regard to self-help, each perspective has a different strategic level of focus. Within the economic development approach, the results of activities are reported aggregatively in terms of outputs achieved within a geographic area, such as the number of jobs created or the number of people trained. This implies that self-help is conceptualized as a group process producing community-level self-sufficiency. In contrast, social development proponents conceptualize self-help as a group process producing individual-level self-sufficiency.

The two perspectives not only diverge on these issues; they also display considerable bias. For example, within the myriad classification schemes used to differentiate the initiatives of each perspective, Fontan's (1993, 4) has become the one most commonly adopted by social development proponents. It uses term "progressive" to describe initiatives that advance social development, and the term "liberal" to describe initiatives focused solely on economic development. In his usage, "progressive" connotes improvement while "liberal" does not, suggesting that progressive approaches are "better" than liberal ones. Bias is also evident among economic development proponents, who typically differentiate initiatives in terms of Community Economic Development and Local Economic Development. For example, Joyal (1994, 14) portrays social development advocates as "people who see housing provision for the homeless as a more urgent priority than improving chances in securing a job so that one day they can house themselves from their own pay packet." His depiction is not accurate, as economic initiatives are often integral in the strategy for meeting the needs of marginalized individuals (Ninacs 1993, 19).

IDENTIFYING AND ADDRESSING THE CONCEPTUAL DEFICIENCIES

The issues remaining to be addressed are inextricably linked to the definition of CED and the understanding of the development process.

After dealing with the fundamental issues surrounding definition, we examine the essentials of the process to identify the factors required in a conceptual framework for understanding how and why communities influence economic development.

Defining Community Economic Development

Central to the understanding of any phenomenon is a definition of key concepts. Community Economic Development encompasses two of these – community and economic development – which each perspective understands differently.

DEFINING THE IDEA OF COMMUNITY

As the idea of community becomes more prominent in the literature, the variety of its meanings is a source of confusion and controversy (Swack and Mason 1993, 1; Brodhead 1993, 2). The term evokes a range of connotations, which have been endorsed in differing combinations and intensities (Lotz 1991, 3; Fontan 1993, 9). For the most part, it is used in describing the focus for activity. However, I argue below that the existing definitions are inadequate for explaining how and why the process can accomplish the desired objectives.

The economic development perspective defines a community according to administrative boundaries. This definition has been criticized not only by other social scientists but by economists themselves, who suggest that it has arisen out of statistical convenience (O'Neill 1993, 4). Those concerned with urban development have been the most critical, arguing that problem areas rarely have an administrative identity (Fontan 1993, 9). Indeed, we saw in chapter 2 that the adequacy of using a region to define the spatial context of a community has been challenged, particularly on the grounds that it usually encompasses a range of needs or circumstances.

A sense of identity is seen as instrumental in mobilizing local resources to address problems, yet its role is ignored when community is defined according to either administrative or statistical boundaries. For example, the OECD (1993, 44) proposed using a labour market or a region to define the local area. Such a definition suggests that identity is not well understood. A sense of identity is considered to emerge from shared economic, social, and cultural experiences, but both a labour market and a region normally include diverse economic, social, and cultural units. *Webster's Encyclopedic Dictionary: Canadian Edition* (1988, 198) defines a community as "a body of people with a faith, profession or way of life in common"; "a body of people living near one another and in social relationship." These interpretations challenge the appropriateness of defining a community according to a labour market area or a region, and suggest a need to augment the criteria used to delimit a community beyond mere geography.

Accepting that collective action is used to influence development and that shared economic and social relations create a sense of identity instrumental in mobilizing this action underscores the importance of social interaction in the process. To be functional in defining community, the geographic dimension must delimit the spatial boundaries within which economic (or indeed social) problems are perceived to be shared as a consequence of a common identity. Administrative boundaries or other statistically derived units do not fulfill this requirement, since they are not drawn up on the basis of identity.

In the definitions adopted by social development advocates, the idea of community as group raises an important point. *Webster's Encyclopedic Dictionary: Canadian Edition* (1988, 425) defines a group as a "body of people with a common purpose." As we have seen, "community" has been defined as a body of people who have *something* in common. Given that "purpose" generally denotes an end to which effort is directed, action is implied. Indeed, social psychologists (Johnson and Johnson 1991, 10–13) argue that one of the fundamental reasons groups exist is to make it possible for people to achieve goals that they are unable to achieve alone. Defining a community as a group indicates not only that people have something in common but that they also have some common purpose, which is fundamental to action. However, the propriety of making marginalization the basis for designating the group boundary in defining a community has been questioned.

Marginalization provides grounds for developing a sense of identity, which in turn is a catalyst for joint action. Implicitly or explicitly, it also incorporates the required geographic dimension. Yet there are problems associated with its usage. Restricting collective action to a specific group within a geographic area may exacerbate social exclusion, as homogeneity fosters differentiation rather than integration. Defining a community as a single disadvantaged group that lacks control over resources would constrain its capacity to access and mobilize those resources, by reason of its homogeneity. Moreover, such an interpretation ignores the fact that a multiplicity of marginalized groups may exist within a given geographic area, leaving the basis on which marginalization is determined and intervened upon open to challenge.

Within a specified locality, individuals – whether considered marginalized or not – may be stakeholders in numerous institutions and activities. Indeed, they establish a multitude of social relationships by virtue of the formal and informal, economic and non-economic, activities and groups in which they participate. Consequently, the effect of problems would not be isolated to one group, but rather would affect many relationships. Defining community as a specific marginalized group ignores the situation and needs of many other individuals and unduly restricts the scope of self-help. Further, it diminishes the possibility of effectively using the notion of self-help in order to capitalize on the range of both intragroup and intergroup opportunities in stimulating collective action to mobilize resources to influence development.

With whole geographic localities becoming "marginalized" as a consequence of economic restructuring, the appropriateness of defining community in terms of a traditionally disadvantaged group is questioned. Because of shared activities, it is not just one group of people who perceive themselves to have a stake in addressing the situation.

Both perspectives, then, display a stark ignorance with regard to identity. Clearly, a person's identity is not exclusively aligned with a single group, nor is it likely to be given focus by the diverse aspects contained within administrative boundaries. On the one hand, while administrative boundaries do provide people with something in common – living space – they do not always provide a basis for some common purpose. On the other hand, marginalization may provide a group with purpose, but defining community in this way excludes consideration of all others within the same geographic area who perceive themselves to be stakeholders in the problems being experienced. Indeed, it is necessary to define community in terms that are inclusive of people who, by virtue of shared economic and social relations, have developed a sense of identity through which collective action can be mobilized to respond to problems affecting the geographic area in which they live. In adopting this definition, we need a clear explanation of identity and its influence on collective action.

Community Redefined

Assuming that development can be influenced in a community, by a community, through collective action, three elements emerge as important in defining community. The first pertains to geography, that is, location. The second is social, reflecting both economic and social interaction. The third concerns psychology: a perception of belonging. Perry (1987, 63) defines a community as "a more or less circumscribed geographic locality in which the residents tend to see their destinies as somehow bound together, and where their destinies are in fact linked together to the extent that the residents share a common view of life and share (or overlap in) membership in most of the institutions in which they participate." The geographic and demographic elements combine the geography and the people; the psychological involves a sense of belonging; the cultural is expressed in common ways of judging, believing, and valuing; and the institutional element involves a network of interrelated organizations and patterned practices within which people live their lives.

Perry's definition has been criticized (Jacquier and Mendes-France 1992, 20; O'Neill 1993, 5) for presuming that "a view of life" or "interests" can be shared by residents of a geographic area, and for failing to identify the aspects of life about which "a common view" would be held. However, sociologists argue (Weber 1947, 136) that a community is a distinctive social unit consisting of people who go about their daily activities in a particular locality and who generally identify with members of that unit. This locality has been conceptualized by some as the "life-world": the boundaries within which people take action that is confined and influenced by dynamic social structures. It represents "the segment of the world which people have formed and interpreted for themselves, in which they interact with and experience their immediate neighbours in space and time" (van Rees 1991, 28). The life-world exists, then, between the individual and society, designating the domain within which concrete life tasks are undertaken. It can be seen to represent a resource for these tasks (van Rees, 1991, 19).

Gerstein (1987, 100) argues that identification affects behaviour in two ways. It standardizes expectations in cases where people are treated the same by virtue of their membership in a community, and it establishes norms of attitude and behaviour in relation to others by virtue of community membership. For Polese (1993, 4), a "sense of place" provides a collective method of "reducing information costs and 'transaction costs'" through the formal and informal network of contacts and shared values and interests. Indeed, it is people's life-world, influenced by the dynamics of social structures, that shapes this sense of identity and can be seen to delimit the boundaries of action.

While it may be unrealistic to assume that residents of an administratively defined geographic area share a common view of life – particularly if the focus is urban – it may not be unrealistic to assume that residents of rural areas, who share a *way* of life by virtue of an undiversified economic base, would also share a *view* of life. The reciprocal influence of social and economic factors is underscored by sociologists (Matthews 1983, 86). Yet the salience of the relationship between the life-world and the development of identity is ignored when community is defined on a regional basis. Assuming that collective action is to be mobilized through shared behavioural expectations, the concept of life-world is pivotal to defining community.

Despite the criticism of Perry's definition, its contribution to a more valid definition of community is significant. It recognizes geographically identifiable interdependencies that may adhere to administrative boundaries; it makes reference to a relative, rather than an absolute, phenomenon; and it incorporates a subjective element – since the boundaries are in part defined by an internalized identity influenced by the interaction of sociocultural, economic, and psychological factors – which is considered instrumental in effectively motivating collective action.

O'Neill (1993, 6) sharpens the geographic element and explicitly retains the institutional aspect in his definition of community: "a geographic area whose residents participate in interdependent economic, social and political institutions and activities, and share a variety of public and private services." While the heightened precision of his definition facilitates testing, it fails to incorporate the cultural and psychological elements instrumental in mobilizing collective action.

Given that both perspectives aim to increase the self-sufficiency of the community through collective action, it is the life-world that shapes and delimits the geographic boundary within which people form a sense of identity and common purpose and that provides the perception of stake or influence in the development of the community. I therefore propose this definition to address the interpretational inadequacies of both the economic and social development traditions. A community is a geographic area whose residents perceive themselves to be stakeholders and share behavioural expectations as a result of social relationships developed while participating in formal, informal, and interdependent economic, social, and political institutions and activities, and while sharing a variety of public and private services. Defining community multidimensionally, according to the concept of the geographic life-world area, provides greater certainty that a shared identity exists and can be utilized in mobilizing collective action. Yet this new definition of community only partially resolves the issue of defining Community Economic Development.

DEFINING ECONOMIC DEVELOPMENT

The debate over the meaning of economic development essentially centres on the understanding of well-being. The social development perspective emphasizes and incorporates various aspects of non-economic welfare. But social development advocates are not necessarily at odds with economists' definition of economic development; rather, they argue that development involves more than economic well-being. The philosophical differences in the understanding of development, in turn, affect the objectives pursued, the nature of the process, and the structures used to achieve the desired ends. Herein lies a key reason for some of the controversy surrounding Community Economic Development. Indeed, practice has not unequivocally established that it is desirable, appropriate, or possible to integrate social and economic objectives or that the objectives of either perspective are in keeping with the perceived needs of the community.

Fundamentally, the purpose of a process is to accomplish a goal or goals. When development is understood in strictly economic terms, goals centre upon employment generation, largely ignoring economic structure. On the other hand, when development is understood in multidimensional terms, goals emphasize aspects of individual development such as empowerment.

The adequacy of the objectives promulgated by both schools in addressing need or circumstance can be challenged. Attaining economic goals does not necessarily mean achieving the desired effect. For example, increases in income and employment can be achieved without helping the unemployed or disadvantaged, or easing the financial pressures on governments dealing with unemployment and poverty. Meanwhile, addressing the needs of one marginalized group ignores the fact that economic hardship may affect many stakeholders in a community.

Social development proponents have been criticized for treating the process as an end in itself. Indeed, it is easy to lose sight of the essence of need if social objectives are concentrated on at the expense of economic goals. Whether individual empowerment can be sustained in the absence of economic self-sufficiency is open to question. While economic objectives now assume a presence alongside social objectives, are the opportunities for increasing empowerment through venture initiation and development recognized and fully understood?

Most important, the capacity of small business to foster individual competencies associated with empowerment – such as initiative, responsibility, decision-making, and problem-solving (Gibb 1993, 18) – has been overlooked. Anecdotal evidence suggesting that social objectives take precedence over economic ones is reflected in the practice of pursuing ventures on a not-for-profit basis in support of job creation, for example. This finding indicates that the contribution of venture profitability to empowerment is not well understood. Indeed, profit is the means by which growth in income and/or employment is achieved. As a matter of course, if ventures are pursued on a not-for-profit basis, the development of independence may be jeopardized, particularly if financial subsidization played an instrumental role in start-up. Indeed, operating a business on a break-even basis means that it lacks a margin for error, making it particularly vulnerable to market uncertainties. It is difficult to understand how individual empowerment would be encouraged under these circumstances. On the other hand, it is quite possible that economic self-sufficiency would contribute to feelings of individual empowerment.

O'Neill (1993, 6) argues that aims such as empowerment and autonomy are inherent in the process when decision-making is community-based. However, community-based decision-making does not necessarily guarantee that those in need will be part of the process. In fact, it is conceivable that participants in the process could belong to the community without being directly affected by the economic crisis. In such a case, one of the main advantages of the collective process – pursuing personal need through joint association – would be lost.

Measurability of success becomes an issue when intangible goals such as autonomy are sought. Moreover, social objectives do not result in financially self-sustaining activities. In fact, the pursuit of social goals has been dependent on diminishing government funding. While it has been claimed that CED has succeeded in achieving both economic and social ends (New Economy Development Group Inc. 1992, 1), this assertion has not been supported by evidence.

Finally, the appropriateness of a long-term focus for objectives amidst an uncertain environment is open to challenge. Given the negative effect of global economic restructuring on the ability of communities to meet their residents' basic needs, it seems reasonable to assume that those affected would have a short-term goal orientation. This is not to deny the value of long-term goals; rather, it suggests that need or circumstance will have an important influence on how development is defined and, consequently, on how objectives and priorities are set.

Although, as noted earlier, people do not necessarily want to maximize their income, economic welfare and quality of life are inextricably linked. However, the relationship is dynamic and contingent upon circumstance. For example, if a community's major employer closes, residents may come to define development in conventional economic terms. Both anecdotal evidence and need theory lend support to this proposition. While empirical work (Wanous and Zwany 1977) suggests that individuals attempt to fill multiple needs at the same time, there is general agreement in need theory (Bartol and Martin 1991, 448–56) that the fulfilment of concrete needs of existence takes precedence over higher level, less concrete needs (which would be inherent in quality-of-life factors).

Fundamentally, if people perceive the fulfilment of their basic needs to be in jeopardy, it is likely that development will be defined primarily in economic terms. Indeed, early social movements adopted this rationale, on the assumption that human development goals would not have priority until the basic economic needs of individuals were met. However, economic development was not the ultimate objective; rather, it was a necessary first step, an element of human development.

The assertion that there is no discernable basis for integrating social and economic objectives suggests that need fulfilment is not well understood. Moreover, the tension between economic and social development objectives may be occurring because communities have not been delegated the responsibility for identifying their needs and expectations and for determining and prioritizing objectives based upon them. Either explicitly or implicitly, CED goals have been determined by interventionists. For example, community stakeholders often define objectives for development initiatives on the basis of programme funding availability (Lewis 1993, 3), rather than according to need. Under these circumstances, dependency, not self-reliance, is fostered.

Economic development programs lack the flexibility to be responsive to a community's needs and competencies. Statements by government agencies and others (ACOA 1992, 122–3; OECD 1993, 15) highlight the extent to which circumstance is overlooked. They claim that the service and information sectors represent a significant part of the global economy and that, because they are not dependent upon agglomeration economies for growth and competitiveness, they present opportunities for economic growth in remote rural communities. This assertion ignores the fact that many of these commmunities lack the skill and education base required for capitalizing on such opportunities, and suggests that the spatial dynamics of the development process are not well understood.

For communities whose economic base can no longer support their residents, structural change in economic activity will be a key success factor in the development process. New socioeconomic relationships are involved here. Since no two communities are identical, economic structure cannot be predetermined, nor can successful aspects of it be transferred from one community to another. Rather, each community will need to identify sources of development and how they can be used in achieving the desired change.

Because communities face different circumstances, needs will clearly vary, as will process aims and priorities. In some communities, the goal(s) may be directed toward social development; in others, economic development will take precedence. If the process is to influence development through self-help, the issue is not defining economic development, nor predetermining the goals to be pursued. Rather, it is making certain that goals are established by the community in accordance with its perceived need(s) and aspirations. If economic goals take precedence, goals and priorities would presumably be established with an orientation toward the formation of new firms or the expansion of existing ones, as these activities provide the means of fulfilling basic needs. Under these circumstances, conventional economic indicators of structural change and growth in income and employment may be useful for measuring effectiveness. However, depending upon the desired goals, it may also be necessary to take into account the distribution of any growth. Fundamentally, the community's needs and expectations must be determined before valid measures of success can be established. When economic development is framed in this way, individual or collective empowerment is not precluded, since the community has stewardship of the process.

On the basis of my earlier redefinition of community and the foregoing discussion of economic development, I can now define Community Economic Development as the process by which a community uses collective action to improve its well-being and self-reliance according to self-defined needs and expectations.

IDENTIFYING THE ESSENTIALS OF PROCESS

While policymakers identify the need for communities to build capacity in order to respond to the effects of economic restructuring, and look to CED for building self-reliance, an absence of conceptualization challenges the efficacy of the process (Neamtan 1989, 16; New Economy Development Group Inc. 1992, 20–1). Philosophical differences present barriers to understanding how the approach can be effective. Because both perspectives pay little attention to the development process itself, the question of why only some communities are able to deal with the effects of structural change, despite seemingly similar circumstances and resources, has not been addressed.

To date, the research emphasis has been on identifying the characteristics of the approach and providing classification schemes for CED activities and organizations, as seen in Table 2 (New Economy Development Group Inc. 1992, 11,18–21; Brodhead 1993, 4; APEC 1994, 11; Ketilson, Fulton et al. 1992, 29). However, these schemes provide no justification for claiming that a particular set of factors is essential to the process, although it is generally agreed that effectiveness is contingent upon using a bottom-up process involving participation by the community, local leadership, local entrepreneurship, autonomy in decision-making, and partnerships among community stakeholders. But the meaning of many of these factors has not been clearly defined; nor have their role and their contribution to development been determined. Rather, their merits tend to be argued on an individual basis. For example, Swack and Mason (1993, 2) are adamant that local control of economic resources is essential if people are to help themselves. Yet there is little evidence to demonstrate that resource control, in itself, will lead to development.

Table 2
Community Economic Development Classification Schemes

Characteristics of CED *Strategies (*APEC *1994, 8)*	*Desired Characteristics of* CED *Initiatives, Policy, and Organizations (Brodhead 1993, 4)*	*Key Success Factors (New Economy Development Group 1992, 11)*
Local participation and empowerment Local leadership Local entrepreneurship Individual and collective skill enhancement Harmonization of social and economic objectives Development of local institutional capacity to provide control over local resources and to achieve community management, evaluation, and control of the development process Questioning of the status quo	Responsiveness to marginalization Building of local capacity to plan, design, manage, and evaluate initiatives aimed at community revitalization Integration of economic, social, cultural, and environmental sectors of the community Medium- to long-term time horizon Community constituted by the disadvantaged Collective (rather than individual) benefit Partnerships between marginalized segments and the rest of the community Empowerment and self-reliance achieved by pursuing economic development	Psychological well-being Entrepreneurial talent and motivation Number and nature of community organizations Educational attainment Nature of skill base with respect to relevance to current and future economic practice Nature and accessibility of financial institutions

Formal planning as the means by which organizations and communities gain more control over their resources and socioeconomic future has been challenged on several grounds. Planning is an activity best suited to dealing with complexity (Kotter 1992, 103) rather than with change. In volatile situations characterizing communities in economic crisis, it is difficult to plan, as the future cannot be predicted. Furthermore, the foundation of planning is past experience – experience that for many communities is no longer relevant as a basis for future directions. As well, planning has a long-term orientation, while a community facing economic restructuring has the opposite. Finally, though public participation is invited and encouraged by local strategy groups, anecdotal evidence and political participation theory (Sharp and Bath 1993, 216; Verba and Nie 1972, 126) both suggest that it is related to social status: those with higher levels of income and education are more likely to participate. This tendency challenges the capacity of communities to involve those people in decision-making who stand to benefit directly from the process. How might they be included?

The organizational arrangements believed to facilitate resource control and empowerment also emphasize institutional partnerships. However, the issue of how these arrangements facilitate effectiveness has not been resolved. Indeed, organizations obtain the behaviour they reward (Kerr 1991, 126). The manner in which institutional policy and procedures encourage partnerships will significantly affect whether community resources are synergistically utilized in capitalizing on strategic development opportunities.

The role of informal arrangements in the process has largely been ignored. Their importance was pointed out by Stöhr (1990, 2) and Johannisson (1990, 84) in studying community-based development in Europe. Their research suggests that the informal sector plays a major role in the success of local initiatives. A significant proportion of leadership in mobilizing collective effort was found to come from the informal sector, where an individual's capacity for results was drawn from personal influence. According to Shapiro (1992, 363), the informal organization is instrumental in encouraging people to work together. With evidence indicating that many of the services provided by economic development organizations are underutilized (Curran, Jarvis et al. 1993, 16; Gibb 1988, 12), the question is whether facilitation of the process is the sole prerogative of the institutional sector. It raises the further issue of the role of the informal sector, especially in relation to the nature of local leadership required. Since collective action is assumed to be the essence of CED, and since people tend to do things through informal channels on the basis of trust in a rural development context, an understanding of this matter is essential.

A related matter is the role of network resources, and whether the effectiveness of the process depends upon the nature of local interaction and support networks. Local network resources have been found to positively influence the formation and development of small and medium-sized enterprises, which play a key role in generating sustainable local development.

Capacity-building also requires examination. While CED does incorporate entrepreneurship and innovation, their role is made indeterminable by a lack of definition and explanation. Indeed, these factors are sometimes implicitly understood to be ends, while at other times they are considered part of the process. For example, some (Economic Council of Canada 1990, 18; O'Neill 1993, 18) claim that development solutions attempt to foster an entrepreneurial culture, entrepreneurial activity, and entrepreneurial capacity; others (Ketilson, Fulton et al. 1992, 30; Lamontagne, APEC 1994, 8) describe entrepreneurship as a characteristic of Community Economic Development; still others make no mention of it (Brodhead 1993). Considering the importance afforded these factors by endogenous approaches, the relationship among entrepreneurship, innovation, and economic development must be clarified. This topic is examined later in this chapter.

It can be inferred that both perspectives have adopted a very narrow interpretation of innovation and entrepreneurship. Most measures to encourage entrepreneurship within regional development involve business service activities, such as providing technical or financial assistance. In representing the social development position, Fontan (1993, 16), describes entrepreneurship as one of four CED intervention activities and defines it as "any measures to assist in the strengthening and development of businesses in a community." Others – for example, Coffey and Polese (1985, 86) – in recommending policies for enhancing entrepreneurial capacities, take a broader interpretation, yet they focus on only one or two dimensions, for example, initiative and know-how. Moreover, while the success of local initiatives is said to depend on instilling "positive attitudes to technical and social innovations" (Blakely 1989, 280; Fontan 1993, 21), the means of achieving this end has not been addressed. Since attitudes are embedded in culture, the meaning of culture and its effect on action need to be clarified before attitudes can be influenced. Indeed, Matthews (1983, 154–5) points out that failure to consider the influence of a community's culture may have unforeseen deleterious consequences.

Culture consists of shared beliefs, values, norms, and attitudes[3] that manifest themselves in observable behaviour patterns. Anthropologist Clyde Kluckhohn (1961, 86) defines culture as "the set of habitual and traditional ways of thinking, feeling and reacting that are characteristic of the way a particular society meets its problems at a particular point in time." A community's culture, then, concurrently defines and reflects the values, beliefs, norms, and attitudes of its members through social interaction processes (Senge 1990). Culture regulates social systems (O'Reilly 1991, 176) as it dictates what is important and expected, which in turn influences behaviour.

In an economic crisis, a community experiences considerable uncertainty. In responding to crisis, Stöhr (1990, 2) and Johannisson (1990, 63) argue, entrepreneurship is the key human resource mobilized to provide the impetus for collective action. Garafoli (1992, 2–10) concludes that some rural communities characterized by an underdeveloped level of economic activity and a perceived absence of entrepreneurship and innovation have little opportunity for endogenous development. While a community's culture may not contain beliefs, values, and assumptions that support entrepreneurial behaviour, it is possible to change cultural components by first changing behaviour (Sathe 1989, 402). This possibility challenges Stöhr's (1990, 7) contention that the solution is to induce self-sustaining local initiatives in the absence of entrepreneurial capacity; rather, it is to stimulate entrepreneurial behaviour.

The desire of policymakers to use CED as a strategy for reducing the demands on social safety nets implies its adoption in communities experiencing economic hardship. The Economic Council of Canada recommends that the support of communities be determined on the basis of need and potential. However, the matter of potential is perplexing. On the one hand, the Council argues (1990, 3) that communities have the potential for improvement by virtue of the fact that they can mobilize underutilized resources to exploit unrealized business opportunities. On the other hand, it proposes (1990, 17) that potential be assessed on the basis of communities' development efforts. However, a lack of effort does not indicate a lack of potential; rather, it may point to a lack of the entrepreneurial skill(s) needed for an effective autonomous mobilization effort. The meaning of those inextricably linked but rarely defined terms, innovation and entrepreneurship, must be established in addressing their role in development (McMullan and Long 1990, 216; Fry 1993, 30–1).

THE ROLE OF INNOVATION AND ENTREPRENEURSHIP

The confusion surrounding the role of innovation and entrepreneurship in CED is exacerbated by a lack of clear definition of these terms. My purpose here is not to engage in a definitional debate but to provide definitions meaningful within a CED context.

Innovation

Kanter (1983, 20) defines innovation as a new idea applied to the introduction or improvement of a product, service, or process. When the idea is perceived as new by stakeholders, it is considered to be innovation, even though outsiders may view it differently (Zaltman, Duncan et al. 1973; Van de Ven 1986). Innovation is a relative concept, as it can result from small, incremental introductions or improvements or from large, discontinuous ones (Nadler and Tushman 1991, 20).

Ritsila (1999) likewise uses a broad interpretation of innovation, arguing that territorial innovation in lagging regions can encompass a range of factors: intersectoral job shifts, application of new technologies to existing forms of production, radical innovations, or new organizational forms. Considered in this way, innovation is not confined to technological advances. Since development involves changes that bring about improvement, a community capable of changing the relationships between socioeconomic elements and actors in order to improve well-being and increase self-reliance and sustainability has arguably created innovation.

Within a business context, groups and teams are integral to successful innovation, as are institutional innovations within the operating environment, which encompasses a social, economic, and political infrastructure (Van de Ven 1993, 214). Stata (1989, 70) argues that because innovation involves originality, learning is an inherent part of the process, which involves not only the use of new knowledge, tools, and/or methods for managing, but also the widespread sharing of new knowledge and insights to modify behaviour. Innovation is achieved by introducing new knowledge within small groups with the power and resources to make the changes necessary for improvements, and by instilling, through reinforcement, cultural values positively influencing innovation, such as a belief in teamwork.

In a community context, innovation will not be achieved by a single individual or entity; it will depend on the collective contributions of a range of stakeholders. Because a community is comprised of various groups with a stake in development, there is an opportunity to share new knowledge and tools in maximizing the available power and resources through collaboration. The multiplicity of ways of capitalizing on existing endogenous capabilities for innovation provides an opportunity to increase both efficiency – by reducing costs and duplication of effort – and effectiveness – by utilizing the collective resource base of stakeholders to satisfy need.

Entrepreneurship

Over time, entrepreneurship has become associated with business initiation or ownership. The term is often used interchangeably with "small business." Indeed, economists typically choose either to equate entrepreneurship with small business or to abstain from clarifying its meaning (Bannock and Peacock 1989, 70). While there are some who consider anyone who launches a new business an entrepreneur (Gartner 1985, 696–706; Low and MacMillan 1988) others have a more limited view, defining entrepreneurship, for example, as the "building of new growth ventures" (McMullan and Long 1990, 17). The fact that a new business is often small has undoubtedly led to the synonymous use of the two terms.

However, a distinction between small business ownership and entrepreneurship can be identified. Generally, "small business" has emerged

Table 3
Entrepreneurial Characteristics

According to Gibb (1987, 6)	*According to Hornaday (1982, 20–38)*	*According to Timmons, Smollen et al. (1985, 151)*
Initiative	Self-confidence	Commitment, determination, and perseverance
Persuasion	Perseverance	Drive to achieve and grow
Moderate risk-taking	Determination	Opportunity and goal orientation
Flexibility	Energy	Taking of initiative and personal responsibility
Creativity	Diligence	Persistence at problem-solving
Independence	Resourcefulness	Realism and sense of humour
Problem-solving ability	Calculated risk-taking	Seeking and use of feedback
Need for achievement	Need to achieve	Internal locus of control
Imagination	Creativity	Tolerance for ambiguity, stress, and uncertainty
Self-confidence	Initiative	Calculated risk-taking and risk-sharing
Leadership	Flexibility	Low need for status and power
Hard work	Positive response to challenges	Integrity and reliability
	Independence	Decisiveness, urgency, and patience
	Perceptiveness	Ability to deal with failure
	Dynamism	Team-building, hero-making
	Leadership	
	Positive attitude	
	Ability to get along with people	
	Responsiveness to suggestions and criticism	
	Profit orientation	
	Perceptiveness	

as a term describing an economic reality: number of employees, sales figures, size of investment, whether a business is owner-managed. Kao (1989, 6) defines a small business as an owner-managed firm with fewer than a hundred employees and sales of less than $2 million.

Because small businesses are usually independently owned and subject to competitive market forces, they often provide the opportunity and the incentive for employing psychological and other attributes that have come to be associated with entrepreneurship. Although the three lists in Table 3 share some common points, between them they indicate the wide-ranging scope of entrepreneurial characteristics, which encompass behavioural elements (e.g., hard work), personality traits (e.g., independence), and skills (e.g., problem-solving).

Many of the characteristics associated with successful entrepreneurs also characterize successful managers, public sector employees, and groups (Brockhaus 1987, 2; Sexton and Bowman-Upton 1991, 11). Therefore, how can it be appropriate to associate these characteristics exclusively with founding or owning a small business? Indeed, Vesper (1990, 12) questions whether the entrepreneurial characteristics differentiating founders from non-founders are a cause or an effect of venture formation. Entrepreneurial characteristics are not the exclusive domain of a subset of society, nor are they necessarily restricted to certain individuals (Stevenson and Gumpert 1992, 22; Gibb 1987, 11). Indeed, the fact that they have been found to be widely distributed in the population (Kyle, Blais et al. 1991, 13) indicates a potential for enterprise in every community (Cannon 1991, 23–4).

The academic focus – particularly within psychology – on identifying personal capabilities diverts attention away from the central issues of what entrepreneurs do and why they do it (Bygrave and Hofer 1991, 14; Sexton and Bowman-Upton 1991, 6). While personality may predispose individuals to entrepreneurial behaviour, Gartner (1989, 33) provides evidence to suggest that situational factors – including the nature of the task and the environment – often have more influence on behaviour than personality traits or other personal attributes. Gibb (1993, 14), for instance, identifies the following entrepreneurial behaviours: making things happen, seeking opportunity, solving problems/conflicts creatively, taking action in uncertain environments, coping with and enjoying uncertainty, responding flexibly to challenges, actively seeking to achieve goals, acting on one's own initiative, and persuading others.

The role of an entrepreneur involves recognizing an opportunity in the marketplace and accessing resources to exploit it for personal gain (Kao 1991, 14; Sexton and Bowman-Upton 1991, 7). Entrepreneurship, then, has an action orientation. In relation to innovation, it involves identifying and acting upon an opportunity by using collective personal capabilities to assemble the resources required to capitalize gainfully on that opportunity. Conceptualized in this way, entrepreneurship is the means by which an end – innovation – is achieved. The circumstances of restructuring require precisely the attributes of entrepreneurs: the ability to identify opportunities, operate with uncertainty, take risks, and innovate.

The entrepreneurial role has four essential requisites: an identified opportunity, ability, motivation, and a supportive environment (Vesper 1990, 334–41). Within the CED context, identifying an opportunity involves generating an idea for creating or modifying a community's resources to capitalize on changes taking place elsewhere, thereby making structural changes to improve the community's production system.

Entrepreneurial abilities include problem-solving, creativity, decision-making, taking action amidst uncertainty, negotiating, planning, and persuasiveness (Sexton and Bowman-Upton 1991, 16–17). While genetics does influence an individual's capabilities, most differences in ability stem from learning experiences and practice (Bandura 1986; Gibb 1993, 15). Assuming that all individuals have a certain level of entrepreneurial attributes and that enterprising behaviour can be stimulated, it can be inferred that each community contains some measure of entrepreneurial capacity which can be actuated or developed.

The economic structure of a community exerts a significant influence on ability, inasmuch as the economy provides a major source of opportunity for acquiring skills. Large enterprises engaged in routine manufacturing provide limited opportunity for developing entrepreneurial competencies. A need for learning or practice exists in communities with this type of economic base, with respect to both entrepreneurial skills and specific task requirements of the proposed innovation. Through the learning of new skills, new organizational methods, and new ways of responding to problems through collective action, behaviour can be modified. When the community begins to see new behaviour as a more appropriate way of dealing with problems, it becomes incorporated into the culture.

Having the requisite skills will not necessarily result in entrepreneurial behaviour: people need to be motivated to initiate action toward realizing an opportunity. Motivation underlies the propensity to persevere and is the force that energizes and gives direction to behaviour (Bartol and Martin 1991, 445). Entrepreneurial motivation is associated with a range of factors (Vesper 1990, 336–9), some of a "push" nature – unemployment, job discontent – others a "pull" – desire for independence, pursuit of an idea. In a community context, economic crisis may be the dominant motivating force.

Finally, the degree to which the environment supports entrepreneurship depends not only upon the nature and volume of the resources and infrastructure available, but also upon the nature of the community's culture and social structures. When the environment is uncertain, unstable, and non-routine, entrepreneurial behaviour has been shown to be effective in achieving objectives (Gordon 1991, 325–6). Vesper (1990, 16) and others (Stöhr 1990, 27; Kao 1991, 16; OECD 1993, 18–19) argue that environmental conditions have a significant effect on the *levels* of innovation and entrepreneurship exhibited.

The strength of the enterprise culture and the extent to which it is shared and internalized will affect the extent to which entrepreneurial behaviour is used in dealing with problems. Given the uncertainty, instability, and non-routine nature of the circumstances produced by economic restructuring in some communities, the absence of an enterprising culture suggests a need for learning entrepreneurial behaviour. Arguably, the development process is a key vehicle for doing so.

Conclusion

To underscore the integral role of entreprise in the development process, I now propose a distinct term. Community Enterprise Emergence is a social action process whereby stakeholders in a community improve economic well-being, self-sufficiency, and sustainability by exercising entrepreneurship in generating and mobilizing resources to respond to identified needs and expectations. Bringing together the arguments in the chapter, this definition reflects the following facts:

- Economic development is influenced by social factors.
- Entrepreneurship is needed to create the innovation required for development to occur.
- "Community" is a multidimensional concept.
- Community self-sufficiency in the face of economic adversity requires economic activity.
- A range of stakeholders have a role to play in defining and improving any current situation.
- Development by a community involves direct stakeholders.

Moreover, the use of a unique term highlights my proposing a different understanding of community-based development than that held in economics or the social development tradition. The community's interpretation of what constitutes well-being is central to this understanding, as it determines the desired development outcomes. When circumstances threaten the established way of life, the development process provides a powerful vehicle for pursuing personal need through joint association. Those affected will not only identify with each other more strongly but also be motivated to draw on existing social relationships to mount a response. These relationships represent a key resource to be mobilized.

For enterprise to emerge as the main strategy used by a community in pursuing its goals, development activities need to satisfy two requirements. First, they must provide opportunities for community members to develop entrepreneurial skills and other abilities; second, they must succeed in improving the economic well-being of participants. The result is an increase in both individual and community capacity, self-sufficiency, and sustainability (this last assumes that a community will not pursue activities detrimental to its long-term survival and growth). Clearly, if people find entrepreneurial behaviour effective in meeting their needs, through time it will be institutionalized in the community's culture.

Given the effectiveness of entrepreneurial behaviour at achieving objectives in an uncertain, unstable, and non-routine environment, as well as the role generally afforded innovation and entrepreneurship in endogenous development, we need to understand how they can be encouraged by the development process. But fostering entrepreneurship in communities lacking an enterprising culture is a daunting task. The challenge is to develop a framework for exploring the relationship of issues identified as important to Community Economic Development and their effect on entrepreneurship and economic development outcomes.

5 A Conceptual Framework for Fostering Entrepreneurship and Innovation

Analytical frameworks of the development process have been eschewed within the Community Economic Development literature, on the assumption that the uniqueness of communities and the situations they face render them inappropriate (New Economy Development Group Inc. 1992, 20). However, the fact that the same distinctiveness characterizes individuals, groups, and organizations has not precluded attempts at explanation of process and behaviour at these levels of analysis. Systematic analysis and interpretation of the development process is essential to understanding the key role of innovation and entrepreneurship.

ENTREPRENEURSHIP AND COMMUNITY ECONOMIC DEVELOPMENT: THE ANALYTIC FOCUS

There has been a proliferation of government policy and discussion papers in Canada dealing with the need for innovation, particularly in addressing local needs and opportunities effectively. Public consultation in the early 1990s reports that "Canadians share a goal of self-reliance, a respect for learning and the full development of each individual..." (Government of Canada 1992, 2). Although the gap between this vision and reality has been widening in many communities, it is assumed that communities are able and willing, and should influence development. This viewpoint is consistent with the resource dependence model's explanation of the relationship between communities and their environments (Ulrich and Barney 1984, 471–81), which argues that there is manœuvring room to respond to environmental change and that aspects of the environment can be influenced.

It is claimed that innovation has been the hallmark of initiatives in communities that have dealt effectively with economic restructuring. Entrepreneurship, the process by which innovation is achieved, represents the fulcrum for explaining innovation and embodies the key to influencing development. Yet the issue of how entrepreneurship is fostered within development activity has not been addressed.

Previous chapters have demonstrated the need to tie together a great deal of currently unrelated knowledge from the fields of entrepreneurship and economic development in order to provide a basis for research, analysis, and policy. The literature tends to adopt either a micro- or macro-level approach in explaining how innovation is created. For example, because innovation is frequently attributed to a specific person, much entrepreneurship research focuses on individual characteristics, behaviours, and roles (Cooper and Gascon 1992; Brockhaus and Horwitz 1986; McClelland 1961). This approach has been criticized for attributing an innovation – whether in a business or another organizational context – to a particular individual (Van de Ven 1993, 212) and for paying insufficient attention to process (Bygrave and Hofer 1991, 16).

The ecological perspective (population/ecology)[1] has been a major contributor of macro-level insights. However, it concludes that organizations have little control over their destiny (Betton and Dess 1985) because survival depends on the extent to which organizational characteristics fit environmental conditions. It fails to address the question of whether innovation results serendipitously or occurs through purposeful entrepreneurial action. The models in this perspective focus on explaining aggregate changes in demographic characteristics; they cannot explain how the entrepreneurial process evolves, since behaviour is not examined.

In considering national variations in economic development, scholars have sought to identify and explain the macro factors that make a nation more innovative, such as its economic, technological, or educational structure (Bennett and McCoshan 1993; Rostow 1991; Schumpeter 1934). However, neither societal influence nor the action of an individual has been shown to create or alter the conditions fostering innovation and entrepreneurship in a particular community (Stöhr 1990, 42–3). Consequently, a gap exists between the micro and macro levels of analysis, which has limited understanding of some communities' enhanced innovativeness.

In studying organizational innovations, various scholars (Van de Ven 1993, 212; Reich 1992, 55) bridge the analytical gap by challenging the prevailing notion that a specific individual is solely responsible for a particular innovation. A supportive cultural context, involving diverse stakeholders who may perform differing key entrepreneurial roles, is seen as having a significant influence. This context evolves over time, shaped by events and relationships affecting the distribution of available resources (Aldrich 1990, 7).

A meso-level focus is required for understanding the factors that make a community more entrepreneurial and innovative. This chapter argues that a variety of events, structures, and actors will, over time, create a set of behavioural expectations for dealing with problems and opportunities that determines the extent to which innovation and entrepreneurship characterize the approach to economic development.

THE CHALLENGE OF LINKING ENTREPRENEURSHIP AND ECONOMIC DEVELOPMENT

A multidisciplinary framework is important for understanding how entrepreneurship and innovation are encouraged. If the framework is based solely in economics, for example, it is likely to be unable to deal adequately with the reciprocal relationship between entrepreneurship and the development process, since economists tend to gloss over the workings of entrepreneurship. The economic models of endogenous development, productive restructuring, or spatial (territorial) development lack the comprehensiveness to explain the development process. They focus on either one aspect of the process or one form of development.

Other social science disciplines, including sociology, political science, anthropology, psychology, and geography, analyse local economic development and entrepreneurship from a variety of perspectives. However, perspectives within independent disciplinary traditions tend to reflect a particular aspect of either economic development or entrepreneurship. For example, political science analyses the role of interest groups, political power, and institutions in the development process. Sociology focuses on the analysis of environmental conditions and contingency factors influencing the formation and structure of relationships (Reynolds 1991, 67), largely ignoring process (Ring and Van de Ven 1994, 91) and outcomes. Psychology's exclusive emphasis on the traits and characteristics of the individual entrepreneur has a pervasive influence on the academic approach to entrepreneurship. But while the relative and situational influences on an individual's propensity to exercise entrepreneurship have been generally accepted, academic inquiry has ignored the collective dimension of the process (Van de Ven 1993, 212).

Altogether, then, while various contributions have been made to the understanding of local economic development and entrepreneurship, no single discipline provides a framework that considers all of the antecedent conditions, actors, tasks, structures, and outcomes involved in achieving innovation. In particular, the collective dimension of entrepreneurship must be explored if entrepreneurship at the community level is to be fully understood. Rooting the framework in any one social science inevitably means emphasizing certain aspects of the process at the expense of others. However, avoiding the effects of disciplinary allegiance without sacrificing academic integrity is no easy task.

The Potential of Organizational Assessment Models

A comprehensive model of community-based development needs to meet a number of criteria. First, it must be able to deal with boundary relations. Unless the model can clearly distinguish between a community and its environment, it can evaluate neither the process by which resources are used to respond to environmental circumstances nor the relationship between the process and its outcomes. Second, it needs a process focus, since one of the main issues still to be dealt with adequately is how the develoment process mobilizes people to take action in influencing development. Third, it must be able to conceptualize a community as a purposive system consisting of interrelated parts, so that the individual and collective actions and influence of various stakeholders can be identified and explained. Fourth, because mobilizing people is largely a behavioural issue, the model must be able to incorporate the various social and economic factors influencing behaviour and to link behaviour and effectiveness; the contribution of innovation and entrepreneurship to CED has to do with the effect of behaviour on effectiveness. Finally, because development has not been shown to result from the actions of a particular individual or organization, the model must be capable of dealing with behaviour and effectiveness at multiple levels.

Frameworks explaining complex patterns of behaviour holistically are scarce. However, one group in the management literature – organizational assessment models[2] (Lawler, Nadler et al. 1980, 121) – does have this capacity. Within this group, three perspectives dominate conceptualizations of effectiveness (Denison 1990, 36–8): goal models, strategic constituencies models, and natural systems models. Goal models assume that organizations are rational, goal-seeking behavioural systems. Effectiveness is defined and assessed according to the degree to which organizational goals are achieved. Constituency or stakeholder models attempt to deal inclusively with the range of stakeholder definitions of effectiveness. However, both goal and constituency models focus on outcomes without adequately dealing with the process of how they are achieved. Natural systems models define effectiveness in terms of system characteristics but offer no specific constructs or relationships that can easily be used or tested in practice. However, they do provide a valuable basis for developing more specific models of organizational functioning, since they incorporate a factor proven to be important in understanding organizational behaviour: the boundary relations within and between organizations.

Synthesizing these models makes it possible to address the major criticisms[3] and to conceptualize how communities can influence development. In so doing, effectiveness must be considered in terms of the achievement of goals seen as important by the major constituents, and the determinants of effectiveness must be considered in terms of how the elements of the organizational system influence members to engage in behaviour contributing to the desired outcomes.

The parallels between organizations and communities afford organizational assessment models considerable validity as a means of understanding behaviour and effectiveness in a community context. Like organizations, communities are complex and dynamic, consisting of interdependent parts that function in relation to one another within a broader environment. As well, communities are unlikely to have similar perceptions of what constitutes effectiveness, given the unique circumstances experienced by each. Moreover, evidence that communities purposively influence economic development suggests it is appropriate to consider them as goal-seeking behavioural systems. Defining effectiveness according to the goals desired by a community delimits the domain of effectiveness under consideration.

Each community's constituents may perceive the main task (goal) of economic development activities differently. For example, goals developed by government agencies might bear little resemblance to those developed by the community itself. However, if the mandate of these agencies is to assist communities indirectly with their development efforts, it would be appropriate to define effectiveness according to each community's goals. Indeed, proponents of goal models use the goals of the most important constituent to define and measure effectiveness. Assuming that the effectiveness of economic development is defined according to the community's goals, outcomes and their determinants must be conceptually linked for the relationship to be understood.

A systems perspective considers the extent to which individuals, groups, formal organizational arrangements, informal organizational arrangements, environmental factors, and the relationships among them affect goal achievement. It thereby offers a more holistic understanding of how outcomes (and therefore effectiveness) are achieved. As in the case of organizations, the primary concern is with explaining the task performance capabilities of a community – how well various components of a community are structured and how well they function to achieve goals – and the effect of the system on behaviour.

Because conceptualizations and emphases vary among organizational assessment models, it is necessary to choose among them. In choosing, we must consider a model's ability to clarify the phenomenon in question (Hausser 1980, 159), to make sound predictions, and ultimately to contribute to the improvement of organizations (Cameron and Whetten 1983, 5). Because the available literature on CED has not dealt with process, the aim here – as a first step – is to develop an exploratory rather than a predictive model. To deal with the complexity of the literature, I reviewed models[4] in light of their capacity to integrate the three organizational assessment perspectives and their appropriateness as a general organizing framework. I judged appropriateness according to a model's capacity to meet the five criteria discussed earlier in the chapter.

THE CONGRUENCE MODEL OF ORGANIZATIONAL ASSESSMENT

On the basis of this review, I have chosen Nadler and Tushman's (1980, 261–78; 1983, 112–24; 1991, 18–34) Congruence Model of Organizational Assessment as a framework for understanding the entrepreneurial process. Founded upon a systems perspective, it offers a holistic understanding of organizational behaviour, encompassing human, structural, environmental, technological, and other factors in conceptualizing organizational functioning (Gordon 1991, 23–4). The model views an organization as a system of process components, focusing on their interaction under conditions of relative balance and consistency. It asserts that a key determinant of organizational effectiveness is the degree of congruence or "fit" among these components: if they fit well the organization functions effectively; if not, problems will arise.

Not only does the Congruence Model meet the five criteria previously outlined; it is also one of the most widely used process models of effectiveness (Cameron and Whetten 1983, 7), with considerable utility as a diagnostic tool in organizations (Gordon 1991, 27–8). Indeed, it has both theoretical and practical applicability in dealing with effectiveness and the process by which it is achieved. The Congruence Model is therefore considered relevant for use in a community context.

While focusing on a *transformation process*, the model also considers the inputs with which a system has to work and the nature of the

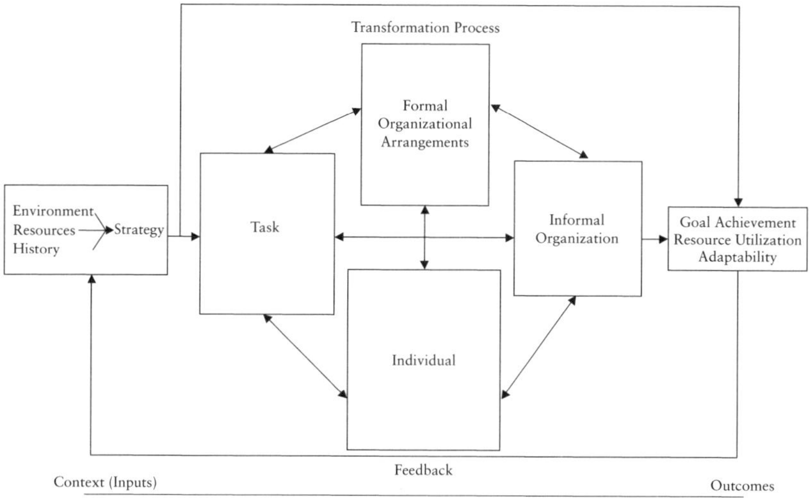

Figure 1
The Congruence Model
Source: Tushman and Nadler 1991, 24

system's outputs. It is therefore a comprehensive approach to both behaviour and effectiveness. Inputs include those factors which, at any point in time, are relatively fixed: the system's environment, the resources available to the system, its history, and organizational strategies. The transformation process consists of the interaction among the four main organizational components: task requirements, individuals, formal organizational arrangements, and informal organizational arrangements. Outputs include individual affect and behaviour, group behaviour, and total system functioning – in terms of goal achievement, resource utilization, and adaptation. Explicit feedback loops connecting outputs to inputs and the transformation process represent information about output(s) and the interaction of system components that can be used to make modifications leading to improvements.

According to the Congruence Model, in the short to medium term, effectiveness is assessed according to the degree of fit or congruence among the four process components and the extent to which the pattern of congruence matches the basic requirements of the strategy. When the strategy fits environmental conditions, congruence is associated with organizational effectiveness. When the variables fit poorly, problems occur, particularly with regard to motivation and performance. In setting out the relevant constructs and testable relationships to be included in describing and explaining effectiveness, then, the Congruence Model serves as a useful framework.

A PROPOSED ADAPTATION OF THE CONGRUENCE MODEL

While the concept of congruence is widely used in the management literature to explain how an organization can influence behaviour and performance, it has yet to be used in a community context. In this section, the Congruence Model is adapted to develop a holistic conceptual framework for economic development. The core premise is that the effectiveness of CED is a function of the extent to which the development process fosters enterprise.[5] The framework, the Community Enterprise Emergence Model, draws on the literature to specify the variables making up the major constructs: the configurations of task requirements, formal organizational arrangements, individuals, and informal organizational arrangements that foster enterprise. The model is a means of exploring how entrepreneurship and innovation are stimulated, and their effect on CED outcomes.

The Inputs to the Entrepreneurial Process

The process inputs (summarized in Table 4) fall into four main categories: the community's environment, the resources available to it, its history and core values, and its strategy for utilizing resources. At any point in time, these factors are relatively fixed. They essentially define the development context.

ENVIRONMENT

A community's general environment includes the economy, technology, political influences, sociocultural factors, and government policy, regulation, and programs, which together provide constraints and opportunities for economic activity. While important, these elements cannot be substantially influenced by the efforts of any community. For example, a single community cannot affect interest rates. However, a community can exert influence on its task environment, which includes any organizations or individuals with whom the community normally interacts and exchanges resources, such as government agencies, businesses, financial institutions, educational institutions, interest groups, non-profit organizations, and individual non-residents (for example, visitors and potential citizens).

For community functioning to be understood, the environmental factors relevant to a particular community need to be identified in terms of how they individually or interdependently create demands, constraints, or opportunities influencing action. The ability of a community to mobilize resources in response to these factors is affected

Table 4
Major Inputs to a Community's Behaviour System

Environment	*Resources*	*History and Core Values*	*Strategy*
GENERAL	Natural	Economic structure	Goals
Economy	Physical	Social structure	Objectives
Technology	Financial	Political structure	
Political influences	Technological	↓	
Sociocultural factors	Human (entrepreneurship, collective identity, skills, abilities, knowledge)	Culture	
Government policy, programs	Informational		
TASK	Educational		
Government agencies			
Businesses			
Financial institutions			
Educational institutions			
Non-profit organizations			
Interest groups			
Individuals			

Source: Adapted from Nadler and Tushman 1980, 270.

by the nature and scope of relationships established with task environment stakeholders (Johannisson 1990, 67). Consider a community that has lost its major employer as a result of a decline in a particular economic sector. In identifying growth industries that would be viable in the community, a former resident who retains close ties to the community through family connections may be persuaded to relocate his or her business there.

RESOURCES

A community's resources can be classified as external or intrinsic. External human, financial, technological, and physical resources can be accessed from various public, private, and voluntary sector agencies and organizations for use in development activities (MacNeil and Williams 1994, 8). The availability of these resources is affected by the nature of government policy and programs and the functioning of the product, service, and capital markets within the broader environment.

The internal resources of a community are either tangible or intangible. The former include natural resources, capital, infrastructure – transportation, social, technological, and institutional elements (services, information, education) – and human resources – entrepreneurship, collective identity, and technical and organizational knowledge, skills, and abilities (Latella 1992, 65). Intangible resources are the quality of life, as well as locational considerations (such as distance from core market areas), which influence the type of activities considered feasible (Garofoli 1992, 54; Pecqueur and Silva 1992, 25).

A rural community whose economy has been relatively stable and based on primary resources or routine manufacturing will generally possess less infrastructure and fewer human and financial resources than an economically vibrant community. The sole exception relates to social capital, the elements of social organization that encourage cooperation for mutual benefit (Putnam 1995). Social capital is known to flourish when individuals within a relatively closed social system interact with one another in multiple roles over a period of time (Coleman 1993; Flora, Sharp et al. 1997).

HISTORY AND CORE VALUES

A study of the effective use of available resources requires consideration of the community's history. The economic and sociocultural structures and events of the past significantly influence present and future action. The relationships resulting from participation in them shape the behavioural expectations of a community and define its culture.

Communities with a stable, undiversified economic base would be expected to have a strong culture[6] because of the duration and intensity of shared economic and social experiences (Schein 1991, 453). Social activities involve many people who also have economic relationships. While a sense of identification and interdependence can emerge on the basis of economic activity (Kerr and Slocum 1987, 103), it is likely that the strong informal relationships have been reciprocally influenced by both economic and social relationships. Economic, social, and personal networks represent perhaps the greatest resource to be mobilized in influencing development. As the density of these networks increases, so too does the likelihood of collaboration, which, in turn, increases a community's capacity for collective action (Aldrich and Zimmer 1986, 14).

However, if networks are to be effectively utilized in influencing entrepreneurship, the content of the existing culture must be considered. For example, an economic structure based on natural resources or routine manufacturing impedes entrepreneurial behaviour (Bennett and McCoshan 1993, 98–9; Anderson 1988, 5). If such a structure collapses, it will be important for development activity to tap into existing networks in providing opportunities to learn and practise entrepreneurship. As noted, entrepreneurial behavioural expectations will begin to be adopted into the community's culture once such behaviour proves effective in achieving desired outcomes.

STRATEGY

Strategy – a way of utilizing resources to achieve goals in dealing with environmental demands, problems, and opportunities – plays a key role in (re)balancing the relationship of a community with its environment.

The strategic decision-making context of a community differs from that of a business in several particulars. First, coordination and control are achieved informally rather than through formal policies and procedures. Communication is through networks rather than through a hierarchical chain of command. Participation is voluntary rather than contractual, underpinned by a strong sense of identity. Finally, cooperation is achieved through trust, norms of reciprocity, and the belief that by acting together, the community can accomplish what is not individually possible.

A strategic goal represents a broadly understood desired future end. The sharing of problems as a result of similar economic or social circumstances creates a powerful basis for establishing a common purpose or goal. The goal in some communities may be to ensure community survival; people may be willing to accept a reduced standard of living to achieve this end. In others the goal may be to moderate the rate of decline; in still others it may be to restore previous income and employment levels. A community may choose from a range of options in attempting to achieve its goal: making the existing productive system more efficient, diversifying the local economy through the production of new goods, or establishing an entirely new productive system. Whatever the choice, a strong commitment to place makes sustainability paramount to success.

Strategic decision-making involves identifying opportunities that are possible within the context of the community's environment, resources, and history and core values. The past and the future are linked thereby (Eccles and Nohria 1992, 102). Paradoxically, building a sustainable economy requires both stability and change; stability in core values facilitates cooperation and collective effort, while structural change and experimentation help create the specific and differentiated resources needed for achieving economic development.

Arguably, the formulation of strategy will be an iterative process subject to social and political influence. Strong ties provide an efficient way of accessing and processing information within the community. The envisioned options for action may initially be limited, since the ties that expand the available resource base are usually underdeveloped in stable rural communities. Over time, some actions will be considered more effective in achieving desired outcomes. When beneficial behaviour patterns are discovered, they tend to be repeated, communicated, and adopted by others (Astley and Van de Ven 1983). Thus, changes to the social system are enacted as prevailing norms evolve. If entrepreneurial behaviour is found to be effective in dealing with uncertainty and ambiguity, over time it will be incorporated into the culture as a behavioural expectation. The fostering of entrepreneurial behaviour by the development process is the focus of the next section.

The Enterprise Emergence Process

To determine the extent to which enterprise is fostered by the development process, we need to establish a set of subcomponents for each of the four variables in the Community Entreprise Emergence Model.

FOSTERING ENTREPRENEURSHIP: TASK REQUIREMENTS

Task component requirements (Table 5) have to do with the nature of the work (Lorsch 1992, 315; Nadler and Tushman 1991, 23) in which a community engages to stimulate economic development. The ends of individual development initiatives become the means by which the community's overall goal is accomplished. The tasks – that is, the specific activities – undertaken by the community to achieve its strategic goal involve several factors: uncertainty, novelty, interdependence, interaction, control, variety, skill, and knowledge requirements (McCaskey 1992, 248). These factors together contribute to a task's structure, which influences innovation (Huse and Cummings 1985) through its effect on entrepreneurial behaviour.

Innovation involves tasks that are more novel than routine, providing opportunities for learning (McMullan and Long 1990, 135). Although the degree of novelty varies, it entails uncertainty, since the outcomes are unpredictable. The task must therefore be broadly defined, providing considerable flexibility (Kanter 1992, 68) and freedom to experiment with a tolerance for failure (Nadler and Tushman 1991, 31). Engaging in new activity develops a capacity for dealing with uncertainty.

Because innovation requires a range of skills (McCaskey 1992, 248), it demands collective effort (Reich 1992, 54; Vesper 1990, 48). A task requiring diverse skills, knowledge, and ability encourages entrepreneurship by bringing a variety of perspectives and competencies to bear on problems or opportunities. The generation of creative new ideas is thus fostered by the collaboration, contribution, and commitment of a range of stakeholders (McCaskey 1992, 248; McMullan and Long 1990, 162).

Giving those participating in an initiative joint responsibility for setting objectives helps to ensure that the objectives are relevant and

Table 5
Task Requirements Likely to Foster Entrepreneurship and Innovation

Broad task definition
Uncertainty of the task
Short-term focus on attaining outcomes responding to community need (with a long-term strategic intent)
Flexibility
Freedom to experiment
Tolerance for failure
Diversity of skills, knowledge, and abilities
Interdependent control and ownership
Holistic set of tasks
Intrinsic rewards
Opportunities for learning by doing

instills a sense of interdependent ownership and control. People working toward shared objectives tend to encourage and facilitate each others' efforts to produce. Shared accountability for performance prompts people to think about problems, issues, and tasks holistically, objectively, and quantitatively instead of subjectively and politically (Stata 1989, 70). For example, collaboration among development agencies increases awareness of the possiblities that would be unattainable through individual effort. People are more committed to what they help to create (Beer 1992, 427); interdependent ownership and control might therefore foster entrepreneurship and contribute to effectiveness.

Indeed, collective activity provides numerous opportunities for learning and practising entrepreneurship. First of all, a capacity to cope with and even enjoy uncertainty can be cultivated through interdependence, as it can bridge the gap between dependence and independence. This may be particularly critical for participants who have had little exposure to uncertainty. Second, collective activity is an opportunity for vicariously learning how to behave entrepreneurially through observation of those who already do so and recognizing the positive consequences of their actions. Moreover, with joint responsibility and control, key task requirements can be flexibly distributed so that new competencies can be learned and existing ones enhanced. For example, in a certain situation one person may be the principal opportunity-seeker, while under other circumstances someone else might take this role.

Acting together in creative or problem-solving efforts aimed at tangible results within specific time frames brings about greater effort, achievement, and productivity than working alone (Kanter 1992, 68; Clark 1993, 4). The attainment of tangible results through entrepreneurial behaviour can alter a community's assumptions about how to deal effectively with uncertainty in a given situation. Adopting a short-term focus on achieving outcomes with a long-term strategic intent inherently involves continuous improvement and helps to ensure flexibility in any future action. Moreover, a common purpose for action increases participants' ability to function effectively (Gordon 1991, 520).

It is much easier to convince stakeholders to collaborate in a short-term than a sustained effort, particularly those among whom collaboration is difficult to achieve, such as development organizations (Huxham and Barr 1993, 1). By integrating planning and implementation (Walton 1992, 490), an action orientation helps to eliminate the risk of activity being stalled in the planning phase. The benefits of collaborative effort and the validity of approaching problems differently are more readily identified when results are achieved quickly (Beer 1992, 426; Clark 1993, 3). It is more likely that people will recognize and respond to changing conditions when time is short (Walton 1992, 490).

Short-term activity fosters high intrinsic rewards; participants are rewarded by a sense of accomplishment and pride in what they have done. Results that are perceived to be positive can provide the motivation required to counter the uncertainty associated with long-term effort; they can also represent tangible milestones on the route to achieving long-range goals. They thereby encourage further commitment, contributions, and collaboration, which will be needed in achieving the overall strategic goal.

FOSTERING ENTREPRENEURSHIP: FORMAL ORGANIZATIONAL ARRANGEMENTS

Formal organizational arrangements (Table 6) include the structures, systems, and procedures developed explicitly to get people to perform tasks consistent with a strategy (Nadler and Tushman 1991, 27). They define the way people work together and indicate the kind of behaviour considered appropriate for solving specific problems or capitalizing on specific opportunities (Eccles and Nohria 1992, 119–33).

Structures that encourage entrepreneurial behaviour are said to be organic: characterized by lateral (rather than vertical) communication; influence based on expertise and knowledge (rather than on authority of position); loosely defined responsibilities (rather than rigid job definitions); few rules, regulations, or controls; and an emphasis on exchanging information (rather than on giving directions) (Burns and Stalker 1961, 119–22; Sexton and Bowman-Upton 1991, 184). Imposing few constraints on behaviour, organic structures stimulate enterprise (McCaskey 1992, 248) by providing the flexibility needed to respond to community need. Flexibility creates manœuvring room for participating in the development process on the basis of what an individual

Table 6
Formal Organizational Arrangements Likely to Foster Entrepreneurship and Innovation

Formal linking mechanisms
Organic structure
Locally based decision-making authority and responsibility
Local democratic accountability

or organization has to offer rather than according to regulations, policies, and procedures (Gordon 1991, 529–30).

Locally based decision-making authority and responsibility provide process participants with considerable flexibility for action and instill a sense of ownership and control of initiatives. Responsibility for program development and delivery not only fosters entrepreneurial behaviour but also helps to ensure that the end justifies the means. In contrast, when organizations are responsible for delivering externally determined programs, considerable time and effort may be spent on rationalizing the demands and results of a program, creating a situation wherein the means justify the end. Moreover, when there is local democratic accountability, efforts may focus on pursuing opportunities aimed at meeting the community's overall strategic goal(s). Typically, the structure designed to accomplish this end would be a local board of directors.

Formal linking mechanisms such as joint or interlocking boards, ad hoc committees, and teams can foster entrepreneurship (Tushman and Nadler 1986) by coordinating interorganizational efforts through communication and problem-solving. As vehicles of communication these mechanisms create high levels of local knowledge and awareness and build relationships among organizations, thereby facilitating the collaboration or resource contributions needed (McMullan and Long 1990). They also serve as vehicles for generating ideas or building broad-based agreement about community goals, priorities, and time scales. The greater the extent to which coordination and control are based on shared goals, values, and tradition, the greater the effectiveness, thanks to the greater commitment of those involved (Walton 1992).

FOSTERING ENTREPRENEURSHIP: INDIVIDUALS

This variable in the Community Enterprise Emergence Model comprises the individuals involved in development activity (Table 7). Its primary characteristics are related to the differences among individuals relevant to entrepreneurial behaviour: skill levels, interests, need strength, learning styles, values and assumptions, and preferences for

Table 7
Individual Characteristics Likely to Foster Entrepreneurship and Innovation

Positive attitudes toward learning by doing
High level of collective community identity
Synergistic strategic vision for economies of action
High level of transferable skills and abilities
High level of formal and informal connections
High levels of trust and respect for competence
Preference for informal, free-ranging work style
Ability to manage interdependencies and deal with multiple tasks

variety, for definition and structure, and for individual challenge (Nadler and Tushman 1986, 273; McCaskey 1992, 247).

Although people want to improve their situation, individuals rarely possess the full range of capabilities needed to perform the entrepreneurial functions (Kilby 1971, 27–8) involved in producing innovation. In addition to certain technical skills, the capacity to innovate is influenced by the entrepreneurial attributes, competencies (McMullan and Long 1990, 309), connections, and resources (Vesper 1990, 118) of those involved.

The skills needed to broaden an individual's entrepreneurial capability – including problem-solving, applying creativity to problems, persuasiveness, negotiating, and decision-making – can be developed through socialization practices and opportunities for learning by doing. Since task performance is affected by differences in individuals, these must be considered in aiming to develop entrepreneurial behaviour.

People learn about and from each other's abilities (Reich 1992, 56): positive attitudes toward learning by doing encourage entrepreneurship. High levels of collective community identity are conducive to collaborative effort; people tend to be more aware of what is being done by others, what resources others have, how each person's competencies can be capitalized on, and how an individual can help others. This situation fosters a synergistic strategic vision (McMullan and Long 1990, 132; Sexton and Bowman-Upton 1991, 17) for economies of action, the ability to envision how available skills and resources can be used to achieve desired outcomes. People with a collective identity are more inclined to persuade others to make a commitment to activities, both directly through involvement and indirectly through a commitment of resources (McMullan and Long 1990, 163; Bartunek 1983, 17).

Persuading others of the advantages of making commitments requires a number of skills and abilities. For example, it takes considerable interpersonal skill and team-building to understand and anticipate other people's situations, motivations, and goals (Kanter 1992, 64). It often involves finding creative solutions in acquiring needed resources from those over whom one has no formal authority. It might also entail taking the initiative (Finley 1990, 25; Gibb 1993, 14) in persuading and negotiating with others to contribute resources. All of this suggests that diversity among participants can serve to increase the effectiveness of the process, as each person is likely to have a unique set of formal and informal connections that expands the range of external sources of information, expertise, and resources which can be drawn upon. People who are trusted and respected for their competence add powerful momentum to the development process (Nadler and Tushman 1991, 26).

If membership in volunteer or social organizations and activities enhances knowledge and skill (Honig 1998) individuals who are actively involved in such organizations would be more likely to have acquired entrepreneurial skills and abilities and managerial experience that could be transferred to economic development activities. Such involvement suggests a preference for an informal, free-ranging work style, associated with entrepreneurship (Sexton and Bowman-Upton 1991, 17). Experience in group activity, as well as shielding against excessive stress and uncertainty (McCaskey 1992, 241), develops the ability to manage interdependencies and deal with multiple tasks.

FOSTERING ENTREPRENEURSHIP: INFORMAL ORGANIZATIONAL ARRANGEMENTS

Informal organizational arrangements (Table 8) are the non-prescribed social structures and processes that define how things get done. Embodied in the culture, they are the shared assumptions and behavioural expectations that emerge from the interaction of the other three variables (McCaskey 1992, 257). While less is known about their significance for effectiveness than about the others' (Denison 1990, 3; Lorsch 1992, 329), research has begun to identify some factors associated with innovation and entrepreneurship.

The work of Putnam (1993) and others (Jacobs 1961; Coleman 1993) on the effect of social capital on economic outcomes draws attention to the features and instrumentality of social organization. Given the view that economic (and other social) behaviour is embedded in social structure, interactions are key to an understanding of the influence of social relations on economic behaviour. Implicit is the notion that each member of a community is expected to contribute to the group while also receiving benefits (Flora et al. 1997). When a community encounters an economic crisis that threatens its very existence, those affected are expected to contribute to solutions.

Table 8
Informal Organizational Arrangements Likely to Foster Entrepreneurship and Innovation

High value placed on supportiveness, trust, and cooperation
Strong collective identity
High level of involvement and participation
High degree of agreement on goals, objectives, time scales, and outcomes
High degree of overlapping formal and informal business and social relationships
Normative integration (shared entrepreneurial behavioural expectations)

The interaction among community members focuses attention on the dynamics of networks, structures that help to determine which persons are available for interaction, what resources are available for use, and whether these resources can be accessed (Wellman et al. 1991). In a community where small firms and entrepreneurs are in the minority, personal networks play an important role in leveraging social capital to encourage enterprise.

In addition, membership in voluntary organizations that successfully initiate diverse activities indicates that many of the norms facilitating innovation have been internalized. It further suggests a capacity for behavioural adaptiveness, a cultural characteristic shown to influence effectiveness (Denison 1990). For example, although an individual may not have opportunities to exercise entrepreneurship during the course of his or her employment, involvement in voluntary organizations may provide numerous opportunities for doing so, thereby supporting behavioural adaptiveness. Arguably, community members who have developed this quality will emerge as leaders of development initiatives and will use their personal networks to involve others.

Individuals in a stable community are more likely to interact with one another in multiple roles over a period of time than those in an unstable community. When formal and informal business and social relationships overlap, they are likely to produce a widespread and timely exchange of information and resources. Relationships structure resource allocation and join into networks (Wellman and Berkowitz 1991). The stronger the ties between people, the more likely they are to trust each other and develop a common value system that promotes economic cooperation in achieving collective outcomes that would not be considered possible through independent action (Curran and Blackburn 1994; Flora et al. 1997). When supportiveness, trust, and cooperation are the principles upon which participation in activities is based, they help instill a strong collective identity in which people perceive their actions to be mutually linked. Not only does participation create a sense of ownership and responsibility (Denison 1990, 7), it also fosters greater commitment.

The common frame of reference that emerges supports the development of agreement as to goals, objectives, time scales, and outcomes. Indeed, a sense of purpose and direction has not only been associated with entrepreneurship (Gibb 1993, 14); it has also been shown to increase effectiveness significantly (Denison 1990, 13).

When activities are non-routine and unpredictable, with few rules and procedures to guide action, informal structures and processes act as the primary means of defining appropriate attitudes and behaviour (Kerr and Slocum 1991, 437). If individuals find an activity satisfying and the values associated with it intrinsically rewarding and consistent with personal values, they will be more inclined to feel obligated to conform to the resultant behavioural expectations (O'Reilly 1991, 181). A few general, value-based principles to guide action enable individuals to "better react in a predictable way to an unpredictable environment" (Denison 1990, 9).

Normative integration – that is, shared behavioural expectations – is strongly associated with effectiveness (Denison 1990, 9). The norms encouraging innovation are quite consistent, irrespective of context (O'Reilly 1991, 178):

- Informal operation
- High expectation for individual and group performance
- Flexibility in decision-making and problem-solving
- Experimentation and learning
- Ownership of the task and commitment to seeing it through
- Tolerance of risk, failure, and mistakes, without fear of punishment
- Development and utilization of strong informal links within and outside the community
- Open communication
- Valuing of ideas
- Challenging the status quo

(Stata 1989, 70; McMullan and Long 1990, 175; Nadler and Tushman 1991, 30–2)

These norms define how things get done. As behavioural norms facilitating innovation are adopted, they can ultimately change the way people think about what is desirable, possible, and necessary (Zaleznik 1992, 89). In the absence of extensive formal organizational arrangements, the informal ways in which things get done significantly influence the extent to which entrepreneurial behaviour is fostered.

The Outputs of the Entrepreneurial Process

Outputs are the result of interactions among the variables, given the inputs. Dealing with the outputs of a community's development process involves addressing the issue of effectiveness. Effectiveness is a multidimensional construct that cannot be completely assessed in any single study. However, Cameron and Whetten (1983) argue that examining limited domains can greatly enhance an understanding of it.

A community's output is undeniably influenced by individual behaviour, particularly with regard to task performance. Indeed, certain individual-level outputs (affective reactions such as satisfaction, experienced quality of working life) may be desired outputs in and of themselves. Because the analytic focus here is on assessing the effectiveness of communities in fostering entrepreneurship, innovation, and economic development, effectiveness needs to be judged according to how well the system as a whole is functioning.

Three factors are important in evaluating the effectiveness of a community's short- to medium-term economic development: goal achievement, the extent to which the community's desired goals are achieved; resource utilization – in relation to goal achievement, the concern is whether resources are sustained or depleted – and adaptability, whether the community is able to accommodate itself to environmental conditions. The criteria used to assess goal achievement cannot be predetermined, since they need to be derived on the basis of the aims pursued by a particular community. Once determined, they serve as the standard for judging the extent to which goals are accomplished and provide one indicator of the effectiveness of the process. As regards resource utilization, the fact that resources have been maintained or increased would serve to indicate that the development process is sustainable. Arguably, if a community characterized by stability is suddenly confronted by an economic crisis and responds by initiating a development process that fosters entrepreneurship in meeting its economic and/or social goals and objectives, it would be considered to have increased its ability to adapt to the environment. Moreover, if the results achieved constitute an improvement, then, according to the definition provided earlier, the process has created innovation.

CONCLUSION

The Community Enterprise Emergence framework proposes a comprehensive understanding of the process by which economic development can be influenced. In addressing the effect of entrepreneurship on outcomes, it links economic development process and outcomes and deals with the issue of explaining effectiveness. To test the framework's capacity for addressing the links among entrepreneurship, innovation, and economic development, the next chapter sets out the methodology and research design I have adopted.

6 Methodology and Research Design

Any empirical inquiry is underpinned by assumptions about how most appropriately to study a particular phenomenon. Despite their differences, the two perspectives underlying Community Economic Development practice share the view that development is not a deterministic process. Both assume that a community has the greatest understanding of the problems it faces and therefore is in the best position to develop solutions making use of underutilized resources. Given this as the key premise, the meanings adopted by a community at any point in time are central to understanding the development process. Acquiring knowledge of the process requires an emphasis on the way people understand and interpret their social reality. This is one of the essentials of an interpretive research approach.[1]

Earlier it has been argued that a community's boundaries are most appropriately drawn on a life-world basis; that a community's definition of economic development and its aims will be influenced by circumstance; that the process and its effectiveness cannot be divorced from these understandings and aims; and that CED needs to be examined holistically. These considerations align the research with a qualitative approach, which carries certain methodological implications.

Qualitative research is firmly committed to contextualism – understanding events, behaviour, etc. in context – and holism – examining and developing an understanding of social entities such as communities as wholes (Bryman 1993, 64). Contextualism and holism engender a style of research in which the meanings that people ascribe to their own and others' behaviour need to be set in the context of the prevailing values, practices, multiple perceptions, and underlying structures (Miles and Huberman 1994, 10).

RESEARCH DESIGN

Research design involves three interdependent considerations: deciding which of the major research strategies – experiments, surveys, archival analysis, histories, case studies – is most appropriate; determining how to link the data to the initial questions of the study; and establishing the quality of the design.

Choosing a Research Strategy

The way research is conducted depends upon the nature of the research question; the extent of an investigator's control over actual behavioural events; and the degree to which current events, as opposed to historical ones, are the focus (Yin 1994, 4–10). Because the present research focuses on the question of "how," case studies,[2] histories, and experiments are all potentially relevant.

A case study "investigates a contemporary phenomenon within its real-life context, especially when the boundaries between phenomenon and context are not clearly evident" (Yin 1994, 13). It is the most appropriate strategy for studying how communities influence development. Experiments require behavioural control and exclude context, a factor important in understanding the development process. Histories are inappropriate, as they deal with situations where there is no access or control. Case study is the most flexible research strategy, since it can involve one or more cases and multiple data collection methods,[3] and can range along the descriptive to predictive continuum. Even more importantly, it has the greatest capacity for contextual and holistic investigation (Hakim 1994, 61–3).

A case study's research design consists of five components: the key question(s), the propositions/hypotheses, the unit(s) of analysis, the logic linking the data to the propositions/hypotheses, and the criteria for interpreting the findings (Yin 1994, 20). The conceptual framework established in the previous chapter addresses the question of how communities can influence development and leads to the following exploratory hypotheses:

- Community entrepreneurial effort is influenced by the extent to which the configurations of the task, the formal organizational arrangements, the individuals, and the informal organizational arrangements maximize the potential for entrepreneurial behaviour.

- An entrepreneurial configuration of any single one of the four variables in the Community Enterprise Emergence Model is not by itself sufficient for effective community entrepreneurial behaviour.
- The greater the congruence or fit among the four variables – when each also maximizes its entrepreneurial configuration – the greater the amount of effective community entrepreneurial behaviour.
- Effective community entrepreneurial behaviour manifests itself in terms of innovation; innovation, in turn, is reflected in stronger economic performance, greater influence of the community on the path of local economic development, closer fit between the strategies and local environmental conditions, higher levels of goal achievement, effective resource utilization (external and internal), and adaptability.

It is hypothesised that, in the short to medium term, an entrepreneurial pattern of congruence will be required for strategic effectiveness within the current environmental conditions.

Defining the community's development process as the main social unit of analysis necessitates addressing a number of related issues to establish the parameters of data collection and analysis: defining the community's boundaries, differentiating the process and its context, determining the participants in the process, and establishing the time boundaries marking the beginning and end of the case. These matters will be discussed in due course.

Linking Data to the Research Question

While the research question(s), hypotheses, and unit of analysis focus on what data are to be collected, the logic linking the data to the hypotheses and the criteria for interpreting the findings emphasizes what is to be done after data collection. These issues heighten the significance of theory development throughout the research process. The qualitative tradition typically develops theory during or after data collection. Yet this is not always the case (Woods 1986, 156–61; Miles and Huberman 1994, 4). Indeed, there is nothing to indicate that the adoption of a more closed and structured strategy is incompatible with a qualitative research approach, or that qualitative data collection techniques are not amenable to testing theory (Bryman 1993, 123).

Theory development facilitates data collection: with a theoretical framework to guide analysis, the inherent selectivity is made more explicit. Within case studies, theory provides a basis for achieving analytic generalization (Miles and Huberman 1994, 29). While statistical generalization aims to make inferences about a population on the basis of data (Yin 1994, 30), the logic underpinning analytic generalization is similar to that used in multiple experiments wherein the empirical results are compared to a previously developed theory. Therefore, the function of empirical research is to bring data to bear on the Community Enterprise Emergence framework. These data are derived from the lives of the people in the communities being studied. Unlike physical phenomena, however, people give meaning to themselves, to others, and to the social environments in which they live (Hughes 1993, 96).

SINGLE OR MULTIPLE CASE DESIGN?

While most studies of communities focus on one locale, according to Hakim (1994, 67) "the strongest designs involve the comparative study of two or more communities." For this reason, I chose a multiple case design. I also decided that two cases would provide an adequate basis for testing the proposed framework. Concentrating on two communities increases the likelihood that they could be matched on a large number of process inputs.

The fundamental logic underlying multiple case studies is either that similar results are expected (a literal replication), or that contrasting results are produced for predictable reasons (a theoretical replication [Yin 1994, 46; Hakim 1994, 64; Sudman 1976, 26]). In the present instance, the concern is with establishing whether the proposed model of enterprise emergence illuminates why communities with similar circumstances and resources realize different levels of economic development. In achieving theoretical replication, the results could be accepted for a much larger number of similar communities, even though further replications have not been performed.

We have seen that CED is not the result of actions taken by a single individual or organization; rather, it results from the collective contributions of a range of stakeholders. Because more than one unit of analysis is involved in each case, the design is referred to as an *embedded design* as opposed to a *holistic design*, which would explore only the global nature of the development process (Yin 1994, 41).

CASE SELECTION

Using theoretical sampling (Glaser and Strauss 1967; Hakim 1994, 141–2), I selected communities on the basis of expecting them to serve as strategic cases in testing the model's capacity to understand how the development process fosters entrepreneurship and economic development. Three main criteria were used to guide the sampling process. First, the communities had to have relatively similar inputs in terms of environment, resources, and history and core values. Second, each was required to have a different level of economic development (outcomes).

Third, the two communities had to have engaged in the development process for a similar period of time.

Prior knowledge is required in selecting cases that test theoretical frameworks in real-life settings (Hakim 1994, 64). I was able to capitalize on my access to the requisite knowledge by sampling within the province of Nova Scotia. Nova Scotia is especially apropos as a source of cases. Situated in Atlantic Canada, it is part of the most economically disadvantaged region in the country. Decades of intervention have been unable to remedy the persisting levels of economic disparity. With government and practitioners alike calling for an alternative development approach, there is much to be gained by learning more about what might constitute an effective community-based development process.

Since most CED research has been urban-based, studying community-based development in Nova Scotia provides an opportunity to gain insight into rural development experiences. Although there are wide fluctuations in economic well-being within the Atlantic region, the greatest development challenges lie in the rural areas. Most of the Nova Scotia communities with the worst economic problems have either a single industry or a natural resource-based economy.

The implications of an undiversified economic base were heightened in 1989, when the Canadian East Coast fishery experienced a crisis that eventually led to the closure of the groundfish industry. This situation had a direct negative effect on several Nova Scotia communities. Those communities with an economic base anchored in the groundfish industry saw the virtual collapse of their economy. The fact that several communities were experiencing a crisis induced by the same circumstances at the same time increased the likelihood of meeting the sampling criteria for testing the theoretical framework. Since I embarked on the research nearly six years after the effects of the crisis were first felt, sufficient time had elapsed for communities to respond to the circumstances by mobilizing a development effort.

To identify possible cases, I consulted a number of economic development policymakers, practitioners, and academics familiar with communities in Nova Scotia. As a result, Isle Madame was chosen for its effectiveness in responding to the negative effects of the fisheries crisis,[4] while the community of Canso was selected for being considerably less effective.

Determining the Relevant Population to Explore

In defining a community as a life-world area, social analysis is needed to determine the boundaries within which people perceive their circumstances to be shared. The primary method for establishing each community's boundaries was to conduct informal interviews with

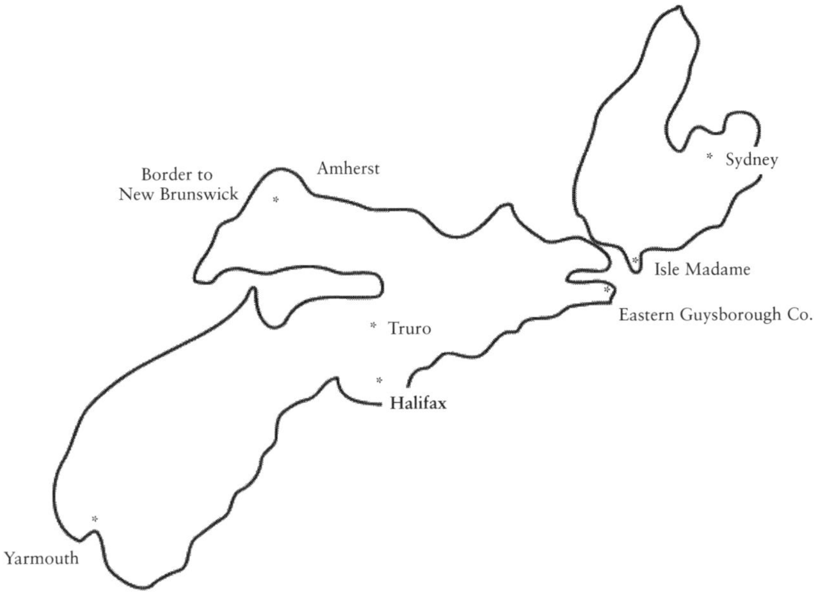

Figure 2
Map of Nova Scotia Indicating the Location of the Two Case Study Communities

various stakeholders regarding the scope of the geographic area affected by the fisheries crisis. Secondary data sources, largely consisting of reports and studies, were also examined. Moreover, it is a basic assumption that, in working together, in belonging to the same church or social groups, in using similar public and recreational services, people know each other. It is on the basis of these relationships that the development process is mobilized to pursue a common purpose in addressing shared circumstances. Accordingly, it was important also to investigate the geographic service area of various socioeconomic institutions and activities where relationships were developed. Each community's boundaries were therefore defined according to criteria of both a short- and long-term nature: the geographic impact of the fisheries crisis is a more recent occurrence, while the relationships developed through mutual participation in activities and services have a long-term foundation.

It was determined that Canso's life-world community extends in a triangle: Queensport to Port Felix to Canso (Figure 2). Here I refer to this community as Eastern Guysborough County. Within this area, people had developed relationships based in joint economic or other activities and services such as grocery shopping, health care, and recreation; outside the area, people were found to shop, work, etc. elsewhere.

Despite the existence of a natural geographic boundary, informal interviews were conducted within and beyond Isle Madame to determine whether all or only part of the island constitutes a life-world. While the investigation did confirm that the natural boundaries define the life-world community, it was not immediately apparent that the fishery crisis affected the whole island, as the fishery was concentrated largely in one of the island communities.

Answering the question of who the development process actors in each community were involved differentiating the process from its context. While some individuals were perceived to be instrumental in mobilizing initiatives in their communities, they invariably acted through organizations. Moreover, private enterprise did not play a leading role in addressing the adverse economic circumstances. For example, in the Business Development Centres servicing each community, loans to small businesses in both locales had actually declined over the preceding two years. A time series analysis of business directories and listings (based on postal code) corroborated this evidence, indicating few business start-ups over the two years prior to the study.

Because the study focused on community-based action, organizations were required to meet the following criteria to be considered process participants. First, they had to service the community, in whole or in part. Indeed, few organizations had service area boundaries corresponding to the community boundaries defined by the research. Second, it was important for an organization to have community representation. For example, while some organizations, such as government agencies, serviced the area and were therefore community stakeholders, any in which the community did not have a membership interest (typically meaning board membership) was not considered part of the community-based development process. Third, it was important for an organization's main mandate to be either economic development or redress of the negative socioeconomic circumstances created by the downturn in the fishery.

Preliminary informal interviews confirmed the assumption that both communities defined development in economic terms. Indeed, job creation was each community's main concern. At the time of the investigation, six organizations were active process participants in Eastern Guysborough County while seven were identified in Isle Madame. Finally, while the development process covered several years, I chose 1 January 1995 to mark the beginning of the study and 31 December 1995 for its end.

DATA COLLECTION TECHNIQUES

The multidimensional nature of the four process variables of the Community Enterprise Emergence Model requires a more structured data collection technique. Semi-structured interviews were chosen, so that interviewees could be encouraged to provide robust accounts of what they considered important or to reveal unanticipated information, while enough structure was preserved to furnish the data required.

One major weakness of interviews lies in their subjectivity. Indeed, there can be marked differences between what is said to have occurred and what actually occurred. Yet objective measures are not necessarily more reliable or valid than subjective measures. In many instances, subjective measures that ask respondents directly and in confidence what goes on within an organization yield more accurate data than objective measures obtained from records compiled by the organization being assessed. Given the limitations of various kinds of organizational records, their data can never be taken at face value; a detailed investigation of their accuracies and inaccuracies must be conducted (Van de Ven and Ferry 1980, 60).

While multiple sources of evidence can provide multiple measures of the same concept, the measures must be compatible.[5] The strategy adopted was to obtain differing perspectives in measuring the elements of process components, thereby bringing multiple sources of subjective evidence to bear on them and so reducing the effects of bias or poor recall.

Because it was decided to interview people from different positions in an organization, all non-support staff and selected board representatives were interviewed. Three interview schedules were required: for employees, for board members of organizations with employees, and for board members of organizations without employees. In addition, non-participant observation at board meetings provided insight into the group's dynamics and verified certain elements of the interview data.

Secondary data, including census data, reports, and documentary evidence, were used to measure objective characteristics of the communities in establishing the process context. They were collected in two phases. Several months before the field work was conducted, public domain studies, reports, and statistical data (primarily 1991 Canadian census data) were collected and analysed. This stage facilitated theoretical sampling and provided background knowledge of the development context. During the field work, additional secondary data, including relevant newspaper articles, agendas, minutes of meetings, and other written reports, were gathered. Where appropriate, secondary data sources were used to verify and augment interview data.

Design Quality

The quality of the research design hinges on its reliability and its construct, internal, and external validity.[6] These matters were dealt with by using multiple sources of evidence, creating a case study database, and maintaining a chain of evidence[7] (Yin 1994, 90–9). Construct validity is dealt with in the next section, in the discussion of the development of the interview questions, while the issue of reliablity is addressed later, in the section explaining the procedures followed in the case study.

CREATING THE INTERVIEWS

The interviews were designed to consider context and emphasize open questions, although they included both structured and semi-structured questions. Additional design objectives were achieving standardization, so that responses could be compared from one organization to another; providing an explicit and consistent frame of reference to guide individuals in interpreting and answering questions; and making sure that the questions were simple to understand.

Time Perspective

Covering an explicit period in a question provides more assurance of reliability than leaving the time frame implicit or unspecified (Van de Ven and Ferry 1989, 58). To discern a normal pattern of behaviour, an account needs to cover a period long enough to include a repetitive cycle of activities (which by definition is a normal pattern of behaviour). The time frames for measures vary with the specific process concepts examined, but most range between six and twelve months and focus on normal patterns of behaviour during the period. Although descriptions of historical events become increasingly unreliable over time thanks to loss of memory and the recency effect (i.e., the tendency to rationalize and distort accounts of past behaviour in light of subsequent events and conditions), a shorter period is inappropriate, given the nature of economic development activity.

Descriptive and Evaluative Measures

Measurements can range along a continuum from descriptive to evaluative. Process elements are defined[8] and measured primarily in descriptive terms, while results are measured both descriptively and evaluatively.

Descriptive measures focus on existing characteristics and behaviours. They are less affected by an individual's frame of reference because they are usually framed in terms of an external or observable standard or norm. For example, in measuring task flexibility, a person might be asked to describe the activities in which the organization is involved; the amount of flexibility is interpreted from these data. Evaluative measures ask for an opinion, for example, whether the individual feels the organization has enough flexibility in choosing the types of activities it undertakes. People are thereby required to invoke their individual standards, norms, or values in making an assessment, making the measure susceptible to different frames of reference (Van de Ven and Ferry 1980, 61–2). Keeping evaluative data to a minimum decreased problems with interpreting the data, since feelings and attitudes did not play a major role.

Individual and Collective Levels of Analysis

There is considerable debate regarding aggregation and disaggregation problems[9] when changing units of analysis. For concepts having a collective unit of analysis, this issue is resolved by indicating whether collective properties are intended to have parallel meaning with individual properties. For example, heterogeneity of skills applies only to the collective; it has no parallel meaning at the individual level.

The Role of Respondent versus Informant

Closely related to the collection of individual- and collective-level data are the roles performed by people from whom data are obtained. When an individual is asked to provide information strictly about his or her own behaviour and perceptions or about personal relations with other individuals or parts within the organization or community, he or she is acting as a respondent. On the other hand, when asked to provide information about the organization, the person acts as an informant by giving information that is global in nature, pertaining to the collective as a whole and having no meaning for any particular individual. While people occupying different organizational positions were interviewed to provide a more balanced perspective on the organization, the informants who were deemed most knowledgeable were relied upon when more objective concepts were being measured.

To avoid confusing people by asking them to alternate between the roles of respondent and informant while answering questions in the same conceptual index, questions pertaining to individual and organizational data were placed in separate sections of the interview. An introduction to each section clarified the specific types of data being requested, to indicate whether an individual was to act as a respondent or an informant.

Validity

The type of validity that must be considered in developing the measurement instruments is construct validity. Criticism of construct validity centres on two shortcomings: a failure to develop a sufficiently operational set of measures, and a propensity for basing data collection on subjective judgments. When the questions are designed to measure the framework's concepts, the data collected are directly linked to the research query. Using multiple sources of evidence also helps in gathering more accurate evidence.

DOCUMENTING THE RESEARCH PROCEDURES

During the preparatory phase of the case study, no contact was made with anyone from either community, to avoid any perception of being aligned with a specific individual or organization. Such perceptions develop easily in a small community, sparking speculation and/or innuendo regarding research sponsorship or intention. For this reason, any contact names that I obtained while collecting secondary data were filed for future use.

In scheduling the data collection activities, two and a half months were earmarked for getting acquainted with the communities, conducting the informal initial interviews, and making requests to attend board meetings. Three months were set aside for conducting the formal interviews.[10] Because of the distance and expense involved in travelling to the case study communities, I decided to arrange as many interviews as possible in two- to three-day intervals. I deliberately chose a five to six month time frame so that I could get to know residents and their perceptions better than I could by conducting an interviewing blitz. This decision is in keeping with the belief of qualitative researchers that considerable involvement is required for proper interpretation of a community's understanding (Bryman 1993, 61). In total, I made over thirty-five visits to the communities.

The final preparation for conducting the formal interviews was to do a pilot study in Pictou County, which was used to provide insight into issues identified as important and to pre-test the interviews. Prior to the pre-testing, I asked academic colleagues to review the interview schedules. On the basis of the information and insight so obtained, I refined the research design in preparation for formal interviewing. The refining process helped in making the study relevant and the questions capable of providing the data required to link to the theoretical issues.

The pilot interviews supplied information about field questions and the logistics of the field inquiry. For example, one logistical question concerned the number of interviews that could be conducted in a day. It was found that, because the length of the interviews varied, only two interviews per day could be scheduled. A related issue was whether some interviewees might obtain knowledge of the questions asked from others. However, there was no evidence of contamination.

It was anticipated that considerable lead time might be required for arranging to be an observer at board meetings. I therefore decided that the request would be made informally during the initial interview, and followed up by a formal request in writing that could be considered at the next scheduled board meeting.

Two recording techniques – note-taking and tape recording – were chosen for the investigation. Notes would be taken during preliminary interviews and board meetings, while formal interviews would be tape-recorded and subsequently transcribed in full. Although transcribing is a lengthy process, it gives the researcher great familiarity with the data. Taping ensures the complete and accurate recording of responses and encourages an informal, free-flowing conversational style in the interview, since it allows eye contact to be maintained. Indeed, note-taking can be very distracting to the interviewee. Freedom to concentrate on the content and process of the interview leads to more accurate follow-up on relevant questions.

DATA COLLECTION

Data collection involved two phases. I first undertook a preliminary investigation to gain first-hand knowledge of each community's development context and to establish the parameters of data collection and analysis. Although both formal interviewing and observation were used in the second phase, the analysis of the development process relies largely on formal interview data.

Preliminary Investigation

A series of interdependent activities was undertaken in gathering information from both secondary sources, which included census reports and documentary evidence, and primary sources, which included direct observation and interviews. One of the first tasks was collecting and reviewing existing studies, surveys, reports, maps, directories, and news accounts of relevant development activities which had taken place since the fisheries crisis began. I also gathered and analysed data from secondary sources such as census reports, for the contextual background they provided. These data related to such matters as population change and characteristics, level of education, economic base, employment, income, poverty and welfare, and natural resources.

Beginning on 27 October 1995, I made thirteen one- or two-day visits to the case study communities before embarking on the formal interviewing on 3 January 1996. Upon my initial arrival, I made systematic observations of each community and the nearby areas to gain insight into the nature and characteristics of its resources, noting their probable influence on community affairs, their use, the goods, and/or services provided by the community, and the nature of the community's focal points. Next, I identified and interviewed people to establish the geographic boundaries of each community; to determine each community's perception of its main problems, needs, and development priorities; to identify development activities and who was undertaking them; and to build rapport.

In Eastern Guysborough County, initial contact was made at Canso's town office, since observation indicated that it was a focal point of activity within the town. This proved to be a fruitful decision, leading to contacts with representatives of two development organizations, the CEO of one and the chair of the other. In Isle Madame, observation did not identify any focal point where contact could be initiated. I therefore decided to contact the local clergy, feeling that they would be well-informed about the community's development problems and any attempted solutions. On the basis of the information they supplied, I compiled a preliminary list of key development actors.

Where possible, first contact was made face to face. For example, I visited organizations with offices without an appointment and typically obtained introductions to several staff members. This approach was effective in establishing rapport, resulting in no interview refusals. I began each meeting by introducing myself, stating the purpose of my research – gaining a better understanding of the Community Economic Development process – and explaining how the communities were chosen. Individuals were *not* informed of the emphasis on entrepreneurship, to avoid the potential risk of bias during formal interviewing.

In determining each community's geographic boundaries, I asked every interviewee to describe the service area of various public and private institutions and activities. For example, individuals were asked where people came from to buy groceries, to use the hospital, to use recreational facilities such as the rink, and so on. In effect, they were asked to delimit the life-world community. People had no difficulty in reaching consensus on this matter.

Generally, the initial interviews were open-ended and couched in descriptive terms, with care being taken to avoid evaluative topics. Notes were kept to a minimum (largely key points and names and addresses of other contacts), in the interest of establishing rapport. Here are some examples of lead questions: How has the fisheries crisis affected the community? Whom has it affected? What do people see as the main development need? (Jobs were confirmed to be the main concern in both communities.) What development activities are currently being undertaken? Who are the people and organizations getting things done? What are some of the priorities for future development? I made a point of asking whom else I should talk to and whether there were any reports or documentation that might be of interest. By cross-referencing the recommendations, I identified the main development actors in each community fairly quickly.

I then compared the evidence from these informal interviews on the characteristics and dynamics of the community (including important historical events, community boundaries, component characteristics, and community resources) to the conclusions drawn from the studies and reports I had gathered earlier. At this stage, some organizations were excluded from the formal empirical investigation, since their activities were not deemed community-based. For example, College L'Acadie is located in Isle Madame, but its programs are centrally determined and administered.

The typical way of gaining access to board meetings was to have my written request forwarded to each board for consideration. While this process took upwards of three months, it enabled me to meet board members prior to making arrangements for formal interviews. In situations where informal face-to-face contact was not possible for an initial meeting, time pressures necessitated making the request to attend a board meeting by telephone. Under these circumstances, I received two refusals. Both organizations were totally volunteer, and because the board chairs did not work in an office there was no opportunity for me to drop in and introduce myself. When initial contact is made by telephone it is far easier for an individual to say No.

With this exception, I encountered no problems in obtaining interviews, establishing rapport, and collecting sufficient data. Indeed, once face-to-face contact was made, people were invariably very willing to cooperate, as indicated by the candidness of their responses, for example. The perceived practical benefit of the research is important. Indeed, at one board meeting I attended, a request from another researcher was denied on the grounds that it would place undue strain on available resources and provide no practical benefit to the organization.

On the basis of the informal interviews, I decided that the chair and one other board member would provide adequate board representation for the formal interviewing, since board members of organizations with employees are not the primary actors in the development process. In organizations without employees, two interviews were also deemed sufficient, because development activities were not pursued full-time.

Formal Interviewing

Once the formal interviewing was begun, the communities were studied in succession, beginning with Eastern Guysborough County. This approach was deemed to provide a more holistic understanding of the development process in each community and facilitated scheduling. These interviews were scheduled entirely on the basis of each interviewee's timetable and availability, which meant that rescheduling was often required. Scheduling a minimum of two interviews per day around any board meetings, which were invariably held at night, helped build in contingency for last-minute cancellations. However, near the end of the formal interviewing in each community, I needed to make single-interview trips in order to complete the data collection within the allocated period.

Having introduced the research during the first interview,[11] I preceded each second interview with an overview of the structure of the interview, explaining that it had two parts, the first asking questions about the organization and the second asking questions about the individual in relation to his or her job. I also assured each interviewee of the confidentiality of the responses, invited the individual to ask any questions about the research that he or she felt had not been clarified previously, and asked permission to tape-record the interview. Staff were generally interviewed before the board. On average, staff interviews took an hour-and-a-half, though they ranged anywhere from an hour to four hours, while board interviews averaged an hour in duration, with some lasting up to three hours.

Non-participant Observation

Non-participant observation was used mainly to gather evidence about board composition, dynamics, and functioning. As well as taking into consideration the two refusals, I decided not to attend any Business Development Centre board meetings, since they essentially focused on lending decisions, many of them involving loan requests from outside the communities being investigated.

DATA ANALYSIS AND INTERPRETATION

The analysis of evidence is one of the least developed and most challenging aspects of case study (Yin 1994, 102–3). It is therefore highly advisable to prepare for analysis by developing a general analytic strategy that sets priorities for what to analyse, and why. The preferred general strategy – and the one adopted in this research – is to follow the hypotheses that led to the case study. Using a technique known as "pattern matching," one analyses the evidence by relating information from each case study to the hypotheses. The logic of pattern matching involves comparing an empirically based pattern with a proposed pattern. The expectation here was that the patterns would contrast sufficiently to test the theoretical framework.[12]

Fundamentally, case study research requires a capacity for interpreting information as it is being collected and recognizing when sources of information contradict one another, calling for additional evidence (Yin 1994, 58). These functions were facilitated by transcribing during data collection. In addition to checking that accounts were plausible, I verified each individual's reliability and accuracy as a reporter by comparing his or her report with those of others. Given the open-ended nature of the interview questions, some responses were more in-depth than others. The range of perspectives obtained by conducting multiple interviews within each organization provided a rich source of evidence to use in developing an understanding of the development process. Indeed, the fact that in no instance was there conflicting evidence suggests that a high degree of accuracy was present in interviewee reporting. Making most of the questions descriptive rather than evaluative undoubtedly helped in this regard.

There is currently no precise way of setting the criteria for determining whether the findings indicate a match. I therefore developed decision rules for interpreting the data (see the appendix). In using multiple embedded case studies, the first step of analysis was to analyse the embedded unit within each case. Next the findings were interpreted at the single-case level. Finally, the patterns for each single case were compared in relation to their theoretical generalizability.

In adopting a qualitative approach, a major issue was how to deal with the research method's vulnerability to error and bias. One way of avoiding bias was to select communities where I had no prior dealings. Additionally, the interviewees confirmed my version of the findings. To help identify any potential bias in interpreting the connection between the data and the theoretical framework (Bryman 1993, 79), I asked academic colleagues to review the link between the instruments and the framework. A further test of investigator bias is the extent to which he or she is open to contrary findings. For example, while the framework proposed that community-based (horizontal) linking mechanisms would stimulate innovation and the synergistic use of local resources, I actually found little evidence that these mechanisms played this role in either community.

The analysis in the next chapter focuses on the most significant aspect of the case studies – namely, process – and illustrates how the interpretations systematically account for and tie together the evidence. While every effort has been made to minimize bias, interpretations are undoubtedly influenced by the researcher's philosophical stance.

7 Analysis and Results

This chapter presents the findings from the two case study communities. In it, I test the theoretical framework by exploring whether the case study evidence supports the proposition that a community's effectiveness in influencing economic development is dependent on the extent to which the process it adopts encourages entrepreneurship, even though its main purpose is to foster economic development. Underpinning this basic proposition is the idea that entrepreneurship takes place when the four key process variables are congruently configured to match those proposed earlier in this book.

Guided by the hypotheses that led to the case study, the investigation makes use of two types of analysis. A within-case analysis compares the pattern of process variables in each community to the pattern proposed to foster entrepreneurship. A cross-case analysis examines the framework's analytic generalization to determine whether the findings make sense beyond a specific case. I use mainly verbatim quotations from interviewees to present evidence of the extent to which a characteristic of a variable was matched.[1]

WITHIN-CASE ANALYSIS

Although my primary interest here is in process, process cannot be properly understood in isolation. The task environment, resources, and history and core values all shape the strategy a community adopts in its development efforts. Analysis of these inputs establishes the context for the development process undertaken. To test the hypotheses, the analysis focuses here on determining the extent to which each of the process variables has an entrepreneurial configuration. The emphasis on each component's configuration is fundamental to the capacity to judge the degree of congruence among the variables and, consequently, the extent to which the process fosters entrepreneurial behaviour and innovation and results in economic development. Examining the outcomes addresses the issue of effectiveness.

Eastern Guysborough County

In the following sections we shall examine the context, process, and outcomes achieved through community-based development in Eastern Guysborough County, and relate the findings to the earlier hypotheses.

THE COMMUNITY ENTERPRISE CONTEXT

Eastern Guysborough County, located on Nova Scotia's eastern shore, has been tied to the fishing industry since the early 1600s. The fishery has shaped a very distinct but stable life-world for its 3,500 residents. The people of Guysborough County are familiar with economic adversity. Over the past two decades the entire County has experienced an economic decline similar to that in other natural resource-based rural areas in industrialized nations. Yet the residents were ill-prepared for the announcement by National Sea Products that it would permanently close its plant in Canso on 2 April 1990 in response to dwindling groundfish stocks. The imminent loss of 1,500 jobs constituted a crisis threatening the community's very survival.

The inputs and the strategy adopted in dealing with this situation are summarized in Table 9. Compared to those of the province and the nation, the community's resources for responding were limited. For example, according to 1991 Canadian Census information, both the province and the country were experiencing population growth, while the population of Eastern Guysborough County had declined by 4.4 per cent from 1986 figures. Moreover, the unemployment rate hovered at 18.7 per cent; 13 and 10 per cent respectively were reported for the province and the country. With such unemployment rates and the fishery directly accounting for almost half the total employment in the area, few would deny that the closure of the fish plant constituted a crisis.

The nature of the area's industrial and occupational structure exacerbated the situation, making it unlikely that displaced workers would start new businesses. Very few residents had the occupational backgrounds associated with people likely to start a business when displaced. First of all, low-skilled processing jobs foster an orientation toward paid employment. Moreover, the residents largely lacked the

Table 9
Inputs to Eastern Guysborough County's Development Process

Inputs	
TASK ENVIRONMENT Single-industry natural resource-based economy facing imminent collapse Industrial structure concentrated in primary and manufacturing categories 18.7 per cent unemployment (10 per cent in Nova Scotia; 13 per cent in Canada) Declining rural population; no population centre over 1,500 Little infrastructure – no rail service, 100-series highways, fibre optic telephone network, or digital switching centre – limiting access to suppliers and markets Few support services traditionally available from government or financial or educational institutions	
RESOURCES Technology base lacking Technically skilled and professional labour force lacking Limited financial resources: Average income, $16,663 (80 per cent of Nova Scotia average; 70 per cent of Canadian average) 29 per cent of tax filers receiving transfer payment income 59 per cent of tax filers with income under $10,000 (33 per cent in Nova Scotia; 28 per cent in Canada) 5 per cent of tax filers with income greater than $30,000 (24 per cent in Nova Scotia; 29.5 per cent in Canada) Low education levels: 26 per cent with less than Grade 9 (13 per cent in Nova Scotia; 14 per cent in Canada) No post-secondary educational infrastructure Access to external resources constrained by limited prior dealings with government agencies, businesses, and financial and educational institutions outside the community High quality of life – 83 per cent own dwelling (71 per cent in Nova Scotia; 63 per cent in Canada)	STRATEGY GOAL: Job creation / maintenance APPROACHES: (1) Maintaining status quo (C) (2) Economic diversification through infrastructure development (O) (3) Diversification through recruitment of business (C)
HISTORY AND CORE VALUES Commitment to place: "Where we are the community is number one." "People ... they've been here forty years; they don't pack up and leave." Low expectations: "[People are] not used to having a lot. They tend to be happy with what they have." Perception of limited opportunities: "Other than that we've got rocks and water." "We have nothing here really." Other-directedness: "You have to bring industry in ... there's no other way." Cohesiveness, cooperation, determination, and honesty (observed)	

Adapted from Nadler and Tushman 1980, 267
Legend: C – Impetus for strategy community-based
O – Impetus for strategy provided by outside government interventionists

financial and educational resources required for establishing businesses: the average income was 80 per cent of the Nova Scotia average and 70 per cent of the Canadian average, while 26 per cent of the residents had less than a Grade 9 education, as compared to 13 per cent of Nova Scotians and 14 per cent of Canadians generally.

The strategy adopted by Eastern Guysborough County was shaped not only by its environment and resources but also by its history as manifested in its culture. The community has a very strong culture characterized by a keen commitment to place, cohesiveness and cooperation, determination, and honesty. However, buried among these essentially positive elements of culture are attributes that discourage entrepreneurial behaviour, including other-directedness, perceived lack of opportunity, and low self-esteem and self-awareness.

Eastern Guysborough County's strategy was *transitional*. While the main goal has been to maintain and/or create jobs, three distinct approaches were chosen in order to achieve it. Beginning in 1990, the community was focused on the economic challenges presented by the crisis in the groundfish industry. The initial approach, championed by the community's residents, was to preserve the status quo; it involved efforts to make sure the fish plant remained operational. Once the future of the fish plant was assured, externally based government interventionists attempted to stimulate economic diversification and expansion through locally managed planning and infrastructure activities. To reverse the plummeting employment rates and address the other consequences of the downturn in the fishery, several community-based organizations were established. The final – and current – approach, while also attempting to stimulate economic diversification, differs from the previous one inasmuch as the impetus for action has shifted from government to the community, and the activities involve more direct attempts to generate business development.

THE DEVELOPMENT PROCESS

Six community-based organizations were actively participating in the development process in Eastern Guysborough County at the end of the twelve-month period studied (December 1995). The summary profile of these organizations in Table 10 highlights the dynamic nature of participation. As the findings will confirm, a community-based development process is complex and involves the collective contributions of a range of stakeholders. With differing mandates and geographically defined interests to serve, not all of the organizations pursued initiatives within Eastern Guysborough with the same intensity of effort.

Table 10
Summary Profile of Eastern Guysborough County's Development Process Participants

	Geographic Service Area	*Mandate*	*Start-up Date*	*Services and Activities*	*Staff Complement*	*Operational Funding Source*	*Number of Board Members*	*Board Function*
Guysborough County BDC	Guysborough County > C	Stimulation of local employment and business development	1990*	Business counselling, loans, loan guarantees, equity investments (maximum assistance $75,000 for BDC; CDF funds $250,000)	2 full-time	ACOA	11	Overseeing operations; resource allocation; investment decisions
Guysborough County RDA	Guysborough County > C	Community economic development	1995*	Business counselling and technical activities; human resource development; advocacy and lobbying; information and research	2 full-time	ERA, ACOA, municipalities	9	Advisory; overseeing operations; resource allocation
CWADC	Canso Town < C	Economic diversification through tourism development	1992	Tourism-related infrastructure projects	1 part-time	CDF, ERA, CEIC, HRDC, Town	9	Advisory; overseeing operations; resource allocation
EGCDA	Eastern Guysborough County	Economic development	1995*	Attraction of small manufacturing ventures	1 full-time	ERA, HRDC	8	Advisory; operational; resource allocation

Table 10 (continued)

	Geographic Service Area	*Mandate*	*Start-up Date*	*Services and Activities*	*Staff Complement*	*Operational Funding Source*	*Number of Board Members*	*Board Function*
Canso and Area Resource Centre	Eastern Guysborough County	Information referral and support for individuals affected by fisheries crisis	1990	Contracted HRDC employment services; community group project proposal assistance	2 full-time	HRDC	6	Advisory; resource access and allocation
LDCDA	Little Dover < C	Economic and social development	1994	Initiation of projects related to employment, health, recreation, and heritage	–	Fund-raising	10	Operational and directional (including resource allocation)

Legend:
ACOA – Atlantic Canada Opportunities Agency
BDC – Business Development Centre
CDF – Community Development Fund
CEIC – Canada Employment and Immigration
CWADC – Canso Waterfront and Area Development Corporation
EGCDA – Eastern Guysborough County Development Association
ERA – Economic Renewal Agency
HRDC – Human Resources Development Canada
LDCDA – Little Dover Community Development Association
RDA – Regional Development Authority

* Incorporation reflects the reorganization of a previously constituted organization.
> C indicates that the geographic service area is greater than the life-world; < C indicates that it is smaller than the life-world.

Tasks
This first of the four variables was not found to have a configuration closely matching the one proposed as fostering enterprise. The findings indicate that the task structure of development activities in Eastern Guysborough County lacked sufficient levels of interdependence, interaction, control, variety, and skill requirements to stimulate significant levels of entrepreneurial behaviour. The results of this analysis are presented in Table 11.

Using the Economic Council of Canada's typology,[2] the development task was judged to be quite narrowly defined, as the majority of activities undertaken in Eastern Guysborough County since the fisheries crisis have been supply-side initiatives. Indeed, when the plant closure was announced in December 1989, *all* activities were centred on attempts to employ the idle human and physical resources. As Table 10 indicated, activities focused on expanding the local resource base by either generating new infrastructure or increasing the supply of capital available to the community. The infrastructure schemes have invariably been tourism-related capital projects.

Initiatives improving the economic productivity of resources in order to increase the community's ability to compete in external markets have been minimal. Perhaps the biggest increase in productivity has been realized from the volunteer services provided by the residents to the various community-based organizations. For example, the Community Development Fund[3] estimated that its board alone averaged 384 volunteer hours per year (GCCDF 4th Annual Submission 1994). For the most part, demand-side activities have focused predominantly on efforts to mobilize the community to act, and have generally been of a planning nature.

Despite its narrow definition, the development task was characterized by a high level of uncertainty, because standardized methods were not used in addressing problems or evaluating results, and the outcomes of efforts were unpredictable. One element of structure deviating markedly from that proposed in the framework had to do with the duration of the focus. Rather than looking to the short term – on getting outcomes from action that responded to perceived community need (with a long-term strategic intent) – the vast majority of activities pursued in Eastern Guysborough County either had a long-term focus (e.g., tourism infrastructure projects) or were developed to influence economic development indirectly (e.g., those providing information or financial services). There is little evidence that, until 1995, the initiatives were formulated to respond directly to the community's understanding of the problem(s), sense of urgency, and desired outcomes. Indeed, none attempted to create employment within a relatively short period (less than one year).

Table 11
Analysis of Tasks

	CWADC*	EGCDA*	*Canso and Area Resource Centre**	*Little Dover Community Development Association**	*Guysborough County* RDA	*Guysborough County* BDC
Task definition	Waterfront infrastructure development	Job creation through the recruitment of businesses (emphasis on manufacturing)	Information and referral centre on support available for East Guysborough County residents	Community improvement: "We work on whatever the community wants us to do."	Facilitating economic development in Guysborough County	Creating jobs by providing financial and technical assistance
Task uncertainty or novelty	High	High	High	High	High: Inherently high as organization formed in current year	High
Time and goal focus	Focus on long-term infrastructure development ("Our role is to attract tourists … to create some more jobs. It's not going to create a big pile of jobs directly but in a couple of years …"); local accountability	Focus on short-term sustainable job creation with a long-term strategic intend ("We set our goals in the first year to create at least twenty jobs. We put measurements in. Our long-term goal is definitely to make us a sounder economy."); local accountability	Short-term time orientation, indirect goal orientation: operational funding conditional upon exclusive delivery of HRD services; involuntary movement away from the organizationally defined focus ("To help anyone that walks through the door, whatever their problems"); mixed accountability – both external (HRD) and local (board)	Long-term focus emphasizing infrastructure development ("To lessen the dependence on the fishery by providing work for as many people as we can … to somehow provide the infrastructure to allow the community to grow."); perceived community accountability	Long-term focus oriented to providing the infrastructure to encourage economic development; helping to expedite individual and community projects (e.g., convincing Mobil Oil to locate in County); accountability perceived to be shared between residents and funding partners; strategic focus for all activities; primary accountability externally based (funding partners)	Short-term orientation toward providing financial infrastructure ("providing technical and financial assistance"); perception of being accountable to both residents and the federal government (funding source)

Table 11 (continued)

	CWADC*	EGCDA*	*Canso and Area Resource Centre**	*Little Dover Community Development Association**	*Guysborough County* RDA	*Guysborough County* BDC
Flexibility	Low: No change in projects pursued since inception	High: Freedom to respond to development opportunities, which fall under a broadly defined need-directed mandate	Low: Programs, services, and activities externally determined	High: No external influence on programs, services, and activities	Medium: Activities not subject to outside influence; however, organization's mandate precluded day-to-day involvement in projects.	Low: Externally determined initiatives (but some flexibility added in acquiring remaining CDF)
Freedom to experiment	Low: Present but not exercised	High	Low	High	Moderately high: Evidence of considerable experimentation	Low
Tolerance for failure	High: "So, there's been disappointment, but nothing to get discouraged about."	N/A: Organization hasn't completed the initial operating period.	Largely unknown: No formal evaluation conducted: "The only way we evaluate our activities and how … they are working is just [to] ask the people and everything seems to be great."	Largely unknown: No formal performance criteria or standards: "The only way we evaluate ourselves right now – by what others say about us."	N/A: Organization hasn't completed the initial operating period.	High: Organization has demonstrated a willingness to take risks in fulfilling its mandate.

Table 11 (continued)

	*CWADC**	*EGCDA**	*Canso and Area Resource Centre**	*Little Dover Community Development Association**	*Guysborough County RDA*	*Guysborough County BDC*
Diversity of skills, knowledge, and abilities required	Low: Operations handled by one individual; project participants have homogeneous skills.	N/A: One employee	Moderate: A large percentage of the skills, knowledge, and abilities required by the tasks for the two positions are quite similar.	High: Making projects operational requires contributions from board members with differing backgrounds and skills; projects themselves have not required diverse skills, knowledge, and ability.	High: Staff members' unique educational, skills, and experience backgrounds are required in carrying out the range of organizational tasks.	Moderate: Both full-time positions require fairly similar skills and abilities, although they have been acquired by different means.
Interdependent control and ownership among community-based organizations	N/A: No strategically focused collaborative initiatives with other community-based organizations	N/A: Majority of informants reported initiatives to be independently pursued.	Low: While there is one perceived joint initiative, it is not strategically focused: "We share a staff person."	N/A: No reported joint initiatives	High: "We [staff] would look at a particular project … then it's taken to the board."	Moderate: Decisions to provide joint financing with other organizations are made independently by the BDC.

Table 11 (continued)

	CWADC*	EGCDA*	*Canso and Area Resource Centre**	*Little Dover Community Development Association**	*Guysborough County* RDA	*Guysborough County* BDC
Holistic set of tasks	High: Waterfront development seen as "a piece of the [economic development] pie."	High: Activities are focused on directly addressing community need.	Low: Increasing external influence creating perception that activities are becoming disjointed and less meaningful.	High: Organization has both authority and responsibility for design and delivery of activities.	High: Organizational activities pursued with regard to achieving goals of strategic plan.	Moderate: While activities contribute indirectly to job creation, they are considered complementary and necessary to the functions of other organizations.
Intrinsic rewards	High: Sole employee and board members find work intrinsically rewarding.	Mixed: Sole employee reported extrinsic rewards; board members found work intrinsically rewarding.	High: Both employees report high levels of intrinsic rewards ("It gives you the opportunity to help people."); board members not highly involved.	High: No permament full-time employees, but board finds work extremely satisfying.	High: "There's a lot of self-gratification … personal satisfaction."	High: Both employees report high levels of intrinsic rewards ("to deal with a client that has his goals achieved is the ultimate reward"); board has virtually no operational involvement.
Opportunities for learning by doing	Low: Employee reported having dealt with similar issues before.	High: "It's been a learning experience."	High: "Yes! Many."	N/A: Didn't ask board members.	High: "The more you talk to people, the more you learn."	High: "Where do I begin?" "Lots! Every day I learn something new."

* Organizations whose activities are focused on Eastern Guysborough County

The nature of the task focus had two main influences: government funding criteria and outside interventionists. Government programs typically target specific sectors; in order to qualify for funding, initiatives must meet certain criteria. Most organizations in Eastern Guysborough County pursued activities that either qualified for government funding or were "off-the-shelf" externally developed program/service options of federal or provincial government programs. Government funding availability, rather than need, determined the nature of initiatives being pursued: "Everyone's pretty well the same – trying to get money from where you can get it. This hasn't changed too much." "What we're doing is trying to get as many grants as we can and give people the little bit of work each year that we can get them." "We're similar to them [other community-based development organizations] in a way because they're out there to get grants to work on."

The provincial government's strategy targeting tourism development is a case in point. Tourism is an extremely seasonal industry, with full capacity achieved only in the months of July and August, though in recent years there has been some success in establishing a "shoulder season" in June and September. It is difficult to reconcile the prominence afforded tourism in Eastern Guysborough County when its potential to provide displaced workers with a substitute means of financial self-reliance is so limited. Most tourism ventures require a substantial financial investment and offer a minimal return. For example, two bed-and-breakfasts were established in the community after the fisheries crisis. According to the proprietors, neither generates enough income to enable them to be financially self-reliant, now or in the future. Indeed, the input analysis clearly indicates that the community has very little money to invest.

While tourism development may be an appropriate economic development strategy for the province, few residents of Eastern Guysborough County considered the pursuit of such initiatives the most appropriate response to the negative economic circumstances: "The way I look upon tourism … it's a band-aid. Tourism's good for now because it's something to build upon." "It's going to have to be something that's part of the life of the community on a day-to-day basis as opposed to something that you create for a visiting tourist. A home for the aged or a retirement community where people come here and live and stay here as opposed to a trail where three people in July will come and stroll. It has to be something that enlarges and enriches the community." Indeed, concentration on initiatives endorsed and financially supported by government programs suggests that the means was justifying the end.

Responsibility for determining what would be done to stimulate economic development was assumed primarily by outside interventionists.

For example, in 1990 the government established the Community Development Fund to stimulate business development. There was no evidence of community consultation. Not only were the main terms and conditions of eligibility unilaterally determined elsewhere; the initiative was not sensitive to the community's inputs: "How it was to be spent was dictated to us because it was a fund of last resort – there was no input. We have some fairly competent people in the area. It's not that we lack in human resources." "We've had other federal programs that have come in place which have had very little consultation with the local level of government."

The implication is that the government assumed a lack of capital to be one of the major stumbling blocks to economic development. Despite the financial resources at the disposal of the community, there was little evidence of their effect. The general opinion is that very little has been accomplished in addressing the community's problems, despite considerable monetary investment from government sources: "It appears that there's been lots of opportunity but very little has worked." "Some people have got money through grants ... to improve their businesses but there's been no new businesses other than ... when this six million come in there was a few started up. Some failed and some – one or two of them – are still going." "There is a certain amount of criticism from the general public."

Because the tasks were narrowly defined and externally determined, they provided little flexibility and freedom to experiment in responding to local circumstances. For example, the Community Futures Committee, a government initiative, stipulated that it could not deviate from its planning mandate. "We didn't have a budget to do projects so all we could do was commission studies ... so, you can do studies until the cows come home ... but until the governments decide they'll allow you to do anything, you can't." These constraints meant that the community did not exercise control over what was done to address its own problems: "If we could create jobs we'd do it." With so little freedom to experiment, it was difficult to determine the amount of tolerance for failure.

The majority of operational tasks were completed through individual effort and required fairly homogenous skills, knowledge, and ability. Indeed, most organizational initiatives fell into one of two categories: professional services requiring administrative or technical business skills and background, or project-based infrastructure development requiring unskilled labour. The one exception occurred when responsibility for operating activities was assumed by volunteers. In this case, the operating tasks required the collective skills of all board members. However, once employees assumed responsibility for day-to-day activities, board members served only in an advisory capacity.

There was a marked absence of interdependent control and ownership of tasks in the range of activities pursued in the community. Generally, organizations saw themselves as acting independently of other community-based organizations. However, a surprising result was the high degree of perceived external interdependence within the majority of organizations. Three of the five in existence prior to 1992 indicated that ultimate control belonged to the federal government, since it was perceived as dictating what was to be done. Informants in all organizations but one reported a gradual increase after 1992 in the decision-making control afforded the community. But despite the devolution of government control, the interdependence between externally based government organizations and community-based economic development organizations – known as vertical interdependence – has remained significant.

As the primary source of financing, government encourages community-based organizations to adopt a more external focus in stimulating development. By taking a non-operational role, government has allocated sole responsibility for the outcome of each initiative to the relevant community-based organization. In consequence, most activities were reported to engender considerable ownership of the tasks. This may explain why a particular activity might be considered an independent venture by some members of an organization and a joint venture by others.

The fact that organizations invariably saw activities through from beginning to end not only made them highly meaningful for both the organization's staff and the board but also created a holistic task structure. Within-community activities were perceived to complement, rather than conflict with, one another. But while little attempt was made to use community-based resources synergistically to achieve strategically oriented outcomes, there was considerable collaboration in their use to achieve administratively oriented outcomes. For example, several organizations shared office space.

Although most of the tasks undertaken by the community-based organizations were structured to require independent individual effort, they did provide those involved – largely staff – with high levels of intrinsic rewards and many opportunities for learning by doing. However, because most of the activities did not require interdependence or diversity of skill, knowledge, and ability, there was limited opportunity for broad-based involvement in day-to-day activity that would expand individual scope of action through the learning of new perspectives, skills, attitudes, and behaviours through collective task performance.

The deviations from the proposed task configuration in Eastern Guysborough County were significant. As a consequence of the task structure adopted, residents obtained few opportunities to learn or practise entrepreneurial behaviour. While quite high levels of uncertainty were inherent in all activities because of their novelty – "Things are not always what you'd like. It's difficult because you don't know if what you're going to do is going to work out or not." – task performance generally involved the individual efforts of a limited number of staff.

When tasks did require collective contributions, participants exercised considerable entrepreneurship in seeing them through to fruition, as in the case of projects pursued by the Little Dover and East Guysborough groups. In both organizations, projects required the active involvement of members. The implication is that in a community where the economic structure has not been instrumental in fostering entrepreneurship in the past, undertaking tasks requiring interdependent contributions of diverse skills, knowledge, and ability could provide opportunities for learning how to use entrepreneurial behaviour in dealing with problems and opportunities.

Formal Organizational Arrangements

An entrepreneurial configuration was also not found among the formal organizational arrangements. Table 12 shows that few formal linking mechanisms for either information-sharing or joint problem-solving were established among the community-based organizations. Interlocking board membership was the most prevalent inter-organizational structure, used by three of the organizations. Officially, this structure is adopted for information-sharing purposes in building awareness of inter-organizational activities. In practice, however, the amount of information-sharing that occurs is often restricted by the confidential nature of board proceedings: "I can't bring that back and report to this group because of the oath of confidentiality I had to take."

Although formal linking mechanisms did not play a major role in furthering information-sharing or joint problem-solving, the sharing of premises was identified as a formal structural arrangement instrumental in encouraging the informal exchange of information. The majority of organizations had either current or past experience with sharing space. For example, the Eastern Guysborough County Development Association (EGCDA) and the Waterfront Development Corporation are both located in the town office, while the Business Development Centre (BDC) and the Regional Development Authority (RDA) share quarters in Guysborough.

Sharing premises can play a key role in shaping positive relationships. "We're doing some accounting and financial management services for them." "I mean the town is good to us – they provide us

Table 12
Analysis of Formal Organizational Arrangements

	CWADC*	EGCDA*	*Canso and Area Resource Centre**	*Little Dover Community Development Association**	*Guysborough County* RDA	*Guysborough County* BDC
Formal linking mechanisms	Absent: "There's no formal structure."	Minimal: Interlocking board	Minimal: Ad hoc committees	Absent	High: Regular meetings with organizations sharing space; ad hoc meetings with others; interlocking board membership	High: Regular meetings with organizations sharing space; interlocking board membership
Type of structure	Organic	Organic	Organic	Organic	Organic	Organic
Authority and responsibility for program development and delivery	Moderate local authority, complete responsibility	Local authority and responsibility	Externally-based program development authority increasing; local responsibility for delivery	Local authority and responsibility	Moderate to high local authority and responsibility	Authority for program development externally based; local responsibility for delivery
Accountability	Community (Town)	Community and funding agencies	External: Funding agencies	Community: "We are accountable to the people themselves."	External: Funding agencies	External: Funding agencies

* Organizations whose activities are focused on Eastern Guysborough County

with an office, telephones, photocopying. Scott and Troy are always helping with computer problems or something like that, the girls take your messages." "We rely on each other." "We've found the Town of Canso very supportive in terms of open information lines as well as they have recently extended office privileges to me. I was previously located in the Resource Centre – and that was a fine arrangement as well – so things come really freely in terms of discussion. Communication is open." "Most of them [organizations] are willing to provide any assistance or information." "We have joint staff meetings. We have interlocking memberships on our boards. We communicate daily." "Any time we needed help, they were right there." "There's not many groups or agencies that we don't exchange information with. We help them and they help us. We were involved with Community Services ... and the BDC Community Development Fund staff shared office space with us for the past five years until October when we moved back here."

Organizational structures were found to be highly organic in nature. Informants reported high levels of autonomy in day-to-day decision-making in conjunction with very open communication, offering no indication that rules, regulations, or controls created impediments to regular activities. Keeping structure and procedure to a minimum provided considerable flexibility at the operational level. However, the same degree of flexibility was not found at the policy level. Rather, it was constrained by the fact that the operating and/or capital funding of most of the organizations came from a variety of federal and provincial government program initiatives stipulating the types of expenditures that could be made.

Inextricably linked to flexibility are authority and responsibility for program development and delivery. Informants indicated that decisions about what activities their organization would pursue were made by the board: "The board makes all the major decisions. Your CEO will come in with proposals and some of the proposals are all laid out but you still have to make the decisions [about] which ones you want to go with." "Most of our direction certainly emanates from the board. The specifics of what we do I guess emanate more from staff." "We deal with all the resources available to the board – time, space, material, and personnel."

Boards see their role as twofold: overseeing operations and setting the overall direction of the organization. "Giving direction in regard to proposals, ideas of staff." "To make sure everything's in order." "[You're] responsible for the funding that you get and that it's spent properly." "They're responsible for directing us in how we spend the funds that HRD provides." "We're just there to make sure everything runs the way it started out and the way HRD allows us." "To provide direction to staff." "Complete management of the BDC." "[To] provide the direction for all the activities of the RDA." The sole exception is the Little Dover Community Development Association (LDCDA), whose board also performs operating functions because it has no full-time employees: "Well, we take a part in all the projects."

From attending board meetings, I observed each board's capacity to be primarily advisory. Meetings typically involved staff reports, proposals, and recommendations about activities; they were not noted to spark high levels of discussion or debate. There was little indication that a board's purview included identifying or facilitating opportunities for action. The exception was, once again, the LDCDA, whose board meeting that I attended had considerably greater informality, involvement, and participation, with a range of perspectives being brought to bear on most issues before a decision was made. This meeting also had a strong action orientation; the group identified what it would do to respond to the community's needs, and the individual members shared the responsibilities associated with bringing the projects to fruition.

While all the organizations hold complete responsibility for the activities they undertake, the matter of authority is not so clear-cut. Indeed, the boards were subject to considerable external influence: "They would like one to believe that the community sets its own direction and the community is responsible for its own destiny but there's always intervention. If the powers that be don't like what they see going on, they will influence that decision." "We're looking for funding. The government wants this here community involvement and diversification. That's what they're big on now." "Everyone's pretty well the same – trying to get money from where you can get it." "Every decision we make is based on how [funding source] is going to look at it. We cannot spend money without their approval."

Although, as we have seen, government has been relinquishing its authority to the community over time, what it retains is by no means inconsequential. This becomes especially apparent when we consider accountability. While the various organizations do consider themselves accountable to the community, the majority assign primary accountability to their funding source(s), whether federal, provincial, and/or municipal: "The town and of course you're responsible for the funding to the funding agencies." "HRD as the main funding source." "As far as I know the board makes the final decision but we're funded through HRD. So that's where the end of the line goes." "To the federal government through ACOA but ultimately I suppose to the citizens of Guysborough County." "In essence it's responsible to the board who are representatives of the community in general. The overall responsibility as far as the federal partner would be ACOA." "The three funding partners – ACOA, ERA, and the three municipal units." "Number one, we're accountable to the taxpayers that fund us." "We're getting funding from HRD so ultimately you have to account to them for where the money's spent and how."

The fairly high level of federal and provincial government involvement in the community's development activity works to reduce community-based accountability. The highest level of community-based accountability was expressed by the organization whose operations were entirely self-financed: "We're accountable to the people themselves." "The entire community is what we look out for and I guess they look out for us as well. When we do work through government funding, we are accountable in some way to each of those organizations."

In conclusion, although the organic nature of the organizational structures fostered considerable individual entrepreneurship, the same did not hold true at the organizational and community levels. A general lack of deviation from activities prescribed by external government programs suggests that the absence of entrepreneurship at these levels was engendered, albeit indirectly, by externally imposed limitations on the community's authority to act.

As we have seen, the use of inter-organizational structures in information-sharing or problem-solving was quite limited. While the sharing of premises encouraged the exchange of information, there was little evidence that it furthered strategic joint problem-solving: "Although we share offices ... we work pretty much independently. We've just gone on our own." Inter-organizational structural arrangements essentially fostered administrative entrepreneurship.[4]

In instilling a penchant for pursuing activities independently, the formal structural arrangements did not encourage strategic entrepreneurship.[5] In essence, they contributed to efficiency by fostering entrepreneurship in "doing things right," but they did little in the way of contributing to effectiveness by fostering entrepreneurship in "doing the right things."

By encouraging individual, independent action, the existing formal organizational arrangements tended to curb the development of a synergistic strategic vision for community-based economies of action. The level of entrepreneurship directed at improving Eastern Guysborough County's situation was affected by the fact that the geographic responsibility of two of the organizations, the RDA and the BDC, extended beyond the community's boundaries. For example, while the RDA exercised considerable entrepreneurship in capitalizing on opportunities that presented themselves throughout 1995, its efforts did not directly affect Eastern Guysborough County's problems.

Individuals

Most development activities were undertaken by staff, rather than board members or others. Since the various boards function primarily in an advisory, non-operational capacity, the behavioural implications of members' attributes were minimal. While the number of individuals actively involved in the development process was limited, participants were found to have attributes closely aligned with those posited to encourage enterprise (Table 13).

Individuals' attitudes toward learning by doing were extremely positive. In acquiring new knowledge and skills through this approach, individuals embraced learning as an integral part of the development process, rather than viewing it as a discrete activity: "Every day I learn something new." "I'm still learning a lot. Figuring out how to get the job done." One of the key learning areas was in dealing with people: "You learn to understand people which is really the key." "I was usually shy. It gave me a lot more self-confidence ... getting used to a board." "I've really learned a lot about fishermen's logic."

Collective community identity had no relevance for employees, since their jobs consisted largely of independent work. Among board members, however, collective community identity was high, with direct behavioural implications for the process. Having either lived in the community all their life or grown up there and returned, board members expressed a very strong attachment to the community. While they represent a fairly diverse cross-section of people in both age and background, their level of community involvement is quite similar. On average, they were actively involved in five community groups, which suggests that they perceived group-based action as the most effective means of fulfilling their desire to help improve the community. "I guess it's because I really want to make a difference. I really want something better for my kids." "Well, I wanted to put something back. I love Guysborough County." "I believe in it." "Ever since I can remember, I've always liked to see some things developed in the community. I like to be a part of it ... to be involved in the community – not only for myself, but my kids who's growing up." "So people are proud of the town." "Just being able to be a part of it. This is a part of my accomplishment, and his accomplishment ... our whole board, our whole community."

Participants in the development process had relatively low levels of strategic vision for economies of action. Although the majority of individuals in an organization were aware of at least half of the other organizations and their activities, few articulated economies of action that were both community-based and strategically driven. Rather, the vision tended to involve either community-based administratively oriented

Table 13
Analysis of Individual Attributes

	CWADC*	EGCDA*	*Canso and Area Resource Centre**	*Little Dover Community Development Association**	*Guysborough County* RDA	*Guysborough County* BDC
Attitudes toward learning by doing	N/A: No learning reported	Positive	Extremely positive	Extremely positive	Extremely positive	Extremely positive
Strength of collective community identity[1]	High	High	High	High	High	High
Strategic vision for economies of action	Low unaided awareness of other organizations; vision of majority of members does not include economies of action.	Unaided awareness of other organizations; future vision includes economies of action but tends to be externally focused.	Unaided awareness of other organizations; little vision for economies of action.	Low unaided awareness of other organizations; some economies of action expressed in future vision.	Unaided awareness of most other organizations; economies of action not significant part of future vision.	Unaided awareness of two organizations (not community-based); economies of action minimally reflected in vision.
Skills and abilities	Interpersonal, team-building, and financial (E); actively involved, member of 4.5 organizations (B)	Corporate background (E); actively involved, member of 6.5 organizations (B)	Interpersonal skills (E); actively involved, member of four organizations (B)	N/A (E); actively involved, member of three organizations (B)	Communication skills, ability to deal with multiple tasks, interpersonal skills (E); actively involved, member of two organizations (B)	Interpersonal and generalist skills (E); actively involved, member of eight organizations (B)

Table 13 (continued)

	CWADC*	EGCDA*	*Canso and Area Resource Centre**	*Little Dover Community Development Association**	*Guysborough County* RDA	*Guysborough County* BDC
Number of overlapping formal and informal connections	N/A: Worked closely with "no-one in particular" over past six months	N/A: Just started in position	Moderate number, high overlap	N/A: No full-time day-to-day operating involvement	N/A: Employees recently hired	Moderage number, high overlap for one employee; other indicated working closely with "no-one in particular" but noted more reliance on other agencies than in past.
Degree of trust and respect for competence	Board expressed high level of trust and respect for staff's competence: "The big thing you would expect if you work for a board is respect."	Board members shared a high level of mutual trust and a great deal of respect for each other's competence as well as for that of the newly hired employee: "We have a nice cross-section of different skills at our table." "He knows a lot more about business than anybody so we have to put a lot of trust in him."	Extremely high among staff ("I can rely on her.") and toward staff by board ("We're amazed at what they've come up with and how they've dealt with situations.")	Extremely high level of trust; perceived competence not relevant as activities undertaken by volunteers	High level of mutual respect for competence and trust among staff	High level of mutual respect for competence and trust between board and employees

Table 13 (continued)

	CWADC*	EGCDA*	*Canso and Area Resource Centre**	*Little Dover Community Development Association**	*Guysborough County* RDA	*Guysborough County* BDC
Preferred work style	Informal, free-ranging: Individual accepted job on the condition that he could determine how, when, and where the work would be accomplished.	Informal, free-ranging: "We give him a lot of leeway."	Informal, free-ranging; increasing restriction on freedom to act by external sources not positively received by employees	Inherently informal, free-ranging	Moderately informal, quite free-ranging	Moderately informal, quite free-ranging
Ability to manage inter-dependencies and deal with multiple tasks	Ability difficult to assess as current employee recently hired	Routinely deals with multiple tasks: "Keeping five others moving along in specific directions at the same time."	Indeterminable	N/A: Individuals are volunteers.	High need to deal with multiple tasks	High need to deal with multiple tasks

* Organizations whose activities are focused on Eastern Guysborough County

[1] Applies to board members only; irrelevant for employees

Legend: B – Board members

E – Employees

economies or strategic economies with externally-based stakeholders: "I think in terms of training opportunities for the Sable-off-shore project ... maybe working in collaboration with the Strait or with Antigonish. We can partner in areas like that." "I think we could do even more joint efforts with the school." "There's a need for all these organizations to come together. Sometimes there's too many organizations and they're all doing the same thing ... administrative work and the actual work doesn't get done." "The only thing, really, that's going to help is more jobs." "We need something to generate jobs." "There's a need for training – for leadership training with community groups because they provide a wealth of experience and energy and they could do a lot more. You know we rely on the private sector but it's just not happening here. But there are a lot of community groups out there that can do a lot of good. But a lot of them don't know what they have to do so there can be some training there."

The findings suggest that a business background plays an important role in developing a capacity for synergistic strategic vision. Indeed, the highest levels of strategic vision for economies of action were found among employees who had business skills and/or knowledge. While the overall capacity to recognize the proposed type of economies of action was judged to be low, individuals were keenly aware of human resource deficiencies: "Helping the work force retool to fill the new positions ... we have to look at bringing back the people that have gone through the education system here, gone away and obtained a university education." "Because we have such a low population base, I guess we would have to come up with ideas or opportunities that we could export." "More involvement." "We need go-getters ... people that have those connections. You have to take a chance." This finding suggests that, while individuals understand the community's problems, the appropriate skills to address the problems effectively may be lacking.

Both employees and board members had skills and abilities closely aligned with those associated with individuals' capacity to innovate. Among employees, for example, high levels of interpersonal, team-building, problem-solving, and business skills were reported to be required for job effectiveness: "A good people person, fairly good analytical skills, some financial skills and background and the ability to get good people to work for you." "Financing, organizational skill, management skills – you've got to be able, particularly when you're dealing with a volunteer board, to recognize what people can add to the mix." "Communication skills, interpersonal skills ... you have to be assertive, compassionate." "Private-sector experience." "Good people skills." "Utility – you have to be able to do a little bit of everything ... to look at things objectively and carry on." "More than anything else, probably people skills – an ability to get along with people." "Not to be confined by what has traditionally happened but maybe having a little bit of vision as well for what you see as being possible for your area over the next number of years." Unlike employees, board members had little experience or training in business and/or economic development, a fact indicating that business and technical skills play an important part in leveraging other skills used in being innovative.

While individuals identified interpersonal relationships as one of the things they liked most about their job, routine contacts were not made with specific individuals when information or other resources were needed. Consequently, the number of overlapping formal and informal contacts was not highly significant in fostering enterprise. Rather, individuals made need-determined contacts to acquire resources. Because needs were dynamic, so were the contacts. The uniqueness of the contacts amounted to virtual networks.

Both within and among organizations, there were high levels of trust and respect for competence, given the open exchange of information among members. In fact, several board members offered unsolicited views on the ability and intention of employees to produce valued results: "The credit goes to our CEOs." "I think staff could operate quite well without us." "He was very much what we were looking for and so far has done quite well in the short time he's been here. He earns their trust and they believe in him and he seems to be doing the right things." "We have confidence in the staff that are there, based on their performance." Indeed, the harmonious rapport observed to exist in a variety of situations – board meetings, the day-to-day office environment, public meetings – indicates mutual trust and respect.

In favouring the challenge, variety, and relational aspects of their jobs, individuals were considered to have a strong preference for an informal, free-ranging style: "It's not boring by any stretch of the imagination ... and there's a huge challenge to it." "Every day there's something different. We have a good staff and everyone gets along." "New relationships." "It puts you in a position where you meet a lot of different people." "Everything's different. It's not humdrum." "Meeting people, dealing with them." "Figuring out how to get the job done." "I like meeting people. I don't like a job that's really routinized. You don't know what you're going to have today." Although employees tended to work independently, they required the ability to manage interdependencies in dealing with funding agencies and the organization's board. Moreover, because most employees' tasks were not specialized, coping with multiple tasks was inherent in their job. With no evidence to the contrary, I assumed that board members were also able to manage interdependencies and deal with multiple tasks. This factor was relevant only for boards directly involved in operating activities.

Individuals were found to have positive attitudes toward learning by doing; interpersonal, team-building, and problem-solving skills; a preference for an informal, free-ranging work style; and the ability to handle multiple tasks. The ability to develop and use virtual networks fostered considerable entrepreneurship in accessing necessary information and other resources. Individuals actively involved in the development process initiated and undertook diverse projects and activities with considerable energy, self-confidence, independence, resourcefulness, intuition, creativity, flexibility, and commitment to seeing things through despite the uncertainty of the outcomes. Indeed, the high levels of trust and support afforded employees by their boards reinforced individuals' propensity to adopt entrepreneurial behaviour as an appropriate way of dealing with problems or opportunities.

Among board members, mutual trust and collective community identity were instrumental in generating entrepreneurship in establishing several organizations. However, in the absence of extensive business experience and/or training, board members were unable to capitalize fully on their interpersonal, problem-solving, and team-building skills to develop a synergistic vision for economies of action. This finding was reflected in a comment from one board member: "We couldn't do it ourselves. None of us were qualified or had the time or just didn't know how to go about it." With limited ability to envision how to generate strategic outcomes through economic activity, the boards tended to set their organizations' direction on the basis of projects, services, and/or activities supported by government programs. When assuming responsibility for day-to-day activity upon inception, collective community identity did seem to encourage entrepreneurship among board members, although the activities pursued did not directly generate sustainable employment: "I had a lot [of involvement in day-to-day activities] because we had no staff. We did everything." "Well, I could see what the group was trying to do and what they were trying to accomplish and whatever help that I could give to do those sort of things, I'm right there, gung-ho."

Given the limited number of people carrying out the development projects and activities, there were few opportunities for community residents to learn or to practise entrepreneurship, as evidenced by a lack of effort by people displaced from the fishery to become more financially self-sufficient through economic activity. Since opportunities for learning by doing encourage entrepreneurial behaviour, the implication is that focusing on projects generating sustainable economic activity would increase people's opportunity for adopting this approach in acquiring business skills and experience. Not only would people therefore learn and practise entrepreneurial behaviour; they would also see how this behaviour can be used effectively in both managing opportunities and problems and increasing financial self-sufficiency.

Informal Organizational Arrangements

With the development process consisting of non-routine, unpredictable tasks and the formal organizational arrangements having few rules and procedures influencing behaviour, informal organizational arrangements constituted the primary means of coordination and control. Overall, they were found to have a highly entrepreneurial configuration, as can be seen in Table 14.

In originally shaping the organizational value systems, evidence indicates that members of the various boards functioned largely on the basis of trust, support, and cooperation, since these values were found to permeate the organizations and to constitute the core principles guiding action. My observations of day-to-day activities and board proceedings confirmed the pervasiveness of these principles. They undoubtedly have had a significant influence on the strong collective identity and high levels of involvement and participation found within the organizations. For example, board meetings were well attended (even one on a night with blizzard conditions), and staff frequently mentioned the willingness of board members to provide advice when needed. Whether individuals were staff or board members, they expressed considerable pride in and ownership of activities. Working nights and weekends, the commitment of staff members was unquestionable.

While there was agreement on aims, time scales, and outcomes within each organization, it did not develop out of a shared strategic vision for the community. Rather, each organization operated autonomously on the basis of a mutually exclusive purpose developed in response to government funding availability. Although representatives from Eastern Guysborough County participated in the county-wide strategic planning process undertaken between 1990 and 1995, the community did not develop a broad-based analysis and strategic vision specifically to address its situation immediately after the fisheries crisis.

This delayed response has major implications. The community's residents were expecting their employment problem to be dealt with, yet organizational activities were not effectively responding to and capitalizing on the community's inputs. For example, in establishing the Community Development Fund to provide financial assistance to new and expanding businesses, the assumption was that a small-business sector would develop if money was made available. Only over time did it become evident that this type of initiative was inappropriate,

Table 14
Analysis of Informal Organizational Arrangements

	CWADC*	EGCDA*	*Canso and Area Resource Centre**	*Little Dover Community Development Association**	*Guysborough County* RDA	*Guysborough County* BDC
Valued principles: supportiveness, trust, and cooperation	N/A[1]: "Trust … we listen to each other." "She expected the board to back her, and we did."	N/A: Sole employee recently hired; board members very cooperative, trusting, and supportive of each other.	Highly evident: "We each do whatever needs to be done."; no strongly valued principles communicated by board	Highly evident: "Everybody put that little extra effort into it; dedication, loyalty."	Highly evident: "We have enough respect for one another and our talents." Board very supportive, trusting, and cooperative: "Respect. That's what I try to give them here."	Highly evident: "Everybody seems to have a really good working relationship … everyone's open to new suggestions." Board is cooperative, supportive, trusting of staff: "We have confidence in the staff … a good working relationship with staff."
Collective identity	High	High	Moderate	High	High	High
Involvement and participation	Low	Low	Low	Moderately high	Moderate	Low
Agreement on goals, objectives, time scales, and outcomes	Organizationally focused	Organizationally focused	Organizationally focused	Organizationally focused	Organizationally focused	Organizationally focused

Table 14 (continued)

	*CWADC**	*EGCDA**	*Canso and Area Resource Centre**	*Little Dover Community Development Association**	*Guysborough County RDA*	*Guysborough County BDC*
Overlap of formal and informal business and social relationships	Indeterminable	Indeterminable	Indeterminable	Indeterminable	Indeterminable	Indeterminable
Entrepreneurial norms	High: "I knew what I wanted to accomplish yesterday and today."; board expects staff to work independently	N/A	High: "We each do whatever needs to be done."	High: Open communication: "If you've got something to say, you should say it." "They knew what they were supposed to do, and they just went on their own and did it."	High: "Let's just do it."	High: "Don't just let things slide."

* Organizations whose activities are focused on Eastern Guysborough County

[1] Applies to board members only; irrelevant for employees

indicating that the effect of a community's occupational and economic structure on economic development was not well understood either by the community or by government.

There was little evidence that the mandates of the various organizations were developed out of a shared understanding of the community's problems and their solutions. Consequently, most organizations did not judge performance on the basis of responsiveness to community needs. Rather, an organization was considered effective by its members if progress was being made in fulfilling its mandate and its activities were making positive contributions to the community. Generally, the extent to which activities were able to address the community's needs by having a positive, measurable effect on employment was not a criterion in judging success.

The use of virtual networks for acquiring resources prevented the extent to which formal and informal business and social relationships overlapped from being determined from the data. No clear boundaries distinguishing formal from informal relationships were evident. Given the size of the community, business and social relationships are inevitably intertwined.

Entrepreneurial behavioural expectations (norms) were found to be highly integrated within all organizations. Individuals involved in operating activities showed the following characteristics and behaviours:

- Informal operation
- Open communication
- Valuing of ideas ("We have a staff meeting every morning at 8:30 ... everybody knows what everybody else is doing and also, when you let people in on what you're doing, they may have some good suggestions that can help you as well ... we just sit down and talk very frankly.")
- Considerable flexibility and ingenuity in decision-making and problem-solving that frequently challenged the status quo
- Learning by experimenting
- Lack of fear of punishment of taking risks, or making mistakes ("Like anything involving human nature, mistakes will be made." "You have to take a chance in order to get what you want." "If we fail at this, at least we can say we gave it our best shot.")
- High individual performance expectations
- High levels of task ownership and commitment to seeing things through ("Everybody will do a little bit more than you figure they should." "It's very common to see people in here in the night-time." [This assertion was confirmed through observation.])

In overseeing operations and setting direction, board members tended to reinforce rather than adopt these norms. However, open communication and task ownership were deeply entrenched in the vast majority of boards: "If you've got something to say, you should say it." "The only thing that we really expect from them is to tell us the way it is." "From the other board members you get suggestions." "Everyone on the board has their own little bit of knowledge on certain things that others may not have. We more or less lean on each other." "If we had something to say to her, we told her what we thought." "We listen to each other." "The board's made up of a good cross-section and I pretty well know who knows what and I'll call them."

While unique informal organizational arrangements developed in each organization, considered collectively they had a highly entrepreneurial configuration. As the main mechanism of coordination and control, they were therefore instrumental in encouraging considerable entrepreneurship. Although trust, cooperation, and support were highly valued principles, "community" was judged to be the most fundamental value stimulating entrepreneurial behaviour and underlying the entire development process. The community was the main motivation for volunteer involvement, lending purpose and meaning to activities: "It took us a couple of years to convince people that we were doing it for the good for the town. We never gave up and it's starting to show now." "Just being able to be a part of it ... this is a part of my accomplishment ... our whole board, our whole community." "We do things without looking for recognition."

With the vast majority of tasks structured to require independent action, individuals did not perceive their activities to be linked with those of other community-based organizations. Therefore, trust, supportiveness, and cooperation did not influence activities in the ways expected. For example, while organizations regularly shared information, they did not attempt to address the community's problems collaboratively. Indeed, in light of the task structure, the degree of involvement and participation, collective identity, and shared goals and expectations were not found to be highly significant in fostering entrepreneurship.

One additional norm was found to have a very positive influence on the amount of entrepreneurship brought to daily activities: the expectation that board members would not interfere with or intervene in those activities: "We give them our mandate what to do." "We expect that each of the staff members know what they're supposed to do." "We have confidence in the staff that are there." "We depend on staff mostly." This expectation, like the rest, was deeply entrenched in all the organizations. For example, when given the authority and responsibility to fulfill their organization's mandate, employees determined how and when their work would be done: "As far as the work is concerned I have a lot of freedom." "We have flexibility. If I wanted to come in and work at 7:00 in the morning, I can." "You have to be a little bit flexible."

Unlike in many businesses, where a core set of contacts is nurtured and relied upon for acquiring information and other resources, the novelty and variety of the tasks associated with Community Economic Development require a dynamic and expansive network: "I guess it would be issue specific." "I just have enough contacts in government and around." "I ask for it." "Make a phone call." "Asking." "You be as resourceful and creative as you can in sourcing it." "It depends on the type of information." "Anywhere and everywhere I can. I don't have any set pattern." "No-one in particular." "Every way we have to. We're not shy. I have a lot of contacts." "I guess you have lots of informal networks. It's not really a formal structure. All of us have informal contacts." "There's no formal structure. You get information by knowing people ... so it's informal." "We do whatever is necessary to get the information." "Usually word of mouth." "You use whoever knows about it." While staff members reported personal contact to be the preferred way of contacting people outside the office, it was also pointed out that because of the size of the County and the distance to other areas, the phone was the most common means of communication: "Depending on what it is, but my way, generally, is to visit people. You've got to look them in the eye. When you ask someone a question the body language tells you a lot." "You see them. Once you have a comfort level with them ... nurturing contacts is extremely beneficial." "Mostly phone with a follow-up letter or if it's in the area ... phone 'em, write 'em, go see 'em ... whatever works." "There's a philosophy that there's no-one on this planet that you really want to talk to that you couldn't get to in less than six phone calls."

The autonomy, variety, and involvement associated with tasks have not only encouraged entrepreneurship but have positively influenced personal motivation, work performance, and satisfaction. This finding was especially evident when an individual was the sole employee, since individual and organizational accomplishments were one and the same: "Just the satisfaction that I did a good job – did what they wanted me to do in the period." "It's nice to know that people think that you can help them. It makes you feel good that people think you're doing something worthwhile, that you're appreciated." "To deal with a client that has his goals achieved is the ultimate reward. Other than that, I guess it's rewarding when you know you've done some good for the community." "I guess the pleasure in knowing that you've helped somebody." "I really enjoy [it], and it's a passion, CED. There's a lot of self-gratification comes with the things that you work on." "Probably more just personal satisfaction than anything else."

In the absence of a formal reward system, the rewards provided through the informal organizational arrangements had a strong positive effect on entrepreneurship. The fact that considerable monitoring and evaluation are done informally also encourages entrepreneurship, as problems or opportunities are responded to when recognized: "I don't think they have any formal structure in place. For the financial administration they do." "I guess we judge our success rate by our clientele and their response to what we do." "We evaluate as we go. If we were doing something and we didn't think we were doing it [well] enough we'd make changes." "From the monthly meetings we have ... the only way we evaluate ourselves right now – by what others say about us or what they tell us." "By the number of businesses that start up and jobs that are created." "All the loans, loan applications are done on a monthly basis." "I think we do a fairly good job of monitoring the activities. We provide the board with a detailed loan analysis each and every month. We provide the board with a monthly progress report for all staff members so they know the meetings we attend, the clients we see. I guess we evaluate to some extent by the general public's perception. Are we getting a lot of negative publicity in the newspapers again? The evaluation procedure looks at how things fit in with the strategic plan."

PROCESS OUTPUTS

Having assessed the extent to which the components of Eastern Guysborough County's development process had an entrepreneurial configuration, in this section I examine the outputs produced by the interaction of these four variables with respect to innovation and economic development.

Innovation

Using the pre-established criteria, I assessed innovation in both the process and its outputs. While some process innovation was achieved, little of it could be directly related to the attainment of desired economic development outcomes.

The principal process innovation consisted of the sharing of premises and personnel, which decreased operating expenses and facilitated timely decision-making through the regular exchange of information. Another was the establishment of interlocking boards, which helped make the various organizations aware of the activities being undertaken in the community. While the implementation of ideas that were new to the process participants resulted in greater efficiency in the application of resources to activities, the innovations did not result in any improvement in the community's economic output, income levels, or employment. The innovation was administrative rather than strategic in nature. As a consequence, although the increased efficiency contributed to organizational task accomplishment, it did not enhance the attainment of community goals, since organizational tasks did not directly influence the creation or maintenance of sustainable employment. It is therefore clear that we must differentiate between administrative innovation and strategic innovation. The former is directly related to internal management, involving the creation of new or improved structures or administrative processes; the latter is directly related to achieving the primary outcomes desired by the community.

Economic Development

To determine the degree to which economic development was achieved, I assessed the outputs according to three criteria: goal achievement, the extent to which the community attains its desired aims; resource utilization – in relation to goal achievement the concern is whether resources are sustained or depleted – and adaptability, that is, whether the community is able to adapt to environmental conditions. Table 15 presents a summary of the six organizations' results during 1995.

There is little evidence that jobs were created or that the community's economy became more diversified. No sustainable jobs could be directly attributed to the development process. However, it appears reasonable to assume that the pending completion of a number of tourism-related infrastructure projects would diversify the community's economy to some degree. As regards resource utilization, resources were invariably depleted rather than sustained. Finally, there is no evidence that the community's capacity to adapt to environmental conditions materially increased. Although it experienced a rise in both the number of community-based development activities and the number of people participating in them, a very small proportion of residents was actually involved. Moreover, the majority of these were either retirees or currently employed volunteers. Left to their own devices, residents took no initiative in starting new businesses to increase personal financial self-sufficiency. In the absence of evidence for significant progress in achieving the aims desired by the community, it can be concluded that the process did not successfully modify the community's way of dealing with problems.

In summary, the innovations were not directly contributing to the fulfilment of the community's desire for employment. Given the lack of significant improvement in the community's economic output,

Table 15
Summary of Results Achieved During the 1995 Operating Year

	Results
CWADC*	Completing the Centre Town park; getting the walkway underway; signage
EGCDA*	Hiring a CEO to be responsible for recruiting businesses to the area; receiving approval for the Community Access Project application; obtaining a commitment from a business to locate in the area[1]
Canso and Area Resource Centre*	Successfully helping TAGS recipients access government assistance; assisting an average of sixty clients per day; high levels of staff productivity and satisfaction
Little Dover Community Development Association*	Black Duck Cove day park ahead of schedule in its completion; constructing a building to house the organization by soliciting donations of materials and supplies
Guysborough County RDA	Making the organization operational; other achievements, including influencing Mobil Oil's decision to locate in Country Harbour, did not involve Eastern Guysborough County.
Guysborough County BDC	Improving the climate of job creation; making financial contributions to county businesses, which created 15 to 25 per cent more jobs than expected; specific results for Eastern Guysborough County not indicated

* Organizations whose activities are focused on Eastern Guysborough County
[1] This commitment did not materialize.

income, or employment, the process was not effective in influencing economic development.

THE RELATIONSHIP OF THE FINDINGS TO THE HYPOTHESES

While the informal organizational arrangements and the individual aspect of the development process were judged to have a fairly strong entrepreneurial configuration, the task component and the formal organizational arrangements did not. Lacking the required levels of interdependence, interaction, control, variety, and skill, the task structure was not appropriate for fostering the behaviour required for achieving the community's intended goals. Indeed, there was no evidence indicating that the activities comprising the development task provided residents with sustainable income-generating opportunities enabling or requiring them to learn and practise entrepreneurship. Lacking the authority to make expenditures on activities that deviated from those for which funding had been provided, most organizations did not have the autonomy needed to respond flexibly to opportunities or problems. Moreover, with most organizations independently pursuing a narrow range of activities, there was little reason or motivation for identifying community-based opportunities for economies of action in responding to community need. Despite the entrepreneurial configuration of two variables, the congruence between them was insufficient to foster behaviour effective in responding to the circumstances.

In light of the evidence, the process's lack of effectiveness stems from adopting a strategy to create and/or maintain jobs that did not fit the local environmental conditions. Rather than being directed by a self-determined vision of how the community's problems, needs, and expectations could best be addressed, the activities undertaken were determined by government or were significantly influenced by the availability of government program funding. Adopting a strategy which implicitly assumes that individuals would start a business if more resources were available indicates a lack of congruence between the development task and the existing behaviours, attitudes, and competencies of the community. In the past, residents of Eastern Guysborough County depended on others for employment and for finding solutions to their problems. The very nature of the community's economic structure meant that people did not require high levels of education, skills, or entrepreneurship to secure financial self-reliance, as reflected in the following account: "When I was going to high school, I knew that I could get out of high school and the next day I could go to work down here and I could come home with probably about $3,000 for just working the summer – just an off-the-street employee." Consequently, when the community's economy collapsed, the majority of those affected lacked the competencies for launching a new venture. Moreover, given that low-skilled processing jobs foster an orientation toward paid employment, residents could be expected to seek employment rather than start their own ventures. To create and maintain jobs by endogenously developing the small business sector would require a strategy providing residents with opportunities to develop those competencies. Pursuing a broader range of tasks with diverse time and goal orientations would produce valued results in the short term that would help convince residents that involvement in the development process could meet both personal and community needs.

Two major assumptions underlay the narrow range of tasks pursued in Eastern Guysborough County: first, that the major barrier to economic development was the lack of capital, and second, that economic development could be achieved through tourism. As we have seen, the lack of economic activity despite all efforts challenges the validity of these assumptions. The strategy was designed to react to, rather than to stimulate, entrepreneurship, despite the fact that previous employment involved the performance of relatively routine jobs that did not require individuals to learn or exercise entrepreneurial behaviour. Since development activities did not create sustainable employment – oriented as they were toward infrastructure development – the process was not perceived to be producing valued results. Residents were seeking jobs that would enable them to earn enough to provide for their basic personal needs. There was no basis for creating broad-based interest and enthusiasm for starting a small business. Indeed, in the absence of successful new venture initiatives that would serve to illustrate how entrepreneurial competencies could be used in establishing alternative means of financial self-sufficiency, there was little motivation for individuals to adopt new behaviour patterns in dealing with their problems.

In conclusion, the main reason the community was not effective in meeting its needs and expectations was that the strategy did not fit the environmental conditions. Several factors contributed to this outcome. First, the strategy was largely externally determined and did not reflect the community's understanding of its problems and how to solve them. It also ignored the behaviours, attitudes, and competencies required for people to initiate economic activity. Third, there were no examples from which people could learn entrepreneurship to cope effectively with their problems. Finally, the time and goal orientation of activities were not sufficiently diverse.

The inability of the development process in Eastern Guysborough County to produce the desired outcomes (as derived from explicit and implicit strategy statements) was related to the lack of congruence among the four process variables. Although two of them were consistent with the configuration posited to foster enterprise, this was not sufficient to stimulate behaviour effective in influencing economic development. Indeed, the lack of community entrepreneurial effort was in direct relation to the extent to which the process variable configurations maximized the potential for enterprise. Moreover, it is important to differentiate between administrative and strategic innovation, since no direct relationship was found between the former and goal achievement. Generally, the findings lend considerable support to the hypotheses.

Isle Madame

As we have just seen for Eastern Guysborough County, the following sections analyse the context, process, and outcomes of Isle Madame's development efforts and relate these findings to the hypotheses.

THE COMMUNITY ENTERPRISE CONTEXT

Situated in the southernmost part of Cape Breton Island in the county of Richmond, Isle Madame is a community whose geographic boundaries and economic base have been carved out by the sea. Historically, the fishery formed the economic backbone of the island's economy. For decades, its two largest settlements, Petit de Grat and Arichat (located three kilometres apart) thrived off the fishery, with the former being the centre of fishing activity and the latter providing the island's social, professional, retail, financial, and municipal services.

The dawning of the pre-millennium decade marked the end of the stability to which the community had been accustomed. In 1990, the effect of the collapsing groundfish industry became noticeable; by 1991, it was taking a swift toll on the community. For example, there were times during 1991 that nearly 40 per cent of fisheries workers were unemployed. Amidst worsening socioeconomic conditions, the closure in 1992 of the island's largest fish plant thrust the community into crisis.

By all accounts, the situation was bleak. As Table 16 indicates, some natural, physical, governmental, and educational resources did exist, but they were fairly limited. While the population of both the province and the nation were growing, at 3.1 per cent and 7.9 per cent respectively, Isle Madame's population of 4,333 (30 per cent of which is francophone) reflected a decline of 6.7 per cent since 1986, with out-migration concentrated among those under forty-five years of age. In 1991, the unemployment rate was 19.9 per cent, compared to 13 and 10 per cent respectively for the province and the nation. Manufacturing accounted for almost 30 per cent of employment – approximately twice the percentage of jobs provided by this industrial sector provincially and nationally. With fish processing constituting virtually all the island's manufacturing employment and fishing itself accounting for most of the employment in primary occupations, the fishery directly accounted for approximately 700 jobs, close to 40 per cent of total employment. Only 6 per cent of residents had management or administration occupations, as compared to 10 per cent in the province and 12 per cent nationwide. The data confirm that low-skilled manufacturing firms provide little opportunity for the development of managerial, professional, or technical competencies. The tendency of routine manufacturing to create an orientation toward paid employment was reflected in the following comment: "Most people don't want to start a business. They want a job." Indeed, there was no evidence suggesting that displaced workers would be likely to develop an endogenous small business sector.

Serving to further constrain the likelihood of new venture formation were income and educational levels significantly lower than the provincial and national averages. The average income of Isle Madame's people was 82 per cent of the Nova Scotia average and 71 per cent of the Canadian average. Indeed, 57 per cent of tax filers reported income

Table 16
Inputs to Isle Madame's Development Process

Inputs

TASK ENVIRONMENT
Single-industry natural resource-based economy facing imminent collapse
Industrial structure concentrated in primary and manufacturing categories
19.9 per cent unemployment (10 per cent in Nova Scotia; 13 per cent in Canada)
Declining rural population
Limited infrastructure for accessing suppliers and markets
Few community-based support services

RESOURCES
Technology base lacking
Technically skilled and professional labour force lacking
Limited financial resources:
- Average income, $16,915 (82 per cent of Nova Scotia average; 71 per cent of Canadian average)
- 29 per cent of tax filers receiving transfer payment income
- 57 per cent of tax filers with income under $10,000 (33 per cent in Nova Scotia; 28 per cent in Canada)
- 7 per cent of tax filers with income greater than $30,000 (24 per cent in Nova Scotia; 29.5 per cent in Canada)

Low educational levels:
- 25 per cent with less than Grade 9 (13 per cent in Nova Scotia; 14 per cent in Canada)

One post-secondary educational institution
Access to external resources constrained by limited prior dealings with government agencies, businesses, and financial and educational institutions outside the community
High quality of life – 88 per cent own dwelling (71 per cent in Nova Scotia; 63 per cent in Canada)

HISTORY AND CORE VALUES
Collective community identity: "The community is absolutely wonderful. When there's a crisis or something, we support one another."
Affection for the community's natural beauty: "Most people here think their island is quite beautiful and most people from the outside think it's quite beautiful too."
High value placed on personal relationships: "People are close together and they talk a lot." "Their relationship is very personal and very detailed."
Parochialism: "The communities on the island can't seem to get together on anything." "Each little community is looking out for itself."
Perceived nepotism: "Here, if you're in a position of power, you hire your relatives and friends."
Low self-esteem: "They always think: 'I'm not good enough. The next one is better than I am.'"
Dependency on government: "People still seem to think that government should do everything for them."

STRATEGY

GOAL:
Job creation

APPROACHES:
(1) Creating sustainable alternative employment for displaced fisheries workers (C)
(2) Providing employment opportunities for island youths who left to futher their education (C)
(3) Providing opportunities to increase education levels (C)

Adapted from Nadler and Tushman 1980, 267
Legend: C – Impetus for strategy community-based

less than $10,000; only 7 per cent reported income greater than $30,000. Moreover, 25 per cent of the population had less than a Grade 9 education, as compared to 13 per cent of Nova Scotians and 14 per cent of Canadians.

In examining the culture to gain insight into the community's history and core values, several key elements surfaced: extremely high levels of collective community identity, affection for the community's natural beauty, highly valued personal relationships, parochialism, low self-esteem, a perception of nepotism, and a belief that government has an obligation to intervene. These cultural characteristics bear little resemblance to those typically associated with an entrepreneurial culture.

Although the total collapse of the groundfish industry was not anticipated when the fish plant closed, the severity of the situation prompted the establishment of an Industrial Adjustment Services (IAS) Committee. In 1993 the committee commissioned a report to assess the current fishery, determine its effect, and develop an action plan for adjustment and economic renewal that reflected community input. It was this that shaped the strategy adopted in dealing with the situation.

Widely read and accepted throughout the community, the report provided a focus for the vast majority of the initiatives pursued. Underlying the action plan was the long-term strategic aim of achieving economic renewal through economic diversification while maintaining the island's current lifestyle and increasing people's self-esteem and perceived sense of well-being. The approach advocated was to create or expand community-based small businesses that would be clean and environmentally friendly and provide meaningful work.

The island's strategy was *evolutionary*. Although there were shifts in short-term priorities, a commitment to the original strategic vision has been maintained throughout the process. Indeed, when the total collapse of the fishery in Isle Madame became known after the report was released, the community was not deterred from following its recommendations. Rather, it embarked on the development process propelled by a strong belief that the community had the capability to deal effectively with its problems. From the outset, then, a very pro-active approach was adopted. Dismissing out-migration and the recruitment of a labour-intensive employer as viable options, in the short to medium term the community set out to rebuild its economy by setting goals of both an economic and a social nature. While economic aims took priority, it was generally understood that any activities that compromised the community's social fabric would not be pursued. The economic aim was twofold: to create employment for the remaining residents so they would not have to leave, and to create employment opportunities for island youth who had left the area to further their education. Socially, the aim was to increase education levels so that residents would have the qualifications required for most jobs and retraining opportunities.

THE DEVELOPMENT PROCESS

The six community-based organizations actively participating in Isle Madame's development process are profiled in Table 17. While there is considerable variation among them, particularly in terms of geographic service area, mandate, date of inception, and services and activities provided, two-thirds of them reported having a common purpose and geographic focus: addressing the effect of the fishery's collapse on Isle Madame. Indeed, the raison d'être of two of the organizations, Development Isle Madame Association (DIMA) and Telile, is to respond directly to the crisis in ways recommended by the IAS committee report. Another organization, La Picasse, decided to incorporate economic development into its original mandate in response to the crisis; still another, the Island Association for Community Awareness, has attempted to address the social and recreational needs of displaced workers. The two organizations with off-island locations and broad geographic areas to service, the BDC and the RDA, did not report initiating any activities to specifically address the fishery's collapse, which suggests that the broader the geographic mandate, the less pro-active and need-focused the organizational involvement.

Tasks

The task component of Isle Madame's development process was found to have a highly entrepreneurial configuration. As Table 18 shows, the only dimension found not to be consistent with an enterprising task structure was the nature of task ownership and control.

In undertaking a diverse set of both supply- and demand-side activities, Isle Madame's development task was judged to have broad task definition. For example, of the supply-side initiatives, some were oriented toward using idle human resources. DIMA, while not assuming direct responsibility for training and skills development, was deeply involved in assessing the educational and skill needs on Isle Madame, identifying programs to meet these needs, and encouraging people to pursue educational opportunities such as employment preparation programs and academic upgrading courses. Telile's activities, designed to combine job creation and training in video production for unemployed fisheries workers, were also instrumental in enhancing human resources. And, in an example of the use of idle physical resources, the Island Association for Community Awareness established the Active Living Centre, acquiring and renovating the building vacated by the Richmond County School Board office.

Table 17
Summary Profile of Isle Madame's Development Process Participants

	Geographic Service Area	*Mandate*	*Start-up Date*	*Services and Activities*	*Staff Complement*	*Operational Funding Source*	*Number of Board Members*	*Board Function*
La Picasse	Richmond County (francophone community of whom 85 per cent are resident in Isle Madame > C)	Addressing the social, cultural, economic, and educational needs of the county's francophones	1991*	Construction of multi-purpose community centre	–	Three levels of government, community, province of Quebec	12	Project implementation and completion
Island Association for Community Awareness	Arichat < C	Social development	1991	Provision of recreational programs and office and meeting space for service groups; operation of tea room	–	Operations	12	Operational
InRich BDC	Richmond and Inverness Counties > C	Increasing economic activity through small business development	1990*	Financial and technical assistance (primary activity considered lending)	3 full-time	ACOA	12	Investment decisions; overseeing operations

Table 17 (continued)

	Geographic Service Area	*Mandate*	*Start-up Date*	*Services and Activities*	*Staff Complement*	*Operational Funding Source*	*Number of Board Members*	*Board Function*
DIMA	Isle Madame	Economic renewal	1995*	Initiating projects to create new jobs; retooling human resources	4 full-time	ERA, HRDC	28 (15 to 20 in regular attendance)	Project review; overseeing operations
Telile	Isle Madame	Fostering a learning culture and an entrepreneurial culture	1994	Operation of a community cable TV channel, community programming, video production	5 full-time	Operations	5	Organizational direction and policy
Strait-Highlands RDA	Inverness, Richmond, and Victoria Counties > C	Regional strategic economic planning	1992*	Assisting communities with planning, organizing, or project development	4 full-time	ACOA, ERA, municipal units	15	Overseeing operations

Legend:

ACOA – Atlantic Canada Opportunities Agency
BDC – Business Development centre
DIMA – Development Isle Madame Association
ERA – Economic Renewal Agency
HRDC – Human Resources Development Canada
RDA – Regional Development Authority

* Incorporation reflects the reorganization of a previously constituted organization.

> C indicates that the geographic service area is greater than the life-world; < C indicates that it is smaller than the life-world.

Table 18
Analysis of Tasks

	*La Picasse**	*Island Association for Community Awareness**	DIMA*	*Telile**	*Strait-Highlands* RDA	*Inrich* BDC
Task definition	Creating infrastructure to facilitate the development of Acadian identity	Providing social and recreational activities to increase people's self-esteem and confidence	Pursuing projects to create sustainable employment opportunities, particularly for displaced fisheries workers	Establishing and using a formal communications medium to help foster an entrepreneurial and learning culture by sharing ideas and opportunities	Facilitating planning; organizing activities in response to requests. (Federal/provincial funding program limits the nature of activities pursued.)	Job creation through loans and technical advice (externally determined service offering)
Task uncertainty	High: "I wasn't sure if we were going to realize it or not."	High	High: "You don't really know where you're going to be in six months."	High: No standardized way of dealing with challenges: "Everything I do is new and I'm still learning."	High: New strategic direction adopted that has refocused activities and involved considerable uncertainty and novelty	High: Difficult to predict outcomes of activities

Table 18 (continued)

	*La Picasse**	*Island Association for Community Awareness**	DIMA*	*Telile**	*Strait-Highlands* RDA	*Inrich* BDC
Time and goal focus	Short-term focus on completing the capital project	Short-term focus on providing social and recreational opportunities responsive to the needs of the community in light of the fisheries crisis	Short-term focus on strategically oriented outcomes: "The reason our top priority is jobs … it gives people money to live with … but also looking at the social impact was another focus." "We try for the short term as much as we can. You have to have some projects that create employment and also you have to have some that will generate revenue in order to sustain our operation."	Short-term focus on economic self-sufficiency to maintain current staffing levels	Long-term; not strategically focused to respond to particular community needs	Short-term focus on providing financial infrastructure
Flexibility	High: Added economic aspect to the concept in response to the fisheries crisis	High	High: "It kind of changed our plans of what we can do for the TAGS people."	High: "We're flexible to do almost anything … We'll do whatever needs to be done."	Low: Activities are reactive and restricted in nature.	Moderate: Within the boundaries of services provided, there is some room for the organization to manoeuvre.

Table 18 (continued)

	*La Picasse**	*Island Association for Community Awareness**	DIMA*	*Telile**	*Strait-Highlands* RDA	*Inrich* BDC
Freedom to experiment	High: Unrestricted	High: Unrestricted	High: "Of course you're going to try projects that are going to fly. You're going to try projects that are going to fail."	High: "I like the challenge of starting someting new."	Inconclusive because of lack of evidence	Low: Organization's activities externally defined
Tolerance for failure	High: "When we only had $3.3 million to work with … we solved that."	High: "Our lessons are tough ones but we'll know better next time."	High: "If there's progress being made, we continue working on a project. If not, let's move on to something else."	High: "He might say 'Well, I tried that once and it didn't work for me. You try it and see.'"	Inconclusive because of lack of evidence	High
Diversity of skills, knowledge, and abilities required	High: "They tried to choose people who had a little more knowledge in different fields."	Moderate: Nature of activities does not require highly specialized skills.	High: Thirty-five projects pursued, requring diverse skills	High: Tasks range from producing to editing to writing.	Low: Most staff have technical business skills and training.	Low: Homogeneous skills required
Interdependent control and ownership among community-based organizations	Moderate: Infrastructure project pursued largely with government partners but several joint ventures undertaken in view of future operations	Low: No joint venture pursued	Low: "The ball has always been carried by DIMA. Every project that we've got off the ground in the past twelve months has pretty well been something we started on our own."	Low: No joint ventures	High: "Our successes have been partnering with others and that's the way we want to go."	Low: No joint ventures reported

Table 18 (continued)

	*La Picasse**	*Island Association for Community Awareness**	DIMA*	*Telile**	*Strait-Highlands* RDA	*Inrich* BDC
Holistic set of tasks	Moderate: exclusively focused on francophone community	High: Social and recreational activities seen as making an important contribution to residents' individual well-being	High: Variety of projects undertaken seen to be making direct contributions to the economic renewal of the island	High: Organization's activities perceived to serve as a model for demonstrating the potential for retooling human resources to create alternative forms of employment.	Low: Organization's activities not associated with any specific development outcomes in Isle Madame	Low: Activities not viewed as a key part of the development process in Isle Madame
Intrinsic rewards	High: "It's gratifying to see that you're helping people."	High: "You learn a lot … management."	High: "I love doing this and my reward is, not the money I make every week, it's that the people that I work for get results."	High: "I love what I do."	Moderate: "It's a very interesting job in a lot of respects."	High: "It gives you a feeling of accomplishment when you see businesses …"
Opportunities for learning by doing	High: "I've learned a lot about the new technologies, economic development. I'm always learning."	High: "We're basically learning as we go along."	High: "It's trial and error method so it's a little sloppy sometimes but you learn that way."	High: "Everybody learned everything."	Moderate: "Certainly I've been exposed to a lot more … business plan developments."	High: "You're always learning day by day."

* Organizations whose activities are focused on Isle Madame

Other supply-side activities expanded the community's resource base in a number of ways. New institutional infrastructure was created by the formation of five island-based development organizations after 1991. Capital infrastructure was created through the construction of La Picasse's cultural, educational, and community centre for francophones. The Active Living Centre augmented the community's capital infrastructure base in 1995 by providing a venue for a number of educational and training programs normally held off the island. Finally, the community's financial resource base experienced a marginal expansion in 1995 through an increase in Inrich's capital funding.

There have also been numerous activities to improve the productivity of community resources. For example, DIMA's Coastal Mapping project is generating a natural resource data bank that can be used to identify value-added enterprise or tourism opportunities. One of the main ways of enhancing productivity in all island-based organizations was the use of volunteer services. In organizations with no full-time employees, unpaid labour kept operating costs to a minimum. Even when boards were not directly involved in day-to-day operations, their members and other people in the community contributed in many respects. For example, staff relied on board members for expertise or used them as a spring-board in sourcing information or other resources: "We have different people that do different things for us on a volunteer basis. The clergy ... businesses ... the school ... the Active Living Centre ... the Municipality." "On occasion, there are things that board members can do, not because they're board members, but because they can do it and the staff can't."

Since the development process began, the nature of the demand-side activities pursued varied over time according to perceived need. When the fisheries crisis was first recognized, they were predominantly informational in focus, aimed at mobilizing the community and including the collection and evaluation of information on market opportunities. During 1995, however, demand-side initiatives were essentially influentially oriented. For example, La Picasse successfully induced individuals in the Acadian community to commit to launching or expanding a number of enterprises, which will be located in its facility upon completion. In addition, two ventures that were originally projects of DIMA – Telile[6] and the Small Options Home – became fully operational self-sustaining ventures in 1995.

While the activities undertaken on Isle Madame were very diverse, they shared the attribute of a high level of task uncertainty. Indeed, the novelty typifying initiatives made for highly unpredictable outcomes. Moreover, all the organizations faced difficulties for which there were no standard solutions: "If we have a problem, we tend to resolve it amongst ourselves." "In some cases [problems were dealt with] clumsily and awkwardly because we didn't know what we were doing."

The majority of organizations engaged in one or more initiatives in keeping with the long-term strategic vision but still focused on addressing the community's needs within one year or less. However, the community may not have fully capitalized on its capacity to respond to its needs. While most activities were true to the community's strategic vision, the decision to proceed with a project was often predicated on the availability of government funding. "These agencies ... they'd be more useful in the community to do what the community wants to do not what they want to do. It's not only the money but it's the support you need." "Instead of getting people to try and get the projects to fit the criteria, you should try to make the criteria flexible enough that it would fit the proposal because we're having great difficulties with that ... a lot of bureaucracy and red tape." "A really good project is altered at somebody else's whim. You can put a lot of work, time and energy in and it might not go anywhere."

More than one informant recounted having to abandon or shelve viable projects as they were not eligible for government support. Nonetheless, several initiatives succeeded in creating sustainable employment during 1995. Others, in successfully increasing the education level of many residents, for example, contributed to the short-term goal of increasing employability and the long-term strategic goal of increasing self-esteem. Once again, for the two organizations with a broad service area, there was little evidence to suggest that their activities were undertaken in order to achieve outcomes directly responding to Isle Madame's needs.

The flexibility and freedom to experiment found to be associated with the tasks were nevertheless subject to external constraints. "The focus was on TAGS people because the money was there, training was available and we could work with these people. Funding is the key to everything. Recently, in the last three or four months, they came down with a directive from Ottawa that there will be no more long-term training. It kind of changed our plans of what we can do for the TAGS people long-term for five years down the road." "I'm saying, strictly on our own, it's going to be difficult." The sentiment just quoted contrasts sharply with the experience of the one organization that was financially self-supporting: "I think we move a lot faster because we're not tied up in bureaucracy. We don't wait for grant money." The influence of external stakeholders notwithstanding, organizations were quite willing to try new approaches in response to opportunities or challenges: "We kind of have to do things in a different way. It's always going to change depending upon who's here or what the resources are."

The high levels of flexibility and willingness to experiment suggest a high tolerance for failure. One organization demonstrated this quality most vividly as it faced imminent demise. Recognizing the need to alter its original vision in order to survive, it undertook major changes and is now showing signs of recovery. "We had to downsize to make it a viable financial organization. It's evolved, [in] that it's meeting both needs right now."

The operating activities of the four island-based organizations displayed highly diverse skill, knowledge, and ability requirements. The two without employees drew on the board members' competencies. In the other two, the broad range of projects undertaken called for employees with disparate skills, knowledge, and abilities. While specific individuals assumed responsibility for particular projects or activities, they were frequently assisted by other members of the organization: "But I still need the other people to do the other things to make it all work." "She's going to be there for me." "If I'm stuck I call and say I need help." The result was a sense of interdependent ownership and control and a shared sense of accomplishment upon completion. However, these perceptions did not extend beyond organizational boundaries; each organization reported having sole responsibility for outcomes. Indeed, the vast majority of joint initiatives were championed by a particular organization that secured partners to finance the project.

While there was little synergy in the use of community-based resources, the activities undertaken made complementary contributions to the achievement of both the community's short-term objectives and its strategic vision. A holistic set of tasks was necessary to seeing projects through from beginning to end. Moreover, they had high levels of intrinsic reward, as the work was reported to be very meaningful: "There's nothing like the feeling when you've pulled off a project and you've created some jobs." "I like doing creative work so I really like the job." "It's stimulating in that every day is different, every assignment is different so you're growing constantly."

The tasks also provided numerous opportunities for learning by doing. All informants reported using this approach to acquire the competencies needed to accomplish tasks: "We were really green. It's just learning as we're going along."

Of all the task structure elements, the only one absent from the proposed configuration was inter-organizational control and ownership. The nature of the task structure was therefore judged to be highly entrepreneurial. Just as the various organizations contributed to the process to differing degrees, the elements of the task had varying levels of influence, as we shall see. Although some were more instrumental than others, there is no evidence to indicate that they were mutually exclusive.

One basic implication of a broad task definition is that the scope of activities serves to increase the number of participants with a wide range of competencies. For instance, DIMA alone was able to initiate thirty-five projects. Furthermore, while the initiatives were quite varied, the majority were undertaken by organizations whose sole focus was to improve the situation in Isle Madame. The activities were therefore highly meaningful to the people involved. Interviewees expressed strong identification with their organization's mandate, suggesting that the variety of tasks provided many options for participating in development activities, which in turn fostered entrepreneurial involvement and commitment: "We believe in what we're doing." "We firmly believe we're an asset to the community." Many participants viewed their activities not only as improving the community's well-being but also as providing opportunities to enhance personal well-being through the exercise of entrepreneurship.

The time frames for accomplishing the desired goals were also diverse. Activities with a range of time and goal orientations gave the process considerable momentum and continuity, which in turn allowed accomplishments to be sustained over time. This result helped to convince the community that it could influence development and also built enthusiasm and support for doing so. Indeed, exercising entrepreneurship in undertaking short-term activities producing immediate and valued tangible results was particularly important, inasmuch as development tends to be long term in nature. People began to see entrepreneurship as an effective way of addressing problems and opportunities. One of the most visible examples was the establishment of Telile, which served as a model for convincing residents that displaced fisheries workers could successfully launch a new, self-sustaining venture. Yet never was short-term activity pursued at the expense of long-term goal achievement. In fact, the incremental contribution to the achievement of long-term goals was found to be a primary consideration.

One characteristic of the task structure that assumed greater prominence over time is the ability of tasks to be financially self-sustaining. Four of the six organizations are presently involved in revenue-generating activities. "You have to have some projects that will generate revenue in order to sustain our operation because this organization has no money." "I have a target of generating $50,000 in twelve months." "I think our first priority is to operate as a well-run business so we can set an example of something that works. Our second job is to develop as quickly and as well as we can so that we can offer more employment." "Self-sufficiency is our main objective. Right now I think our main objectives are to try to get revenue to pay off our mortgage, to be able to support the building, and be able to support at least a couple of staff members." "We're getting to the point where it's a fee for service. In that way, it'll lead to sustainability." This attribute not only fosters entrepreneurship but also has a very positive influence on individual self-esteem.

Because of the novelty of the initiatives, considerable uncertainty was associated with the tasks, requiring individuals to exercise initiative, judgment, and interpersonal skills in acquiring the expertise and resources needed to bring projects to fruition. Moreover, dealing with this uncertainty enhanced people's capacity to cope with ambiguity.

Although organizational flexibility and freedom to experiment were subject to external constraints, these limitations were not found to inhibit entrepreneurship. Indeed, high levels of entrepreneurship were encouraged by task flexibility and freedom of experimentation: "I have a lot of freedom. I'm sort of like my own boss in one sense. I think we all are; I come in and pretty well decide on my own what I do that day." Determined to create jobs and rejuvenate Isle Madame's economy, organizations took considerable initiative in accessing resources to fulfill their mandate.

Moreover, the tasks afforded countless opportunities for learning by doing. Of all aspects of task structure, this one has the most influence on entrepreneurial behaviour: "I didn't think I could ever do it. I had a lot of really good response. It surprised me. I think if you push yourself a little bit to do things ... you never know what you can do 'til you try." "You're always learning day by day; I had to kind of train myself. Everything I do now is new and I'm still learning." "I learn every day ... it's that kind of job. There's always different things coming up." "I probably learned more in the last two years about that than I have in my whole life, and more than I probably ever could in school because I'm applying it now." In addition, there is no evidence that individuals had any fear of punishment for making mistakes, indicating that the high tolerance for failure encouraged people to try new things.

The tasks undertaken by the two organizations serving a broader geographic area tended to require a fairly homogenous skill set, unlike those undertaken by the other four organizations. Entrepreneurship was also stimulated by the high levels of interdependent control and task ownership within each organization, as all members identified strongly with the various projects and were willing to do anything to help bring about success.

As we have seen, however, little collaboration existed among organizations. Informants were of the opinion that collaborative tasks would limit responsiveness, since reaching agreement among participating boards would be extremely time-consuming. Because the majority of organizations considered financing to be their most pressing need, they saw little advantage in partnerships with other community-based organizations when relationships with government could provide the needed resources. This evidence suggests that inter-organizational collaboration could actually discourage entrepreneurship.

In providing high levels of personal satisfaction, the work itself – being holistic in nature – becomes a strong motivator for exercising entrepreneurship. For example, being able to make tangible contributions to the community's overall goals builds tremendous commitment and attests to the effectiveness of entrepreneurship in achieving the results expected. "If I had money, this is what I'd be doing the rest of my life without pay – just to make sure that the island would recover and the people would be well off." The sheer number of development activities provided wide-ranging opportunities for community members to learn and practise entrepreneurship.

Formal Organizational Arrangements

Analysis of this variable revealed that the process lacked highly developed formal organizational arrangements. In the absence of formal policy and procedure, coordination and control were achieved informally. While the organizational structures were very consistent with an entrepreneurial configuration, formally developed inter-organizational structures were lacking. Indeed, evidence suggests that formal linking mechanisms may be time-consuming and therefore detrimental to entrepreneurship.

As Table 19 demonstrates, there were virtually no formal mechanisms bringing the community's various economic development organizations together, even for information-sharing. Regular scheduled meetings, the most commonly used inter-organizational structure, served an information-sharing function in bringing together similar groups from different communities. Other formal inter-organizational arrangements tended to be contractual in nature. Some informants viewed these as joint ventures or partnerships: "All our projects have been in partnership with someone else – HRD, ACOA, different organizations." "I think most of our initiatives tend to be joint." However, they have generally been established to formalize funding arrangements from government sources rather to facilitate joint action. Indeed, most community-based organizations report having initiated their projects and bearing sole responsibility for their outcomes.

The organizations' structures were highly organic in nature; there were very few rules, regulations, and controls governing day-to-day activity. Individuals reported having complete freedom to decide how and when their work would be done. The boards of directors constituted the principal formal means of coordination and control, since

Table 19
Analysis of Formal Organizational Arrangements

	*La Picasse**	*Island Association for Community Awareness**	DIMA*	*Telile**	*Strait-Highlands* RDA	*Inrich* BDC
Formal linking mechanisms	Information-sharing and problem-solving meetings with provincial Acadian federation, other Acadian organizations	None	None	Member of Chamber of Commerce (off-island) and Technology Advisory group in Sydney; largely serves information-sharing role	Meetings and information-sharing; quarterly meetings with other RDAs; dissemination of information to community groups	None
Type of structure	Currently organic, but policies and procedures have been established for time when facility is operational	Organic	Organic: "We really have no set policies or procedures. I guess we felt things have been running smoothly enough so that we haven't had to do that."	Organic: "It's such a small outfit here that I don't know if policy wouldn't spell more danger." "Basically we all have our own little jobs and we all support each other's jobs. As far as Tony's style of management ... he empowers us."	Organic	Organic: "We never had it until last week. They (ACOA) wanted to see our policy and procedures but our organization doesn't run on policies and procedures."

Table 19 (continued)

	*La Picasse**	*Island Association for Community Awareness**	DIMA*	*Telile**	*Strait-Highlands* RDA	*Inrich* BDC
Authority and responsibility for program development and delivery	Community-based authority and responsibility for services and activities	Community-based authority and responsibility	Community-based program development authority and local responsibility for delivery; organization's activities not subject to externally imposed conditions and restrictions	Local authority and responsibility: "The major decisions are made by the board." "If the organization is in chaos or paralysis, it's the board who has to deal with it."	Nature of activities subject to external authority, but local responsibility: "We're not allowed to fund projects. We're not allowed to provide funding for somebody else's project. All our funding is basically operational funding."	Authority for program development externally based; local responsibility for delivery
Accountability	The Acadian community	"The public" and the board of directors	Majority indicated community accountability: "DIMA is accountable to the community itself."	"Ultimately to the board"	Primarily the municipalities: "Financially we're accountable to the funding groups."	"We're accountable to the community first and foremost, then … to our funding agency (ACOA)."

* Organizations whose activities are focused on Isle Madame

responsibility for policy rests with them. The nature of government funding has had an effect at the policy level, as reflected in the following account: "Once we contacted different governments and saw what their criteria were, in terms of what they thought would work or the programs that were available at the time, then we kind of married our idea to what they had to offer." However, as the organizations developed, they assumed greater authority by increasing their focus on mounting initiatives that would be financially self-sustaining.

Ranging from five to twenty-eight, the average number of the organizations' members was thirteen. With their shared understanding of the community's problems, board members brought their knowledge, skills, and abilities to bear in determining what their organization would do to resolve them. In organizations with staff, the boards see their main responsibility as twofold: overseeing operations, and setting the overall direction of the organization. The monthly meetings are used to bring forward important issues, usually of a non-operating nature; they also serve as a forum for overseeing action and determining what the board and/or staff need to do in the future. It is explicitly understood, but not formalized in written policy, that day-to-day operations are handled by staff and are not to be meddled in by board members: "Decisions are guided by the organization's objectives and are made more by consensus." "It's the community people themselves who decide what's important and how we're going to go about it." "Historically the core group of the board have been making the decisions. Now the decisions are much more made by the staff and brought to the board for ratification." "Big decisions go to the board. Everything else is left to staff." "It's made at the board level. Generally, a paper's produced by staff which is presented to the board, a committee is struck at the board level, and they respond to that draft with a final policy or procedure put in place." "I guess it's up to him [the executive director] and staff to identify the needs and to bring it to the board. Often, from the board, ideas come up as well." "Any kind of radical departure from our mandate is made at the board level."

Although the vast majority of those interviewed saw themselves as accountable, first and foremost, to the community, informants from two different organizations pointed out the problematic nature of ill-defined accountability: "In one sense to the community but in another sense the community doesn't really know enough about the organization so I think the accountability is amongst ourselves." "It's easy to say the community but what does that mean? I think it's accountable to the board and I think the board has been, thus far, accountable to its own conscience to a very large extent."

We have seen that, with their lack of formality, the organizational structures were consistent with an entrepreneurial configuration. The deliberate avoidance of inter-organizational structures was viewed as a positive influence on the community's capacity for action: "It's hard enough to get things done when you just have one board to answer to, let alone two." It is possible that the complexity of these relationships would be detrimental to entrepreneurship, given the structure of community-based development organizations. However, it is also possible that links with externally-based government agencies act as a deterrent to seeking opportunities for community-based economies of action.

Informal coordination and control are conducive to entrepreneurship. One informant contrasted the nature of the present structure with that of the past: "It's not 'I'm behind you and I'm watching' like it was before. It wasn't a happy work environment for a long time. It was more restricted then. Creative ideas were more squashed than allowed to develop. It was a very authoritarian management. Nothing was allowed before. Everything needed special permission. You had to get on your knees and beg."

Community-based responsibility and accountability, coupled with a significant increase in community authority, also had a very positive influence on entrepreneurship in Isle Madame. In particular, the majority of groups exercised considerable creativity in initiating projects to achieve greater financial self-sufficiency. The board meetings, as a venue where individuals publicly commit themselves to undertake particular tasks, played a key role in stimulating action. While individuals assumed responsibility for initiatives, they also shared responsibility and accountability.

Board meetings also function as a mechanism by which individuals acquire entrepreneurial attitudes. For example, at one of the meetings I attended, a particular project was the subject of considerable debate. Participants held differing positions, with one individual adamant that the project should proceed. In the course of the discussion, various short- and long-term implications of pursuing the project surfaced. In the end, a decision was made to place it on hold until further knowledge of critical contingencies could be obtained. The participants were able to learn from each other and discover some of the shortcomings or strengths of their position through this exchange, which contributed to effectiveness by helping to develop "big-picture" thinking in decision-making.

Individuals

As Table 20 indicates, the collective attributes of development process participants in Isle Madame were closely aligned with the proposed

Table 20
Analysis of Individual Attributes

	*La Picasse**	*Island Association for Community Awareness**	DIMA*	*Telile**	*Strait-Highlands* RDA	*Inrich* BDC
Attitudes toward learning by doing	Extremely positive: "I'm always learning!"	Extremely positive: "You learn a lot! … oodles and oodles of knowledge and human awareness."	Extremely positive: "Learning every day!"	Extremely positive	Extremely positive	Extremely positive: "You're always learning day by day."
Strength of collective community identity	High	Moderately high: High community identity tended to be the primary motivator for one member, while the other was motivated more by collective identity.	High: Board members had been involved in community organizations for years.	High: Board members traditionally very involved in community	N/A: Elected to the board	Moderate to low: "Just to get involved and to try to help out in any way I can. I'm not involved that much."
Strategic vision for economies of action	High unaided awareness of other community-based organizations; broad future vision lacking in specific economies of action (B)	Low unaided awareness of other community-based organizations; future vision lacking in specific economies of action (B)	Unaided awareness of other organizations and their approaches; some strategic vision for economies of action (B); future vision does not include specific economies of action (E).	Unaided awareness of most community-based organizations; some economies of action expressed in future vision (B); broadly defined strategic vision for economies of action (E)	High unaided awareness of all community-based organizations; no specific vision of economies of action (B); no specific vision for economies of action (E)	Awareness of other community-based organizations; vision of future development possibilities lacking (B); economies of action not reflected in future vision (E)

Table 20 (continued)

	*La Picasse**	*Island Association for Community Awareness**	DIMA*	*Telile**	*Strait-Highlands* RDA	*Inrich* BDC
Skills and abilities	Varied project-specific expertise; high involvement in other community organizations suggests high levels of team-building, creativity, and interpersonal skills, particularly persuasiveness and persistence (B)	Organizational skills, interpersonal skills: "Each member … has a talent … the experience overall of dealing with people." (B)	Employee skills: Flexibility, tenacity, decision-making, time management, written and oral communication, interpersonal skills, business savvy, self-confidence, willingness to take risks; board members actively involved in community organizations.	Employee skills: Creativity, persistence, problem-solving, openness to learning, being a "people person," communication, writing, and listening skills; board members actively involved in other organizations; business and management experience	Employee skills: Technical business skills, interpersonal and communication skills; board members actively involved in various community organizations	Interpersonal and financial skills and "an appreciation of the potential of the rural economy" (E); some involvement in community organizations; business background (B)
Number of overlapping formal and informal connections	N/A: "Whoever I need … whatever I have to do, I do." "We get a lot [information] through personal contact." (B)	Little evidence that formal connections overlap with informal connections (B)	Staff has developed both formal and informal relationships with the board: "Cultivate your contacts." "Along the years I've made a lot of contacts." "Generally staff don't work closely with particular individuals." (E)	N/A: "I always work with somebody different outside the office." "No, essentially I haven't worked with anybody closely except people within the organization." "I have a big network of friends." "The board." (E)	N/A: Employees recently hired	Moderate to high: "I don't know. In the type of business we're involved with … we're very much in a personal relationship with our loan clients." (E)

Table 20 (continued)

	*La Picasse**	*Island Association for Community Awareness**	DIMA*	*Telile**	*Strait-Highlands* RDA	*Inrich* BDC
Degree of trust and respect for competence	High: "We always knew what had to be done. We just made sure things were done the right way. The board of directors is very strong." (B)	Currently developing, as the board is new; evidence indicates that members trust each other to carry out their assigned responsibilities.	High: "I think people do their own job but there's a lot of respect around the table." (E) The board considers it important to provide support to staff. Observation of meetings indicated high levels of mutual trust and respect for competence between staff and board.	High: "I think we've got some real quality people there. They've proved to themselves and to us that they can … When I disagree, I disagree with a certain depth of respect." (B) "We respect and heed management's decisions." "We trust each other." (E)	Developing, but evidence available suggests it is high: "He just puts his sights on it and does it. Lisa's very good in the communications." High level of mutual respect for competence and trust between the executive director and board chair (E, B)	High mutual respect for competence and trust between board and employees (E)
Preferred work style	Insufficient data; nature of communication suggests informal, free-ranging (B).	Informal, free-ranging; personal contact emphasized in getting things done: "If I can go, I usually go talk to them in person." (B)	Informal, free-ranging: "I keep in touch with people on a regular basis." (E) While structured, board meetings observed to have a distinctly free-ranging air found to stimulate high levels of opportunity identification	Informal, free-ranging: "I enjoy what I do … the freedom." "There's always something different and I like doing different things." (E) Board meetings observed to be quite free-ranging, which stimulated a great deal of discussion and debate	Moderately informal, free-ranging: "I like the flexibility. I like the opportunities that I have to do things." (E) Board proceedings observed to be extremely formal, administratively oriented	Informal, quite free-ranging (E)

Table 20 (continued)

	*La Picasse**	*Island Association for Community Awareness**	DIMA*	*Telile**	*Strait-Highlands* RDA	*Inrich* BDC
Ability to manage interdependencies and multiple tasks	Extremely well developed, as demonstrated by individuals' ability to initiate multiple components of project (B)	Inherently required by volunteer nature of organization (B)	"It can't fall on one person or … on one board member to keep things together." "Any of our accomplishments [hasn't] come easy. We've really worked for them." (E)	Well developed: Individuals thrived on producing results through collective effort (E)	Individuals constantly dealing with multiple tasks and stakeholders (E)	Individual constantly dealing with multiple tasks (E)

Legend: B – Board members
E – Employees

* Organizations whose activities are focused on Isle Madame

entrepreneurial configuration. Individuals held extremely positive attitudes toward learning by doing. With continuous learning a hallmark of the development process, the vast majority not only adopted but enthusiastically endorsed an active learning style.

Collective community identity was particularly strong among board members. Individuals reported forming or joining their organization out of a desire to positively influence the community: "My philosophy is really 'if I can help one person, it's worth it'; I see that my community, Isle Madame, is really in despair right now. Helping people is what motivated me." "I've been involved in a lot of community things over the years. I felt that the community had been very good to me. Although I'd been doing it before, it's kind of repaying for all the graces they've put on me. I just felt obligated to do that." "Just to get involved and to try to help out in any way I can." Moreover, the active involvement of the majority in various community groups over the years suggests that collective action is considered effective in accomplishing objectives: "The main aim was to get people who had a fair amount of knowledge in different fields." "We came together and tried to find people who were interested." This longstanding involvement has heightened individual awareness of the resources available in the community.

People's visions of the future reflected the perspective of the organization with which they were associated, and tended to be rather broad. The fact that economies of action were seen as including contributions from individuals or external resources rather than from other community-based organizational stakeholders was the main point differentiating the posited and existing strategic visions: "Government resources have to be allocated proportionate to need." "I think business people in Isle Madame have to come together as well." "The future of the island depends on getting more and more people involved and creating more leaders." "We need to be smarter at keeping our resources where they are. It's important that someone takes the bull by the horns and leads it in a certain direction. Education ... and new ideas. Tourism, definitely."

I examined the skills and abilities of both staff and board members to determine the extent to which individuals possessed and exercised the competencies that broaden the capacity to innovate. They were a diverse collection, many of them without much business experience. However, board members shared a fairly distinctive demographic profile. The majority of those interviewed (65 per cent) had a professional and/or educational background. While there was no evidence to indicate that gender affected participation, age, educational background, and employment status did seem to be factors. In general, members were over forty years of age, university educated, and employed. This background, combined with considerable volunteer experience, provided the boards with strong interpersonal, team-building, and problem-solving skills, which were evident at the meetings I attended. Several of those interviewed reported drawing on their organizing and writing abilities in fulfilling their role as a board member.

In addition, members were typically long-time residents of Isle Madame who share an interest in improving the community's well-being. An impressive amount of involvement and commitment was evident: "I don't have a hobby. This is my hobby. I would not be able to estimate but I would say that unless you're prepared to set aside three or four of your evenings a week at least for two hours and a sizeable chunk of your Saturday afternoons and Sundays, don't get into this game." "I have no idea how many hours it takes. There's no way I could even track it." The chairs of the boards reported spending, on average, eleven hours per week on the organization's business, while members spent from three to forty hours a month. Most members reported that starting up an organization demands a huge time commitment, which tends to diminish as the organization develops – either because staff are hired to handle operations or because the organization becomes better organized. On average, members reported belonging to three organizations.

The extent of involvement in various community activities and groups suggests that members have developed rather extensive team-building, decision-making, interpersonal, and creative problem-solving skills. However, in the absence of relevant experience, they lacked the specific business or technical competencies required for economic development: "We were really green. Still getting our feet wet. It's just learning as we're going along." "If you look at the members of the organization, we were all pretty green about this type of work." For the most part, the skills that broaden the capacity to innovate were not only considered equally important for staff, but their importance was considered to far outweigh technical competencies.

The extent to which individuals' formal and informal connections overlapped was not found to be a highly relevant factor, owing to the novelty and non-routine nature of the tasks undertaken. Indeed, people reported having dynamic and diverse relationships, rather than working closely with specific individuals: "I always work with somebody different outside the office." However, employees frequently drew on their informal relationships with board members to establish the necessary formal contacts.

Whether staff or board members, participants were highly trusted and respected for their competence in dealings amongst themselves and between staff and board members. Individuals also demonstrated considerable ability in managing interdependencies. Moreover, most performed several tasks in fulfilling their responsibilities.

To sum up, individual attributes were found to be highly consistent with an entrepreneurial configuration. They have significantly influenced the nature of the community's development efforts. The skills, interests, preferences, values, and assumptions of the individuals involved in CED activities in Isle Madame have been conducive to entrepreneurship in a number of ways. Among staff, a positive attitude toward learning by doing and a preference for an informal, free-ranging work style encouraged individuals to take the initiative in successfully completing their projects and responsibilities: "I think if you push yourself a little bit to do things ..." "I think if you're willing to learn and change ... if you don't think your way is the only way but ... try and always learn from somebody else." "Openness to learn."

The evidence suggests that collective community identity has its strongest effect on entrepreneurship during an organization's start-up. Driven by a desire to make sure that the community not only survives but thrives, people in Isle Madame formed groups to achieve together what they felt could not be achieved separately. "It came to the point with the IAS committee where we realized there wasn't going to be any more government funding but the people who were involved felt so strongly about what we were doing we decided to continue as a board anyway." This statement vividly illustrates individuals' commitment to making things happen.

Mutual trust and respect for each other's competence played quite a powerful and unique role in this context. Trust had been established prior to the formation of an organization, on the basis of personal relationships. This, in turn, formed the basis for role relationships within the organization – a reversal of the way trust typically develops in organizations: organizational role relationships usually form the basis for developing the personal relationships from which trust develops. Aware of each other's skills and abilities prior to embarking on development activity, those who formed the various organizations had mutual respect and high regard for each other's competency. Individuals' confidence in their collective ability to achieve what they set out to do not only enabled them to respond effectively to challenges and opportunities but also allowed them to learn a great deal from each other in the process.

While the nature of their vision for economies of action generally differed from that posited as entrepreneurial, individuals were encouraged, nonetheless, to seek opportunities to acquire external resources for various activities and projects. In following through on opportunities, they frequently brought considerable creativity and interpersonal skill to bear in convincing others to contribute resources. The members of one organization were noted for exercising considerable initiative in creating economies of action. On further investigation, the board was found to play an instrumental role in this regard. Unlike in most organizations, where the CEO or manager is the only staff member to attend board meetings, all staff regularly attended and provided the board with a report on the projects and activities they were responsible for. Both employees and board members routinely brainstormed to identify resources suitable to fulfilling the organization's mandate. The individual accountability and collective responsibility characterizing these meetings were judged to be highly instrumental in encouraging staff to exercise entrepreneurship in fulfilling the organization's mandate by creating economies of action.

With regard to skills and abilities, a professional background and previous active involvement in volunteer organizations were key attributes of individuals who initiated action. Despite their lack of prior experience with development activity, individuals' skills and abilities proved to be highly transferrable, and instrumental in establishing the various CED organizations. While the skills and abilities of staff were quite varied, interpersonal competency emerged as pivotal in fostering entrepreneurship among both staff and board members, particularly in relation to the acquisition of information and other resources from outside the community. For example, board members reported having a wide network of personal and professional contacts that collectively form a vast resource bank: "The networking mechanisms are what enable us to stay on top. There's nothing like personal contact." "Here we have the overlap with the other organizations." "From every source possible ... we're scavengers." "We're very well informed as to what the other groups are doing because we're often sitting on those boards." "A friend of mine in Halifax used to say there's nobody in the country that's more than three phone calls away. So you find out with your three phone calls ... who is the expert on this subject in the country? That's $10 in phone calls to the expert saying 'What are the key things that I need to know about this? What are the key documents that I need to read?' Then you are there. Generally, they're very happy to share it."

While individuals did not rely on a well-defined network of overlapping formal and informal connections to gain access to information and other resources, strong networks did have a role to play in facilitating entrepreneurship. The relationships that developed between staff and board members were often the starting point in the quest for resources. "Depending on what I'm looking for ... we have very resourceful people on our board. I'd probably start there if I needed anything I couldn't find." "He knows so many people involved in various agencies that he could probably save me a lot of time." "He can usually tell me where to go from there." These relationships formed the cornerstone for the development of virtual networks: "I guess it's networking ... because we find out all kinds of things that help us in other things." "We talk – that's the main way we do it." "I'm not afraid to call people. I get information all over the place." "I don't have any problems gathering information." "You get to know people all the time, all over the place." "It's not a problem to get information from anywhere."

The findings indicated that strong mutual trust and respect for each other's competence encouraged individuals to undertake activities with highly unpredictable outcomes. The extent of individual commitment to projects and activities indicated a considerable capacity to cope with and enjoy uncertainty in actively pursuing goals: "Everyone comes in and volunteers their time." "We all do volunteer work on that after hours. I'm used to doing that." "Now he's not funded any more but he still keeps on doing it. People get into it and they do whatever they can. If there's funding, there is. If there isn't, if they're able they still keep on doing it." In managing interdependencies and dealing with multiple tasks, individuals adopted a very informal work style that encouraged flexibility in responding to challenges and opportunities.

Informal Organizational Arrangements

While every organization has a unique social structure, the six in our study possessed informal arrangements that had common elements and also formed the principal mechanism of coordination and control. Uncovering shared beliefs and values provided clues as to what was considered important, which in turn formed the basis for determining what action the organizations considered appropriate. Table 21 shows that the informal organizational arrangements had a highly entrepreneurial configuration.

Trust, supportiveness, and cooperation were among the main founding principles of the four island-based organizations. Collective action indicates that cooperation is an important value in the resolution of problems and the grasping of opportunities. The initiative taken in establishing the organizations indicates that the status quo – relying on the government for solutions – was no longer considered appropriate. Individuals in all the community-based organizations held a strong belief in being masters of their own destiny.

"Community" was perhaps the most highly valued principle: "At that point, we had a vision that it would be a community centre where people would come ... and would not have to pay a lot." "We have a social fabric to protect – a way of life in these communities which is quite good." "Most Acadians ... are very attached to their community. We need an infrastructure of which [*sic*] we can identify ourselves as Acadians." "The function is to serve the community." At board meetings,

Table 21
Analysis of Informal Organizational Arrangements

	*La Picasse**	*Island Association for Community Awareness**	DIMA*	*Telile**	*Strait-Highlands* RDA	*Inrich* BDC
Valued principles: supportiveness, trust, and cooperation	Trust and support, preservation of the Acadian culture, independence	Supportiveness, trust, and cooperation the guiding principles for the organization's formation	Community, cohesiveness, optimism, mutual respect, shared responsibility, open communication: "I'll tell him and if he has anything to say to me he'll tell me." "We try to share information." "You kind of get that sense of a team – that you can depend on people. If it's something you can't do, you don't have to worry about it." Board members believe staff expects support from them.	Independence, initiative, achievement, open communication, trust, empowerment: "If you enjoy what you're doing, you're doing to do a better job at it."	Accessibility and cooperation emerging as important organizational values	"Staff-wise things are done very much by consensus. We'll help anything that's going to create a full-time job or work."
Collective identity	High	High	High	High	High	High
Involvement and participation	High	High	High	High	High	Low

Table 21 (continued)

	*La Picasse**	*Island Association for Community Awareness**	DIMA*	*Telile**	*Strait-Highlands* RDA	*Inrich* BDC
Agreement on goals, objectives, time scales, and outcomes	High	High	High	High	High	High
Overlap of formal and informal business and social relationships	Indeterminable	Indeterminable	Indeterminable	Indeterminable	Indeterminable	Indeterminable
Entrepreneurial norms	Insufficient data	N/A: Board hasn't been together long enough for norms to develop.	Highly integrated	Highly integrated	Indeterminable: Staff recently hired	Indeterminable

* Organizations whose activities are focused on Isle Madame

the implications of action for the community were frequently discussed, indicating that the idea of community was a strong guiding principle and not simply rhetoric: "You have to look at everything project by project ... what would it do for the community?" Improving community well-being was the basis for establishing the various organizations, determining the role each would play, defining its aims and deciding how to achieve them, and determining the appropriateness of action.

While the involvement and participation levels in the operating activities of most organizations were high, the stage of development was a major factor in determining who the actors were. During the pre-start-up and start-up stages of organizational development, board members were very actively involved, dedicating an average of twenty-eight hours per week: "At the beginning it was almost a full time job organizing, fundraising." Consequently, a strong collective identity developed, propelled by a belief that the participants could "make a difference." Over time, staff involvement supplanted that of the board. Within all island-based organizations there was an implicit but clear understanding that membership required high levels of involvement and participation: "Everyone comes in and volunteers their time. You forget that you don't necessarily have to do that."

The members of each group had a strong sense of purpose and generally agreed as to goals and outcomes, even though objectives and time frames tended not to be specifically defined: "If you're specific you can spend a lot of years banging your head against the wall and miss half a dozen other opportunities." "It's hard to set a target date." "Apart from that we haven't set too many specific objectives." "That's what we want to do – have specific, attainable, realistic, and timely goals; self-sufficiency is our main objective."

The degree to which formal and informal business and social relationships overlapped could not be determined, as a result of the dynamic nature of the relationships established in carrying out the work of each organization. As discussed previously, in creating virtual networks individuals indicated that they did not tend to work closely with a particular set of people outside the organization.

Finally, members of all the organizations adopted a set of behavioural expectations that were highly entrepreneurial in nature. One universal expectation was that staff act and the board advises. "I think at this stage, the staff expects the board to keep their nose out of the day-to-day operations. When we've delved into that before, there's been problems." The emphasis placed on informality was indicated in behaviour, dress, language, relationships among members – both staff and board – and the development of linkages outside the organization. For example, on one of my visits to a certain organization, I found the staff preparing for an afternoon meeting with federal and provincial government agencies and politicians. The dress code had not been altered for the occasion. Generally, communication was not by memos or other formal means but by personal contact, either by phone or face to face.

In contrast, one of the off-island organizations had much more formal arrangements, best illustrated by comparing its board meeting with one held by the most informal island-based group. Most of those present wore suits, seating was predetermined, proceedings were taped, and I was not given a copy of the agenda, although the chair formally welcomed me when the meeting was called to order. Agenda items were presented by the executive director, with very little input or debate from board members. For the most part, the proceedings had an administrative focus. At the island-based organization's meeting, dress was casual, people sat wherever they wanted, and the agenda, minutes, and other supporting documentation were distributed to anyone who did not have a copy. In addition to board members, all staff were present. On calling the meeting to order, the chair welcomed the four guests and explained that they could become board members if they attended two meetings. While some of the agenda items were purely informational in nature, others were substantive, with, for the most part, an action focus. In presenting project reports, staff raised key issues that evoked numerous ideas, opinions, and potential sources of contacts from the board. Besides highlighting the impetus that informality provides for entrepreneurship, this account also points out another factor facilitating entrepreneurship: open communication. Indeed, evidence suggests that the more open communication is within an organization, the more opportunities are identified and acted upon.

Individuals involved in day-to-day activities held an expectation that each person would assume general responsibility for tasks he or she finds meaningful and would be given the freedom to make decisions about how and when to do work: "It doesn't always happen that way but that's what we try to do when we divvy up the work – who's good at this? Who likes doing this?" "I'm sort of like my own boss in one sense. I think we all are." "Total freedom." "For example, I come in and pretty well decide on my own what I do that day. It gives me complete freedom. I'm allowed to work all the time I want!" "I'm free – if I want to take an afternoon off, I do. If I want to come in late, I do as long as I don't have a deadline to meet." This flexibility encouraged considerable entrepreneurship, since it fostered high levels of task ownership and commitment to seeing an activity or project through. People felt their contributions are valuable as well as equitable: "I think it's just a sense of responsibility that I have to do this. When you have other people who are the same way, you don't mind doing it. If I was the only one that came in here and did all the work, I'd be upset but everybody's putting in a lot of time."

Another expectation was that individual responsibilities would vary with conditions and therefore be highly changeable. The number and variety of projects and activities indicate broad-based support for experimentation and learning, associated with the expectation that risk, failure, and mistakes will be tolerated. In fact, several people commented on the fact that it was generally understood that not all projects or activities would be successful.

Still another identified expectation was voluntarism, as indicated by the extra effort made: "In my time off, in my nights, weekends, I'm still going to work to help sustain and develop the organization because we have to survive." "Pulling together for one cause – preservation of culture." "The volunteer commitment." Although voluntarism is inherent in community organizations, the actual time commitment by individuals was found to far exceed what was formally required. For example, staff all reported that they regularly worked nights and weekends. Indeed, while the basic time commitment required of board members was one evening a month for regular meetings, almost all reported a far greater contribution.

Opportunities or problems were handled in a timely way through informal monitoring and evaluation, especially since people had the authority and responsibility to take action: "I'm in and out all the time so I see what's going on." "The board evaluates based on whether there is progress being made on a project as reported on by staff." "They monitor them hands on." "All we can base the success of them on is the feedback from the community." "I would have to say by the achievements – if it creates jobs, [that's] good for the community ... depending on the project." "I don't think we evaluate. We work flat out and if it works we keep doing it. If it doesn't work we have a meeting." "Most of the things we do are easily monitored. They're generally evaluated by the community." "The real evaluation for each project would have to be by the people who are working on it. You know when things aren't working." "That's how we evaluate, I guess – by looking at what's happening."

While entrepreneurship was not formally rewarded, the informal rewards functioned as a powerful reinforcement at both the individual and collective levels: "Every time you achieve something, everybody shares in the achievement." Indeed, when employees were asked what rewards their job provided, they reported high levels of intrinsic rewards: "When people appreciate what you're doing it makes you feel good. It's nice to work with people you like to work with and I like doing creative work so I really like the job." "Knowing that I can do a good job and get things done." "It gives me a feeling of accomplishment." "It's exciting, it's adventurous, it's stimulating in that every day is different, every assignment is different so you're growing constantly." "I do what I want to do, what I like to do." "I guess the satisfaction in knowing that you might make a difference. The satisfaction in doing a job and getting it done." "My reward is the satisfaction of at least having movement. Something is happening for people. My reward is not the money I make every week, it's that the people that I work for get results and they do get results."

The informal organizational arrangements were very consistent with an entrepreneurial configuration and influenced the community's development efforts in several ways. Trust, support, and cooperation were collectively shown to be a *sine qua non* in dealing effectively with the uncertainties associated with undertaking development activities for the first time; that is, they were highly conducive to entrepreneurship in all six organizations. "They support each other in presenting projects, proposals." "You kind of get that sense of a team – that you can depend on people. If it's something you can't do, you don't have to worry about it, you can call somebody to help you out. Every time you achieve something, everybody shares in the achievement." "We're a family. I expect a great deal of myself and I expect a great deal of my staff and I've been very fortunate." "We trust each other. We do a lot on our own. We can depend on each other for support or help." "At the staff level a proposal might be brought forward for discussion in regard to what others think of it ... comments, questions. If the group seems to be in favour and it appears that the project is worthwhile ... can be done in a short period of time and can create results, then it's brought to the board." "If DIMA is asked to attend a board meeting or something like that, we have a great showing." "Here you're expected to pitch in."

Individual task accomplishment was typically found to require interdependent contributions; working cooperatively with others allowed the pooling of individual commitment, knowledge, and competence. People were able to acquire and develop skills through both learning by doing and learning from each other. Because people trusted and supported each other, they were not intimidated in proposing new ideas; indeed, the fact that new projects and activities were constantly being launched indicates that ideas were valued.

High levels of involvement and participation were also instrumental in fostering entrepreneurship. The non-routine nature of the operating activities gave people displaced by the fisheries collapse numerous chances to learn and practise entrepreneurship. The short-term focus and diversty of many activities significantly increased the number and attributes of participants. Active recruitment had a significant effect on participation, since residents generally lacked the self-confidence to take independent action to improve their situation. Once involved, people found the activities rewarding, reporting a great sense of accomplishment that enhanced self-worth, which in turn encouraged them to adopt entrepreneurial behaviour as an effective means of facing opportunities and problems.

However, the idea of community provided the greatest stimulus for development participants to exercise entrepreneurship. Driven by the desire to be masters of their own economic destiny, they worked tirelessly to make their vision a reality.

Mutually reinforcing each other, the norms that form the basis for action produced highly entrepreneurial behaviour patterns facilitating decision-making, cooperation, and commitment in organizations and, ultimately, task performance. In adopting these patterns of behaviour, people embraced the challenge of learning to deal with ambiguity and uncertainty, along with the stress associated with changing habits and attitudes: "I think it was the sense that I had to step out of the comfortable ... because it wasn't comfortable sometimes."

PROCESS OUTPUTS

Here I examine the outputs produced by the interaction of the four variables as they existed in Isle Madame, with respect to innovation and economic development.

Innovation

In a development context, both economic development outcomes and the means of achieving them can constitute innovation. Generally, the majority of innovations in Isle Madame involved process.

Process innovation was created in four main areas: the planning of activities, recruitment of participants, accessing resources, and board structure. The approach to planning involved ascertaining residents' understanding of the problems and possible solutions associated with the fisheries crisis. Local residents used surveys and focus groups to research the issues, and a team of consultants then outlined the community's common vision for the future. This exercise proved to be instrumental in unifying and providing direction for the community's subsequent activities. The key innovation was that the vision was created *by* the community, not *for* the community by interventionists.

With regard to recruitment, organizations devised several innovations: giving preference to job applicants who had demonstrated a commitment to the organization and its aims through volunteer efforts;

undertaking projects that provided a positive employment experience to motivate individuals to remain involved in the organization in a volunteer capacity on completion of a project (usually by becoming board members); recruiting board members who had a fairly well developed external network that could be utilized in accessing resources; drawing upon project-specific expertise within the community on an *ad hoc* basis; and recruiting former community residents with skills that would help bring projects to fruition.

The various organizations were established by highly educated professionals who therefore were not representative of people experiencing unemployment as a result of the crisis. The founding members deliberately involved more members of the community in organizational activities, either through employment or by joining the board. Once involved, people became very committed to the organization and its goals. For example, DIMA recruited and hired a number of university students and graduates possessing skills ranging from marketing to legal to technical, to develop a fairly diverse set of employment generating proposals and initiatives. In attending one of DIMA's board meetings, which was held during the same week that university students were home for their February break, I noted that most of the students who had worked for the organization the previous summer were in attendance – an impressive indication of the level of commitment the organization was able to generate.

With respect to accessing resources, two major innovations were noted. First, rather than abandoning a venture opportunity when the necessary financing could not be obtained, in two organizations the board members pledged personal assets to borrow the money required to bring the ventures to fruition. Second, board members frequently drew upon their personal networks to access or expedite the receipt of monetary or other resources.

Finally, as regards board structure, DIMA's design was innovative in several respects. Meetings were open to anyone who wished to attend, regardless of the agenda, unlike most organizations' meetings, which were held *in camera* on the grounds of confidentiality. Moreover, any resident who attended two or more meetings could become a board member. Third, all staff were expected to attend board meetings. Their inclusion not only promoted a shared understanding of the decision-making rationale but also ensured that employees were not simply carrying out the directives of others. As partners in the decision-making process, staff expressed high levels of commitment to the resulting activities. Finally, board meetings had an action orientation facilitated by an agenda that focused on results. The meetings dealt directly with problems and opportunities in current projects and with the identification of potential activities.

Several innovations were directly related to the desired economic development outcomes. One was the creation of ventures integrating training and skill development with the creation of employment. For example, government funding was obtained to train unemployed fisheries workers in video technology and television production. The next phase of this project involved forming a community television channel and a video production company (Telile) operated by graduates of the course. A second innovation was the Active Living Centre, a facility that could serve as focal point for social development. A third was DIMA's strategy of developing short-term projects that could be spun off as self-sustaining ventures, thereby increasing the opportunities for broad-based community involvement. Another was securing a base of "anchor" tenants in an organization's facilities so that sufficient revenue could be generated to cover operating expenses and subsidize services identified as community needs. For example, La Picasse allocated space for a youth centre to serve the francophone community, while the Active Living Centre provided meeting facilities for youth and service groups. Still another innovation involved pursuing diversified employment-generating activities. For example, La Picasse brought together a diverse set of stakeholders to provide new services and resources to the francophone community and convinced two local residents to set up small manufacturing ventures in a space designed for the purpose.

Considered collectively, the various process and outcome innovations outlined above are similar in that they all relate more directly to the achievement of the community's overall aims than to the internal management of the various organizations. That is, the innovations are strategic rather than administrative in nature.

Economic Development

In determining the extent of economic development achieved by the process, I assessed the outputs according to goal achievement, resource utilization, and adaptation. The results achieved by the process during 1995 are summarized in Table 22.

Significant progress has been achieved in creating employment for displaced fisheries workers, and for the island's youth who have pursued further education, as well as in increasing the community's educational levels. As regards resource utilization, there was little evidence of effectiveness in the initial stages of the process, since most resources were being depleted rather than sustained. However, there is a growing

Table 22
Summary of Results Achieved During the 1995 Operating Year

	Results
La Picasse*	80 per cent completion of the building, which is partially operational
Island Association for Community Awareness*	Increasing the number and nature of social, recreational, and educational programs; increasing community involvement in the organization and its programs. Survival was considered a very important accomplishment.
DIMA*	62 per cent participation rate among the 350 TAGS recipients, with 64 (20 per cent) finding full-time or part-time employment and 90 (28 per cent) involved in training 20 people working on Senior Care projects 22 people in the Older Workers Adjustment program Six people involved in the Coastal Mapping Project Creation of five full-time jobs through the Small Options Home Six TAGS clients employed by the Coastal Mapping Project Literacy Outreach project employing one person Home-page Internet project employing one person Recruitment of seven or eight new board members Increasing the organization's financial self-sufficiency Helping to convince people to try new things
Telile*	Achieving organizational survival and financial self-sufficiency through restructuring; maintenance of five positions; providing community programming that satisfies the community
Strait-Highlands RDA	Projects with some effect on Isle Madame: Undertaking a regional strategic planning process; organizing a trade show; supporting and encouraging groups such as DIMA and Telile – perceived to add credibility to the projects these organizations undertook
InRich BDC	Lending approximately $1 million to 50 businesses; assisting in the start-up of 45 to 50 small businesses through the administration of HRD's Self-Employment Assistance (SEA) program. Currently, the organization is turning over 35 per cent of its loan portfolio – well above the desired 25 per cent. However, the BDC has reported very little involvement in Isle Madame.

* Organizations whose activities are focused on Isle Madame

awareness of the need to become financially self-sustaining. As discussed earlier, all four island-based organizations are or will be involved in revenue-generating activities. Finally, with respect to adaptation, the process has been quite effective in initiating broad-based cultural change, as indicated by the growing number of people becoming involved in development activities. The degree of involvement is significant considering that, prior to the fisheries crisis, community-based development had been virtually non-existent. Moreover, the residents of Isle Madame are beginning to endorse entrepreneurial behaviour as a more effective way of responding to problems or opportunities than the behaviour associated with a culture of dependency.

To sum up: The innovations created through Isle Madame's development efforts can be directly linked to job creation and have also been instrumental in diversifying the island's economy. Even though the residents had not engaged in any prior economic development activity, their endeavours created an improvement. While DIMA has been responsible for most of the jobs generated thus far, the community's accomplishments represent the results of collective organizational efforts.

THE RELATIONSHIP OF THE FINDINGS TO THE HYPOTHESES

The findings indicate that the development process achieved considerable success in producing the behaviour fostering higher levels of strategic innovation, goal achievement, and adaptation. The analysis revealed that, in Isle Madame, all four process variables possessed – to varying degrees – an entrepreneurial configuration and therefore exhibited some congruence. Given the outputs achieved, this congruence led to more effective entrepreneurial behaviour. The consistency between the actual process outputs and the desired outputs, as drawn from explicit and implicit strategy statements, indicates that the innovation and economic development achieved are attributable to congruence among the process variables.

Structuring the tasks towards achieving self-sustaining strategic outcomes within a short time and requiring broad-based participation encouraged numerous individuals to exercise entrepreneurship amidst highly informal organizational arrangements, which induced them to adopt a very hands-on approach. One organization vividly illustrates the consequences of a lack of fit among variables. Prior to its restructuring, which had taken place during the previous year, the formal organizational arrangements did not correspond to those proposed in the framework, although the other variables were quite closely aligned. Instead, formal rules, policies, and procedures were used to coordinate and control behaviour, not only inhibiting enterprise but almost resulting in the organization's demise. When an organic structure was adopted, individuals exercised considerable entrepreneurship to see to it that the various tasks were carried out. Although this evidence is specific to one of several embedded units of analysis, it does support the proposition that congruence is associated with the effectiveness of the process.

The community has been effective in influencing its economic destiny because it adopted a strategy well suited to or congruent with the environmental conditions it faced. It was convinced that the development of a small business base would require residents to acquire new competencies. The development process emerging from this strategy involved undertaking activities that gave residents an opportunity to learn and practise entrepreneurship to enhance their existing knowledge, skills, and abilities in order to develop alternative means of becoming financially self-supporting. Guided by a common purpose which made certain that efficiency did not take precedence over effectiveness, the various organizations focused on proactively undertaking initiatives that enabled residents to learn how to modify their behaviour to influence the community's economic situation. In adopting a process that stimulated enterprising behaviour, the community's development efforts were successful in generating innovation and influencing economic development.

In summary, the community's effort was influenced by the extent to which each process variable was entrepreneurially configured, thereby supporting the exploratory hypotheses linking entrepreneurship, innovation, and economic development.

CROSS-CASE ANALYSIS

As noted earlier, previous analyses had confirmed that the fisheries collapse threatened the survival of these two single-industry communities. The general economic climate exacerbated the situation. A lack of economic growth in the province and the country was accompanied by a decline in the traditional manufacturing and natural resource export market. Competitive conditions called for flexibility, responsiveness, and specialization in skills and technology as well as a heightened role for small businesses in the economy. Meanwhile, government policy was undergoing rationalization of programs and funding for economic and social development. As Table 23 shows, neither Eastern Guysborough County nor Isle Madame was well endowed with resources to deal with the new circumstances.

Both communities initiated a development process aimed at creating jobs that would enable residents to remain while preserving the quality of life. Both were found to have similar understandings of what had to be done. In Isle Madame, the need to develop a small business base was expressed as follows: "We didn't see a big company coming in here and creating 500 jobs. That would have been a dream. We figured, if we are going to create jobs, it would be on a small scale – two of this, one of that. We don't want development on Isle Madame at all costs. We have a social fabric to protect." "Employment ... should be clean; that doesn't affect our environment, that doesn't

Table 23
Comparative Context Summary

	Eastern Guysborough County	*Isle Madame*	*Nova Scotia*	*Canada*
POPULATION				
1991 Census	3,500	4,333	899,942	27,296,859
Percentage change, 1986–1991	–4.4	–6.7	3.1	7.9
EMPLOYMENT				
Unemployment rate (%)	18.7	19.9	13	10
Percentage employed in primary industry/manufacturing (%)	49	37	19	21
Percentage in administrative/ management occupation	4	6	10	12
INCOME				
Average income	$16,663	$16,915	$20,706	$23,891
Percentage with transfer payment income	29	29	15.7	11.4
Percentage with income < $10,000	59	57	33	28
Percentage with income > $10,000	5	7	24	29.5
EDUCATION				
Percentage with less than grade 9 education	26	24	13	14
Percentage without high school completion	37	31	30	24
QUALITY OF LIFE				
Percentage owning dwelling	83	88	71	63
Percentage of total single detached households	89	91	68	57

Source: *Profile of census divisions and subdivisions in Nova Scotia*, Ottawa: Industry, Science and Technology Canada, 1994. 1991 Census of Canada. Catalogue number 95-313.

change our way of life." In Eastern Guysborough County, a similar need was defined: "If you have 500 people employed in 100 small businesses, no one of them can disable the community." "Seafreeze is doing great down there but that's all your eggs in one basket. It's one industry, one plant, one everything. If it's gone, everything's gone. Smaller things ... if one goes, sure it hurts but it doesn't kill you. So that's what we're working on now – trying to create new business ... whether there are ten people or twelve people. We're not looking ahead to 1,500 jobs – the Seafreezes. We're looking to start small."

Despite their similar aims and resources, the communities adopted two very distinct approaches. The differing levels of effectiveness achieved by the two communities attest to the role played by the development process in shaping effectiveness. To develop a better understanding of how the process influenced outcomes, in this cross-case analysis I examine each variable in the framework as a basis for drawing further conclusions about the research hypotheses, and the scope of analytic generalization provided by the framework.

Tasks

Isle Madame's task structure had a higher entrepreneurial configuration than Eastern Guysborough County's. Table 24 indicates that several attributes were evident in both cases, while others were exclusive to one community. The extent to which interdependent task ownership and control fostered enterprise was indeterminable, as there were virtually no community-based inter-organizational initiatives being pursued in either case.

The weak entrepreneurial configuration characterizing Eastern Guysborough County's task structure was related to the rather narrow definition and long-term orientation of its development task, as well as a goal focus emphasizing infrastructure development. It is probable that these factors would influence the nature of the skill, knowledge, and ability requirements, the degree of task flexibility, and the amount of freedom to experiment. Nonetheless, owing to the nature of the tasks undertaken, few opportunities were provided for residents who lacked entrepreneurial experience to acquire it through development activities.

The evidence suggests that the characteristics of the task component exert interdependent but unequal behavioural influences. Since both communities possessed high levels of task uncertainty and novelty, intrinsic rewards, opportunities for learning by doing, and a holistic set of tasks, these factors were deemed necessary but insufficient for stimulating community-level entrepreneurship. Flexibility, freedom to experiment, and tolerance for failure varied to some degree. Task definition, time and goal focus, and diversity of skill, knowledge, and ability were judged to be the primary determinants of whether entrepreneurial behaviour would emerge more broadly within the community. It is these factors that facilitated greater involvement in learning and practising enterprise.

Formal Organizational Arrangements

Table 25 presents a cross-case comparison of the formal organizational arrangements. In both communities, the development of formal linking

Table 24
Cross-Case Comparison of Tasks

	Eastern Guysborough County	*Isle Madame*
Task definition	Narrowly defined; mostly supply-side initiatives (expanding the local resource base either by generating new infrastructure – particularly tourism related – or capital available to the community)	Broadly defined; diverse set of both supply-side and demand-side initiatives
Task uncertainty and novelty	High	High
Time and goal focus	Long-term focus; largely indirect attempts to influence economic development; responding to government funding availability rather than need	Short-term focus; propelled by an emphasis on achieving strategic outcomes. However, goal focus was partially influenced by government funding availability.
Flexibility	Low	Moderately high
Freedom to experiment	Low	Moderately high
Tolerance for failure	Indeterminable	High
Diversity of skills, knowledge, and abilities required	Low	High
Interdependent control and ownership among community-based organizations	Absent (encouragement for vertical synergy and interdependence)	Absent but high within organizations
Holistic set of tasks	High	High
Intrinsic rewards	High	High
Opportunities for learning by doing	High	High

mechanisms was negligible, so the extent to which this factor positively influenced enterprise could not be verified.

The organizational structures in both communities were highly organic. While such structures have been shown to be conducive to entrepreneurial behaviours, the findings suggest that enterprise at the organizational and community levels is contingent on the presence of

Table 25
Cross-Case Comparison of Formal Organizational Arrangements

	Eastern Guysborough County	*Isle Madame*
Formal linking mechanisms	Few: Mostly for information-sharing or administrative economies of action	Lacking
Type of structure	Organic	Organic
Authority and responsibility for program development and delivery	Local responsibility, external authority	Local responsibility, moderately high authority
Accountability	Funding agencies, community	Community

community-based authority and accountability. Although Eastern Guysborough County's organizations were found to have quite organic structures and high levels of local responsibility for program delivery, primary accountability and authority for program development resided elsewhere. In contrast, organizations in Isle Madame perceived primary accountability to be community-based and assumed far greater levels of authority for program design. Although this authority was subject to considerable outside influence, that influence has been declining. Thus, while both communities possessed organic structures and community-based responsibility, only Isle Madame's formal organizational arrangements showed community-based accountability and authority for program development.

Individuals

As Table 26 indicates, the individuals involved in day-to-day development activities in both communities fulfilled their organizational responsibilities through behaviours highly aligned with those posited as being entrepreneurial.

Collective community identity had the greatest influence on the process during start-up, since it was the key factor prompting people to take action. Prior to the formation of an organization, a high level of trust and mutual respect for competence had developed on the basis of personal relationships, which served to encourage considerable entrepreneurial behaviour because it made people highly supportive of one another.

While both staff and board members had fairly well-developed interpersonal, team-building, and problem-solving skills, individuals'

Table 26
Cross-Case Comparison of Individual Attributes

	Eastern Guysborough County	*Isle Madame*
Attitudes toward learning by doing	Highly positive	Highly positive
Strength of collective community identity[1]	High among board members; provided impetus for organizational start-up	High among board members; provided impetus for organizational start-up
Strategic vision for economies of action	Low in terms of strategic economies; high in terms of administrative economies	Organizational, as opposed to community-oriented
Skills and abilities	Strong interpersonal, team-building, and problem-solving skills among employees; board members do not fit a particular demographic profile, as occupations, age, and educational backgrounds vary.	Strong interpersonal, team-building, and problem-solving skills among employees; majority of board members have strong managerial and professional background experience and a university education, and are over forty.
Number of overlapping formal and informal connections	Not relevant	Not relevant
Degree of trust and respect for competence	High	High
Preferred work style	Informal, free ranging	Informal, free ranging
Ability to manage interdependencies and multiple tasks	High	High

[1] Applies to board members only; irrelevant for employees

capacity to capitalize on these competencies was predicated upon having technical, business, and/or managerial skills. In the absence of a business background, an individual's future vision possessed few economies of action, strategic or otherwise. Moreover, the extent to which formal and informal connections overlapped was not a significant factor, as individuals reported highly dynamic information and other resource requirements. There was no evidence to indicate that people differentiated between formal and informal contacts. However, given the non-routine nature of the tasks, individual ability to establish and utilize virtual networks was a key factor in identifying and accessing resources.

In summary, the attributes of individuals participating in the development process in both communities were consistent with those of an entrepreneurial configuration: positive attitudes toward learning by doing, collective community identity, high levels of trust and respect for competence, a preference for an informal, free-ranging work style, and an ability to manage interdependencies and cope with multiple tasks.

Technical, business, and managerial skills, as well as the ability to develop and use virtual networks effectively, are attributes that encourage enterprise. Prior business experience and expertise enabled individuals to capitalize fully on their strong interpersonal, team-building, and problem-solving skills. The one individual attribute that was conspicuously absent in both communities was a strategic vision for economies of action. Rather, people's vision tended to be oriented toward either organizationally focused or administratively focused economies of action.

The findings suggest that a number of factors may discourage individuals from engaging in community-based inter-organizational collaboration. In some cases, greater opportunities for acquiring resources from external government sources may prompt organizations to pursue organizationally-based vertical economies rather than community-based horizontal economies. In other cases, organizations may pursue administrative economies because they lack the autonomy to undertake a broad range of tasks. Finally, it has been suggested that community-based inter-organizational collaboration would reduce responsiveness, since approval from several boards would be required before an activity could be undertaken. While each of these explanations has merit, the evidence remains inconclusive.

Participants in both communities possessed attributes consistent with those posited to be enterprising. There appear to be several reasons, however, why enterprising behaviours were found to be more broad-based in Isle Madame. First, given the nature of the tasks undertaken, there were more people involved in the process. Second, because that community's organizations were shown to have more authority, individuals had greater autonomy to act. Third, because more board members there had a business and/or managerial background, they were better able to capitalize on their skills and abilities to innovate.

Informal Organizational Arrangements

As Table 27 indicates, the informal organizational arrangements that developed in both communities are generally consistent with those posited to foster enterprise, with one exception: the extent to which formal and informal business and social relationships overlapped. This

Table 27
Cross-Case Comparison of Informal Organizational Arrangements

	Eastern Guysborough County	*Isle Madame*
Valued principles: supportiveness, trust, and cooperation	Extensively adopted guidelines for action	"Community" found to be an additional value guiding action
Collective identity	High among board members but largely irrelevant, as work done independently	High
Involvement and participation	High	High
Agreement on goals, objectives, time scales, and outcomes	No evidence of a shared broad-based community understanding	Shared broad-based community understanding of goals and outcomes
Overlap of formal and informal business and social relationships	N/A	N/A
Entrepreneurial norms	Highly integrated into behaviour patterns	Highly integrated into behaviour patterns

factor was indeterminable, but was also deemed irrelevant because of the nature of the relationships required by the non-routine tasks.

Two additional behavioural expectations surfaced to foster enterprise in both communities. The first is the expectation that board members would not interfere with the day-to-day activities of staff; the second, the expectation of high levels of voluntarism among an organization's members. In Isle Madame's organizations there was a further expectation that individual areas of responsibility would be determined on the basis of individual interest.

The one factor differentiating the two communities is the degree of agreement on goals. In Eastern Guysborough County, there is no evidence that organizations shared a strategic vision of what was to be achieved in the community. In contrast, in Isle Madame development activity rested on a strategic vision prepared as part of the GTA report. With broad-based acceptance from the community, it implicitly provided a common purpose for the various initiatives. Although each organization operated autonomously, members were keenly aware of how their activities contributed to the economic and social goals described in the aforementioned report. Indeed, the consensus achieved was instrumental in establishing "community" as an important value for guiding action. While development process participants in Eastern

Guysborough County valued the idea of community, its effect on action was not pervasive. Most activities were either initiated by government or undertaken in response to the availability of program funding rather than in strategic response to identified needs.

Conclusion

The consistency of the findings derived from the cross-case analysis with the research hypotheses provides compelling support for the theoretical framework. Neither case indicates that matching the configuration of any one of the model's variables was sufficient to stimulate effective entrepreneurial behaviour. For example, although in Eastern Guysborough County two of the process variables – individual attributes and informal organizational arrangements – were consistent with the proposed configurations, the behaviour generated by the process did not increase levels of strategic innovation or economic development. This finding indicates that community entrepreneurial effort is influenced by the extent to which the four process variables are configured to maximize the potential for enterprising behaviour. With greater total congruence among the four, and a greater consistency with the posited entrepreneurial configurations, Isle Madame's development process was more effective in stimulating entrepreneurial behaviour at multiple levels.

Isle Madame achieved greater levels of innovation in utilizing available resources to meet strategic goals. For example, DIMA's Small Options Home accomplished both economic and social goals by creating several full-time jobs and enabling residents requiring this type of care to remain in the community. The venture required considerable entrepreneurship. Moreover, not only did Isle Madame achieve more innovation; it attained higher levels of effectiveness in goal achievement, a finding which indicated that a relationship between entrepreneurship and economic development does, in fact, exist.

Innovation in Isle Madame was not generated in the way expected – by focusing on the synergistic use of community-based resources – but, for the most part, by deriving resources from external sources. In Eastern Guysborough County, some innovation was generated at the community level, but it was administrative in nature rather than strategic.

Neither community was highly effective in sustaining resources. However, in Isle Madame, an awareness of the need for activities to be financially self-supporting established a direct link between self-reliance and effectiveness in resource use. This finding suggests that we need to reconsider how community organizations typically perceive the role of profit. Indeed, the more revenue exceeds expenses, the greater the margin for error, which in turn encourages learning by doing and provides opportunities to make mistakes without fear of punishment. If some activities with a high profit potential are pursued, the profit generated can be used to launch other job-creating ventures that can help both individuals and the community become more self-sufficient, as well as to undertake initiatives that may only be viable on a break-even basis but nonetheless would fulfill important community needs.

Isle Madame undertook a far greater number of activities within a shorter period and achieved greater participation levels. Its boards had a higher average number of members (12.6) than those in Eastern Guysborough County (8.8), who tended to belong to fewer organizations (an average of 3.3 versus 4.6 in Eastern Guysborough County). As a result, more people dedicated more time and attention to the various initiatives in Isle Madame.

Overall, effectiveness in influencing economic development was contingent upon the extent to which the community's strategy fit the environmental conditions. Indeed, the assessment of the development context in both communities indicates that opportunities for residents to learn and practise entrepreneurship are needed for stimulating economic development. In providing more such opportunities, Isle Madame was far more effective in influencing economic development than Eastern Guysborough County was, thereby supporting the final hypothesis.

Theoretical replication was established by demonstrating that different levels of effectiveness are attributable to the development process. It is significant, as it suggests results for similar communities. With comparable circumstances and resources, each community in the case study generated a different level of enterprise and economic development, a finding which implies that the main reason for the discrepancy lies in the process. Furthermore, as the process undertaken in both communities was quite effective in stimulating enterprise at the individual level, it was easier to identify the attributes most instrumental at the community level: broad task definition and a short-term need-oriented goal focus for tasks, community-based authority and accountability in the formal organizational arrangements, business experience for individual board members, and agreement on goals and outcomes in the informal organizational arrangements.

The findings highlight the importance of adopting a strategy that fits environmental conditions as it shapes the tasks undertaken, which in turn have a pervasive effect on the other process variables, and ultimately on effectiveness. While the accomplishment of goals is an important measure of effectiveness, resource utilization cannot be ignored if both individuals and communities are to achieve self-sufficiency. Finally, adaptability is predicated on the extent to which the development process fosters entrepreneurship. The final chapter provides conclusions and recommendations in light of these findings.

8 Conclusions and Recommendations

In this book I address a fundamental question: How can local development be induced in areas identified as lacking entrepreneurial capacity and organizational and administrative skills? In light of the aim to contribute to a better understanding of community-based development, it is important to consider what has been accomplished thus far.

In exploring the connections among entrepreneurship, innovation, and endogenous development, I have shown that an inclusive framework is essential in studying a complex phenomenon such as development. The Community Enterprise Emergence Model represents the first effort to incorporate the various factors that research has identified as important to development. As such, it takes an exploratory role in identifying the interactive influence of the process, its context, and its outcomes. Unlike other frameworks, it has the capacity to incorporate the effect of industry-level factors, as well as endogenous economic and sociocultural factors, on the development process. Moreover, it can deal with the effectiveness of the process by using the context analysis to identify the expected results. Within the context of rural single-industry communities similar to those studied here, the findings serve as a basis for refining the model from exploration to explanation.

The evidence directly challenges the position that development is possible only where innovation and entrepreneurship are firmly entrenched in the local value system. The issues explored in this research are particularly important in the Canadian context. Although government has provided monetary backing and support "in principle" for community-based economic development, it has done so without knowing how or why community-based efforts can be effective. Previous studies had established that Canada's unemployment problem is largely centred in smaller, more remote communities whose natural resource base is depleted or is facing declining prices. In focusing on this context, the findings demonstrate that these types of communities, too, are willing and able to influence economic development. However, for a community to capitalize on its development potential, individuals need the opportunity to learn and practise entrepreneurship.

Endogenous development assumes that local circumstances are best understood and responded to locally. The fundamental unit of analysis must therefore be defined in spatial terms. With no-one outside the life-world communities directly involved in the development process, the findings highlight the necessity for shifting the unit of analysis from the region to the life-world, which serves as a more appropriate basis for understanding and endogenously influencing regional differences.

I have avoided much of the ambiguity caused by inadequate definitions by clearly defining terms. Demonstrating the validity of the definitions makes my conclusions regarding the role of entrepreneurship in endogenously-based development far more defensible. These definitions can be made use of in future research on endogenous development.

Clearly, the debate over whether economic or social goals, or both, should be pursued is ill-founded. Neither community in the study had any difficulty developing a shared understanding of the nature of the goals it wanted to achieve in response to the circumstances. This observation supports the fundamental assumption of endogenous development, that local circumstances and responses are best dealt with by those experiencing them. The primary goals of endogenous activity need to be oriented toward sustainability rather than the reduction of disparities. However, the findings challenge the assumption of economists that people will seek to maximize income as a goal.

Quality of life is important in both communities. Community members' judgment concerning this factor is very different from that of outsiders. Indeed, there was unanimous agreement in both places that residents enjoyed a very high quality of life even though both had the dubious distinction of having employment and income levels far below those of the province and the country. Perceptions of well-being vary among communities; the goals of the particular community must therefore be used as the principle criteria for judging the effectiveness of development activities. While this approach does not necessarily suggest the abandonment of conventional meanings and measurements of economic development, it does question the appropriateness of applying the same standards in judging the success of endogenous development in different communities.

The subjective judgments of endogenous stakeholders play an integral role in the process. Indeed, there was little evidence that exogenous decision-making can empower a community to take action to address its circumstances. Eastern Guysborough County's development process was subject to significant external influence. The assessments and judgments made by people from outside the community were found to be very different from those made endogenously. For example, government interventionists responded to the fisheries collapse by establishing a Community Development Fund to stimulate small-business development. Because it was to be a fund of last resort, several interviewees were of the opinion that this project was setting them up for failure, as it meant that only companies that could not get financing elsewhere were eligible to apply for assistance.

There was little evidence that Eastern Guysborough County's people were given a major role in determining any response to the circumstances. Although government agencies involved the residents in development activities, they did not afford them autonomy in strategic decision-making. This approach, which implies a belief that the best decisions are made by specialists in centralized locations on the basis of economic considerations, is very much in keeping with a traditional policy perspective. In contrast, the findings from Isle Madame indicate not only that internally generated ideas are powerful in creating change but also that decisions not based strictly on economic factors or made by centralized specialists can be effective.

While both communities were attempting to develop their small business sector, they did so with the deliberate aim of diversification – a strategy in direct opposition to the specialization characterizing autonomous endogenous development experiences reported in the literature. The decision to pursue diversification was based on two key considerations. First and most important was the desire to avert the recurrence of the current situation. Second, the nature of each community's economic base in concert with the absence of a technically trained or uniquely skilled work force rendered specialization impractical. Specialization is clearly but one way of influencing economic development.

Although the goals of both communities were quite similar, Isle Madame's notion of how development would take place differed from Eastern Guysborough County's. In assuming far greater control in deciding how to influence economic development, Isle Madame can be characterized as more a development maker and less a development taker. It not only exercised greater levels of entrepreneurship but also achieved greater effectiveness in influencing economic development than Eastern Guysborough County. Even so, there was still considerable emphasis on pursuing initiatives funded by government programs

– the means justifying the ends. The implication is that an opportunity to increase effectiveness will result from more emphasis being placed on the ends justifying the means.

The attainment of self-sufficiency requires a clear focus on how resources can be used to capitalize on market opportunities. The ability to increase or sustain resources significantly expands development capacity. On the other hand, a focus on reducing disparities is no guarantee of increased self-sufficiency.

It is useful to reflect on the relationship of these findings to the four aspects of local development outlined by Stöhr: the origin of the initiative, the resource inputs, the control mechanisms, and the destination of the benefits. Although he prefers all four to be local, he stresses the primacy of local control and benefits. There is fairly strong evidence that neither community considered development to be local when the origin of the initiative was external. The active pursuit of external resources suggests that it was not considered necessary for the resource inputs to be community-based. Indeed, the evidence challenges the position that the main way in which communities influence development is by using their own resources to seize opportunities. While both communities mobilized considerable human resources to address their problems, there was a conspicuous absence of effort to use other local resources synergistically to initiate business activity. Next, that local control is a necessary but insufficient factor was highlighted in Eastern Guysborough County. While the community was given operational control of the Community Development Fund, it did not possess strategic control. As a result, it did not develop a sense of ownership or empowerment through its involvement. This result suggests that development will not be considered local unless control goes beyond the operational level. Finally, owing to the nature of the activities undertaken, all benefits were destined for the community. Overall, the findings suggest that it is particularly important for the initiative and strategic control to be community-based in order to foster entrepreneurship in single-industry communities.

Related to the formal organizational arrangements are the type of structure adopted and its effect on the process. While confirming that organic structures facilitate innovation, the results also indicate some distinctive features of the organizational structures studied. Though decentralized structures were highly conducive to timely decision-making at the operational level, the same level of responsiveness was not noted at the strategic level.

Mechanisms that support local interaction and cooperation have been proposed in the literature as a requirement for effective response to market challenges. However, my research indicates that such mechanisms encouraged interaction and cooperation with external stakeholders, particularly government agencies, to the detriment of opportunities for local synergies. In both communities, formalized relationships were established with externally based joint venture partners. While the partners had no operational involvement in activities, they did have a significant influence on strategic decisions. For example, the vast majority of organizations reported having delayed, postponed, or cancelled activities as a result of decisions made elsewhere. This finding indicates that there is still considerable dependency on government, although its nature has changed.

The collaborative ventures pursued by government agencies or by organizations with government funding focused on generating administrative rather than strategic innovation. Since proactivity is not part of the mandate of many of these organizations, the nature of the activities undertaken may be affected. The growing number of projects involving all three levels of government, coupled with program criteria both requiring and favouring partnerships, suggests that the desire of all levels of government to avoid duplication of services among their agencies is prompting these groups to see collaboration as an end rather than a means of achieving economic development.

The present research provides considerable insight into the influence of individuals on the process and its outcomes. CED proponents argue that effectiveness in building a community's self-reliance requires the active involvement of its members. During the initial stage of the development process, the most active and instrumental individuals were found to be those whose employment status was not directly affected by the crisis. Subsequently, the number and nature of the individuals who became involved was largely determined by the task(s) undertaken. The greater the number of individuals required for initiatives, the greater the amount of entrepreneurship, innovation, and economic development. For example, because most of Eastern Guysborough County's initiatives were infrastructure projects, the operating activities required few people. The opportunities were therefore limited for learning and practising entrepreneurship as well as for fulfilling personal need (for income) through joint association.

Indeed, the interviewees noted how to involve more members of the community to avoid the problem of volunteer burn-out as one of the top challenges of community-based development. One organization's approach was deemed highly effective. Once individuals had demonstrated a willingness to volunteer time and effort to its pursuits, they were encouraged to identify and work on projects that would create sustainable employment for themselves and/or others. This strategy encouraged individuals to join the organization because it gave them opportunities to meet personal needs through joint association while encouraging them to adopt entrepreneurial behaviour in doing so. Involving people with diverse skills and abilities gave the organization a large resource pool to draw on. Not only has it created the largest number of sustainable jobs, it also boasts the largest membership of all the organizations studied.

An important contribution made by this investigation has to do with the role played by community identity in the process. Although others have noted its importance in mobilizing action, no-one has examined its effect once economic development activities become operational. This factor was found to have an extremely positive effect on entrepreneurship during start-up but a potentially detrimental influence once the organization was operational. For example, board members in one organization were unwilling to act on a need for a staffing reduction, relenting only when a financial crisis threatened the group's survival. In retrospect, board members indicated that their desire to maintain the jobs created for the benefit of the community was the major factor clouding their judgment.

This research builds a bridge between the economic development perspective and the social development perspective in considering how entrepreneurial capacity can be developed. It provides a defensible basis for dealing with issues that have divided the field of CED activity: the definition of community, the main participants in the process, the role of empowerment and resource control, the nature of the initiatives required for achieving the desired ends, and the understanding of self-help.

The evidence supports most of the assumptions shared by the two approaches. Crisis provides the stimulus for engaging in development activity, communities can influence development, and communities have the clearest understanding of the problems they face and are in the best position to develop solutions making use of underutilized resources. A shared sense of identity creates a common purpose prompting people to mobilize resources in response to perceived problems. However, contrary to the position advanced in the literature, the focus was found to be on mobilizing external resources. While planning provides a direction for activities, too much emphasis on formal strategic planning can decrease the capacity to respond to change. The strategic planning process in Eastern Guysborough County took five years and encompassed the whole county. In contrast, Isle Madame initiated its own strategic planning process, which was completed and acted upon in less than a year. While confirming the importance of local leadership, the findings indicate, moreover, that development does not result from the leadership or efforts of one person or one organization, underscoring the appropriateness of conceptualizing entrepreneurship as a collective phenomenon.

The research also demonstrates that economic and social development are not mutually exclusive. Initiatives enabling individuals to reach greater individual and organizational financial self-sufficiency positively influence empowerment and self-esteem. Isle Madame's Telile perhaps best exemplifies the capacity of small business to foster individual competencies associated with empowerment. All of its employees reported exercising high levels of initiative, responsibility, decision-making, and problem-solving ability when afforded the authority and responsibility to act in response to a financial crisis threatening the firm's survival. They recounted a great sense of accomplishment in securing the financial viability of the organization and providing more permanent paid employment for themselves. This example illustrates that profitability can make a very positive contribution to both economic and social development.

THE CONCEPTUAL FRAMEWORK: A RETROSPECTIVE

Using the Congruence Model of Organizational Assessment as the basis for developing a conceptual framework, I have considered the various antecedent conditions, the actors, tasks, structures, and outcomes, and the relationships among all these factors. In the Community Economic Development literature, there has been much emphasis on structure, but my research clearly indicates that structure is but one component in the process. I have incorporated the various factors – both economic and non-economic – identified by the literature as contributing to entrepreneurship, innovation, and economic development into a single framework, which makes it possible to examine systematically how the elements of the development process interact to facilitate entrepreneurship.

As it identifies regularities in the process, this research challenges the view that there is little utility in developing analytic frameworks directed at understanding process. Owing to the complex nature of community-based development, there are benefits to be gained by using a theoretical framework to guide the analysis. Since inquiry into community-based development is in its infancy, the set of standards used in this case study may be of assistance in future research.

No framework is without limitations. In the present instance, the first has to do with measuring effectiveness. The fact that neither community had established measurable objectives in order of priority diminished the capacity for using community-defined criteria to judge the achievement of goals. A second limitation relates to the definition of the unit of analysis. In using the life-world as the main criterion, the framework is precluded from being used in an urban context since, for the most part, people in that context do not share common life-world elements.

RECOMMENDATIONS

In the following sections I offer recommendations concerning further research, practical uses for the framework, and measures to increase the effectiveness of policy.

Further Research and Development

The results of this investigation suggest there is merit in adapting the framework to accommodate other contingencies. For example, could it accommodate communities that lack entrepreneurial capacity but define their needs in primarily social rather than economic terms? Could it be adapted for communities where entrepreneurial capacity has already been developed? Where individuals have had the opportunity to learn and practise entrepreneurship, there would be far less need for proactivity and for a collective focus in stimulating entrepreneurship, innovation, and economic development. The extent to which the assumptions of the literature on these three subjects are applicable to other community contexts merits further research attention.

It is important to differentiate clearly between strategic and administrative entrepreneurship and innovation. The framework provides a useful starting point in doing so. Its exploratory nature has made possible the identification of the salient factors of the development process leading to strategic outcomes. Simplifying the framework and the measurement instruments to reflect the relative influence of the variables and their attributes heightens its practical utility.

Other issues for further research come to mind: the effect of a closer focus on resource utilization on the process; the means of initiating the process in the absence of crisis; and the changes in the nature of the process through other stages of development. If longitudinal research were undertaken in the two communities under investigation, the process outcomes could be more accurately assessed because the results could be used as the standard for determining the amount of improvement achieved.

Practical Uses for the Framework

First of all, the framework provides guidance in assessing the development process that is not only descriptive but also diagnostic; that is, it can be used to identify opportunities as well as problems and their possible causes. For diagnostic purposes, it establishes how inputs would be identified, described, and measured. Such an appraisal would be particularly useful during the initial stage of the development process, since it serves as a method for identifying a community's development needs by determining its propensity towards entrepreneurship and economic development. Second, the framework outlines how outputs can be identified and measured. The emphasis is on specifying not only what the outputs should be but also what they actually are. Ascertaining the discrepancy between desired and actual outputs helps in identifying problems. Finally, it facilitates the description and measurement of the four key process variables, and aids in assessing their congruence. Patterns in the variables and interactions that appear to be related to output problems can then be identified.

Towards More Effective Policy Development

This research has tackled one of the primary challenges facing Canadian regional development policy, since it is disadvantaged rural communities that depend most heavily on social safely nets. Holistic study of a community's development process provides a more realistic understanding of the endogenous development process than what has been provided by previous research, which has centred on a single organization and its activities.

On the basis of the case study, I make the following recommendations intended to enhance the effectiveness of policy:

1 Policymakers need to abandon their current definition(s) of community in order to be successful in supporting endogenous development.
2 Policy measures need to encourage communities to take action in response to needs rather than to the programs available. Replacing off-the-shelf program options with tailor-made activities would give communities the authority and responsibility to determine the most effective action, which in turn would encourage them to consider a greater range of options.
3 Few reactive initiatives were found successful in motivating individuals to launch new ventures. It is important for policy to promote proactivity in communities. Encouraging business ventures that enable individuals to learn collectively how to be entrepreneurial can make communities more self-sufficient in guiding their own development. Moreover, ensuring diversity within the group gives individuals more opportunities to learn from each other. It is important for support to be provided on the basis of the fulfilment of

needs rather than of quotas for targeted groups of disadvantaged individuals. People need not be excluded from an initiative on the basis of their employment or other status. For example, the start-up of a business may require very specialized skills. However, once it is operational, that expertise either may be unnecessary or may be developed by others within the business. Indeed, the expertise of the few may be necessary to help the many acquire the skills and abilities needed to operate successfully. Support must be flexible to assist people in learning to help themselves.

4 To show there is no single best way to achieve economic development, policy needs to encourage communities to define the development task more broadly to include a diversified mix of supply- and demand-side activities. For example, while an increase in the availability of financial resources can make an important contribution to community-based development, there is no evidence that this factor alone is effective in stimulating entrepreneurship; it may be a necessary, but not a sufficient, condition of development. Also, infrastructure development does little to give people the skills they need to respond to negative economic circumstances. However, a capacity to produce results fairly quickly can give the process momentum, as individuals are encouraged to participate on seeing that personal needs can be met through joint association. The suggestion is that policy measures can be far more effective if a contingency approach is adopted.

5 Learning *how*, as opposed to learning *what,* is instrumental in fostering both entrepreneurship and economic development. This fact points to a need for policy to encourage profit-oriented projects and ventures, so that people will acquire new skills and abilities by learning how to do things *in situ* rather than through training in an isolated classroom setting. In the former situation, participants see the learning as meaningful because its relevance is perceptible.

6 Multiple measures of success are needed for assessing the effectiveness of community-based development. No single factor is responsible for generating development. Outcomes must be directly linked to the factors influencing them through the use of multiple measures. Goal achievement, resource utilization, and adaptability can all be used in judging the effectiveness of a community's efforts to influence development. While resource utilization has received the least attention in this study, it is a very effective measure of self-sufficiency. However, there is a caveat. While profitability is one of the main ways of sustaining or increasing the resources used in maintaining existing ventures and funding new ones, it must not become an end in itself. In many single-industry rural communities,

the degree of adaptation indicates the extent to which an entrepreneurial culture has begun to replace the community's traditional ways of thinking about and reacting to problems and opportunities, in what has been characterized as a culture of dependency.

CONCLUSION

This book has explored the link between entrepreneurship and effectiveness in influencing economic development. Its focus on providing a conceptual understanding of the development process is a radical departure from the plethora of descriptive narratives on the topic of community economic development. If anything, I hope it has shown that more rigorous research is not only possible but essential if this field is to develop.

Although entrepreneurship, innovation, and economic and social development have not been ignored by scholars, there is a scarcity of frameworks for understanding the relationships among them at a meso level. The process theory (as opposed to content theory) developed here conceptualizes entrepreneurship as a collective phenomenon and so offers a different perspective. While non-traditional for this field of enquiry, the research design leads to a far more thorough understanding of endogenous development than would otherwise be possible. Indeed, Ibarra (1993, 497) notes that, in most research, factors are studied as if they were unaffected by or unrelated to each other. In contrast, the interactive influence of the four process variables is an integral part of the present research.

In lending support to the proposed framework, the empirical work also gives considerable insight into the needs and interests of people in peripheral rural areas experiencing economic stagnation or decline. It provides a basis for policy aimed at fostering entrepreneurship, innovation, and economic development in communities judged to be lacking an entrepreneurial culture and a capacity for endogenously influencing economic development. We know that entrepreneurship can be learned, and that the development process is the key vehicle for doing so. The challenge is to encourage communities to adopt a development process appropriate to their needs and circumstances.

APPENDIX
The Community Enterprise Emergence Model

To make my data analysis and interpretation more readily accessible, in this appendix I provide definitions for the sub-elements of each of the four process variables comprising the Community Enterprise Emergence Model and set out the decision rules used in interpreting the data at the community level of analysis.[1]

TASKS

The eleven sub-elements comprising the task variable are defined below, with an explanation of the criteria applied in determining whether a match exists between each actual and proposed dimension.

Broad Task Definition

Broad task definition exists when the precise means of achieving the established goal(s) of an organization are not specified, although the time frames for achieving them generally are. When tasks are broadly defined, they require more individual involvement, creating greater enthusiasm for learning.

At the community level, determining whether the development task is broad or narrow runs the risk of being perceived as a highly subjective, criteria-dependent process, unless it is founded upon a generally accepted classification scheme. To reduce subjectivity, I adopted the typology used by the Economic Council of Canada (1990, 5). Essentially, I classified the activities of the various community-based organizations according to whether they are supply-side or demand-side initiatives, although some are both. In this schema, supply-side activities are defined as those aimed at improving development capacity by enhancing or expanding local resources, particularly human resources, by employing idle human and physical resources, expanding the community resource base, and increasing the productivity of local resources. Demand-side activities are aimed at responding to market opportunities and fall into three categories: *informational*, providing information to mobilize the community to act and/or giving existing businesses or potential investors information about market opportunities; *promotional*, encouraging investment in the community; and *influential*, generating economic activity by inducing individuals to start or expand businesses or by directly launching ventures.

Broad task definition at the community level was judged to exist when the nature of activities undertaken by the different organizations represented the range of supply and demand initiatives, that is, when more than two types of activities were undertaken. All things being equal, the more diversified the activities, the greater the likelihood of stimulating broad-based entrepreneurial action. For example, while initiatives that increase access to capital may prompt some people to exercise entrepreneurship, it may do nothing for others, who have not had the opportunity to learn or practise entrepreneurial behaviour.

Narrow task definition	◄——►	*Broad task definition*
Focus on one or two types of supply- or demand-side programs, services, and activities		Diversified mix of supply- and demand-side programs, services, and activities

Task Uncertainty

Task uncertainty is defined as the unpredictability of task outcomes. The greater the amount of uncertainty, the more expertise, discretion, and face-to-face contact are required to perform the tasks.

Task uncertainty at the community level of analysis was assessed by considering the novelty of the various programs, services, and activities in which community development organizations engaged, and the aggregate predictability of outcomes. Programs, services, and activities were considered new if they were initiated subsequent to the fisheries crisis. If the majority of organizations were pursuing new activities and initiatives whose outcome could not be predicted, then task uncertainty was considered high.

High task certainty	◄——►	*High task uncertainty*
Most organizations have been providing the same activities, programs, and services since before the fisheries crisis.		Most activities, programs, and services have been initiated in response to circumstances created by the fisheries crisis.

High task certainty	◄——►	*High task uncertainty*
The outcomes of most of the activities, programs, and services can be predicted.		The outcomes of most of the activities, programs, and services are unknown.

Short-Term Focus

A short-term focus on getting outcomes from action that respond to community need (with a long-term strategic intent) has to do with the extent to which the task is oriented towards effect – as opposed to output or activity – in relation to improving the community's current situation while also contributing to its strategic long-term goal (instead of undermining it) in as short a time as possible.

At the community level of analysis, a short-term need-based outcome focus was considered to exist if the majority of organizations had pursued at least one initiative during the current calendar year that was aimed at directly meeting perceived community need within a twelve-month period or less. An initiative was judged to contribute to the achievement of the community's long-term strategic goal if a direct and apparent link existed between the activities undertaken and that goal, and if the activities were undertaken with the intent or the potential to be sustainable, as opposed to being finite projects. When the majority of organizations perceived accountability as primarily community-based, the intensity of the focus was considered stronger.

Flexibility

Flexibility is defined as the degree of versatility in the overall task at both the individual and organizational levels. The task has considerable flexibility when it involves a large number of broadly defined sub-tasks. At the individual level, this means that various broadly defined tasks, issues, or problems occupy the majority of a person's time.

Community-level task flexibility is considered to exist when the majority of organizations are free to pursue whatever programs, services, and activities they wish. In effect, they have the flexibility to respond to the various needs that might arise. Each community's task flexibility was determined by aggregating the task flexibility of the different organizations. Three conditions must be met for task flexibility to be high: more programs, services, and activities; more of them unique to the community; and the more that are new.

Freedom to Experiment

Freedom to experiment refers to the amount of discretion an individual or an organization can exercise in trying new things. Together with flexibility, it is part of the larger concept of control, as high levels of flexibility and freedom to experiment imply that the task structure gives an individual or organization considerable empowerment.

A community was deemed to have considerable experimental freedom when the majority of organizations had control over the design and delivery of programs, services, and activities.

Tolerance for Failure

Tolerance for failure is defined as the acceptance of failure when it is a result of risk-taking or experimentation rather than incompetence or inadequacy. It encourages people to behave entrepreneurially, since they see relatively few risks in trying something new and failing or in making mistakes.

Tolerance for failure was considered high at the community level of analysis if the majority of organizations were found to possess a high tolerance for failure.

Diversity of Skills, Knowledge, and Abilities

Highly diverse skill, knowledge, and ability requirements have to do with the extent to which a task or activity calls for a range of skills, education, or expertise. The more varied the skills and competencies needed, the greater the capacity for problem-solving and response to uncertainty. The greater the diversity among participants, the higher the level of heterogeneity. These attributes generate economies of action and a sense of joint ownership and control (responsibility), which serves to stimulate entrepreneurial behaviour among participants as they learn with and from each other. A task requiring heterogeneous skills and abilities also presents more opportunity for skill development.

At the community level of analysis, the overall task is considered to have diverse skill, knowledge, and ability requirements when the initiatives pursued by the various organizations represent at least three categories of supply- and demand-side activities, and when the majority of those initiatives require diverse skills, knowledge, and abilities.

Homogeneous skills, knowledge, ability	◄──►	*Diverse skills, knowledge, ability*
Spectrum of initiatives is concentrated in one or two types of supply or demand activities.		Spectrum of initiatives represents at least three types of supply or demand activities.
Individual participants in the majority of activities utilize similar competencies.		Individual participants in the majority of activities utilize different competencies.

Interdependence of Control and Ownership

The concept of interdependent control and ownership is defined as joint control over what is done and how it is done, which instills a sense of mutual ownership of the project or activity. When decisions concerning what work is to be done and who is to do it are made jointly by those who will be responsible for carrying it out, a sense of shared ownership develops among participants. The greater the sense of ownership, the greater the sense of commitment, as people tend to feel more responsibility for what they help create. The frequency and direction of communication between the participants in an initiative serve as a measure of interdependence, for if most of the communication between two people is initiated by one of them, less interdependent ownership and control are considered to exist because interdependence inherently involves reciprocity. Additionally, when the actual resource input into an initiative is perceived to be equitable – commensurate with the contribution expected of each participant – the greater the sense of interdependent ownership and control that will be felt by each individual.

Interdependent control and ownership are considered to be present when two or more community-based organizations collaborate on an initiative and all indicate that they had a role to play in deciding what would be done and how.

Independent control and ownership	◄──►	*Interdependent control and ownership*
No community-based organizations collaborate on initiatives.		Community-based organizations collaborate on two or more initiatives.
Participants in joint initiatives do not perceive mutual decision-making responsibility.		Participants in joint initiatives consider decision-making responsibility to be mutual.

Holistic Set of Tasks

A holistic set of tasks is defined as a group of tasks perceived to contribute collectively to a tangible result that is considered meaningful. The greater the variety and harmonization in the tasks in which an individual engages, the greater the horizontal integration. Vertical integration is indicated by the amount of responsibility the tasks involve: the more levels of responsibility associated with the tasks, the greater the vertical integration. The more horizontal and vertical integration present, the more holistically the tasks will be perceived. When an individual views tasks holistically, problems and opportunities are more readily recognized and dealt with. By definition, if an individual is the sole employee, then he or she will enjoy a holistic task structure.

At the community level, a holistic set of tasks is judged to exist when the majority of organizations synergistically use community resources to make a direct contribution to the community's needs and when their efforts have been complementary.

Unrelated set of tasks	◄──►	*Holistic set of tasks*
Accomplishments of various organizations are unrelated.		Majority of accomplishments of various organizations complement each other.
Majority of organizations have not made synergistic use of community resources to directly address community need.		Majority of organizations have made synergistic use of community resources to directly address community need.

Intrinsic Rewards

The concept of intrinsic rewards refers to the satisfaction obtained from the work itself. Jobs and activities providing substantial amounts of freedom, variety, and individual involvement generate inherent motivation to experiment and be creative through the satisfaction obtained from doing the work.

At the community level of analysis, the work is judged to be intrinsically rewarding when the majority of organizations are engaged in tasks that the participants view as intrinsically rewarding.

Learning by Doing

Opportunities for learning by doing exist when the task provides occasions for acquiring new knowledge or skills by actually doing things rather than being instructed in how to do so.

At the community level, opportunities for learning by doing are deemed to exist when the majority of participants report learning many new things and/or acquiring many new skills and doing so through hands-on work as opposed to formal training sessions.

Few opportunities for learning by doing	◄──►	*Many opportunities for learning by doing*
Few things learned and/or skills acquired		Many things learned and/or new skills acquired

Few opportunities for learning by doing	⟷	*Many opportunities for learning by doing*
Most learning accomplished through formal training sessions		Most learning accomplished through learning by doing

FORMAL ORGANIZATIONAL ARRANGEMENTS

In this section, the six sub-elements of formal organizational arrangements are defined, with an explanation of their assessment.

Formal Linking Mechanisms

Formal linking mechanisms are structures that have been put in place to bring people in different organizations together for information-sharing or problem-solving. The focus is essentially on creating lateral communication networks within the community.

At the community level, formal linking mechanisms were measured by aggregating the number of these structures found in organizations. Their use is considered significant if common to the majority of community-based organizations.

No formal linking mechanisms	⟷	*Strategic use of formal linking mechanisms*
Formal linking mechanisms not used between any community-based organizations for problem-solving and/or communication	*Ad hoc* use of formal linking mechanisms, mostly for information sharing	Majority of organizations using formal linking mechanisms for problem-solving and/or communication

Organic Structure

An organic structure is characterized by the imposition of relatively few rules, regulations, and controls on activity.

At the community level, minimal levels of structure and procedure are considered to exist when the majority of organizations report that policies, procedures, and rules do not interfere with organizational activity.

High levels of structure and procedure	↔	*Minimal levels of structure and procedure*
Majority of organizations' activities are constrained by policies, procedures, and rules.		Majority of organizations' activities are not constrained by policies, procedures, and rules.

Locally Based Decision-Making

The concept of locally based decision-making authority and responsibility has to do with the right (authority) and the obligation (responsibility) to make decisions in the community about what programs, services, and activities will be offered and how they will offered, without requiring externally-based approval.

At the community level of analysis, a high degree of locally-based decision-making authority and responsibility is considered to exist when the majority of organizations are found to possess autonomy in decision-making.

Local Democratic Accountability

Local democratic accountability is defined as responsibility to the community for actions taken. It typically involves being answerable to a board of directors or other body that represents a community's interests.

At the community level of analysis, if the majority of organizations are found to exhibit local democratic accountability, then it is considered to exist in the community.

External accountability	↔	*Local democratic accountability*
Some organizational members report accountability to be externally based.		All organizational members report accountability to be primarily community-based.
No attempts are made to generate public awareness, interest, or involvement.		Attempts to generate public awareness, interest, and involvement provide opportunities for community input.

INDIVIDUALS

This section provides definitions for the eight individual attributes expected to positively affect entrepreneurial behaviour, then discusses the basis for determining whether they are manifested among the community's development process participants.

Positive Attitudes

Positive attitudes toward learning by doing express a preference for hands-on, as opposed to instructional, learning.

At the community level, individuals involved in the development process are considered to prefer this style of learning when it is the preference in the majority of organizations.

Collective Community Identity

A high level of collective community identity exists when an important element of an individual's identity (how the person defines who he or she is) involves both being a member of a particular geographic community and sharing that membership with others. Membership in a group or groups that seek to have a positive influence on the lives or work of other residents suggests a high level of collective community identity.

At the community level of analysis, a high level of collective community identity is considered to exist when it is present in the majority of organizations.

Synergistic Strategic Vision

A synergistic strategic vision for economies of action is defined as the ability to consider comprehensively how various resources can be integrated in order to deal effectively with the challenges and problems faced by the community. Essentially, it is a capacity for envisioning possibilities for the attainment of a common purpose – for achieving together what could not be achieved individually.

At the community level of analysis, when individuals in the majority of organizations recognize opportunities for economies of action, a synergistic strategic vision is deemed to exist in the community.

Transferable Skills and Abilities

The concept of transferable skills and abilities has to do with the application of those competencies that broaden an individual's ability to innovate in response to environmental conditions: in particular, interpersonal skills, problem-solving, and team-building. Making a significant time commitment as a member of a community group or groups implies that an individual board member has team-building, decision-making, and interpersonal skills (which include persuasiveness and the ability to negotiate), as well as the skill of creative problem-solving, since such organizations are typically required to function with scarce resources. Those employees were assumed to have these skills who indicated that they were necessary for job effectiveness.

At the community level, individuals participating in the development process are considered to possess high levels of transferable skills and abilities when the majority of individuals in the majority of organizations are found to have them.

Low level of transferable skills and abilities	⟷	*High level of transferable skills and abilities*
Most board members are not actively involved in the organization.		Most board members are actively involved in two or more organizations.
Employees require specialized technical skills for job effectiveness.		Employees require interpersonal, problem-solving, and team-building skills for job effectiveness.

Overlapping Connections

Overlapping connections are defined as contacts having both a personal and a professional aspect. Having more connections, formal and informal, implies readier access to resources and a greater likelihood of developing economies of action. For example, the most innovative organizations maximize their ability to acquire and process information, while valued resource transactions tend to be worked out by people from complementary organizations who are personally acquainted and who communicate frequently.

Participants in the development process are deemed to have cultivated a high level of overlapping formal and informal connections when the majority of individuals and organizations receive information or other resources from more than five people and report having established personal relationships with most of their professional colleagues.

Few overlapping formal and informal connections	⟷	*Many overlapping formal and informal connections*
Few people relied on in obtaining information or other resources		Many people contacted in obtaining resources
Sources known for a long time in either strictly personal or professional capacity		Sources known for varying lengths of time; professional relationships tend to have developed a personal element

Trust and Respect for Competence

A high level of trust and respect for competence exists when others perceive an individual as having the ability and the intention to produce valued results. It is related to perceptions of character and ability. Perceptions of character can be based on an assortment of factors, including integrity (honesty), motives (intentions), consistency (reliability and predictability of behaviour), openness, and discretion (safeguarding of confidences). Perceptions of ability likewise can be based on several factors: the specific competence required for a task or activity, the interpersonal competence needed to accomplish the task, and the general competence needed to manage in a business environment. Evidently, a broad range of criteria may be used in concluding whether another person is to be trusted and considered competent. Irrespective of how the assessment is made, a high degree of trust in others and belief in their competence is key to fostering innovation, since behaviour is primarily coordinated and controlled on the basis of these factors.

At the community level of analysis, participants in the development process are considered to be trusted and respected for their competence if the majority of organizations are comprised of trusted, competent people.

Not all individuals are respected for their competence and trusted to produce valued results.	⟷	*Individuals are respected for their competence and trusted to produce valued results*
Organizational members do not share positive expectations and/or assessments of one another.		Organizational members express positive mutual expectations and/or assessments of one another, regardless of whether they are staff or board members.

Work Style Preference

A preference for an informal, free-ranging work style refers to the extent to which an unstructured work environment is favoured. It is measured by means of a content analysis of an individual's likes and dislikes with respect to the job; how contacts are made – whether formally by memo or pre-arranged, structured meetings or informally by face-to-face meetings or telephone; and observation of the work environment and board meetings.

At the community level, when an informal, free-ranging work style was used by the majority of participants in the development process, it was considered to be the general preference.

Formal work style preference ⟷	*Informal work style preference*
Reliance on formal means of communication (letters, structured meetings)	Reliance on informal means of communication (impromptu meetings, spontaneous phone calls, unplanned visits)
Individual preference for job with well-defined job description and duties	Individual preference for loosely defined job

Managing Interdependencies and Multiple Tasks

Managing interdependencies and multiple tasks is defined as the capability to produce the expected results while participating in a project or performing a job that involves relying on the contributions of others. In conducting this analysis a distinction has been made between independent, dependent, and interdependent action. Independent action is individual or organizational action that does not rely on input from other sources for completion of the task(s). Dependent action occurs where another individual or organization largely determines action. Interdependent action is action that is determined jointly.

At the community level of analysis, participants in development activity are considered to possess the ability to manage interdependencies and multiple tasks when the majority of people in the various organizations demonstrate this ability.

Individuals lack the ability to manage interdependencies and multiple tasks. ⟷	*Individuals possess the ability to manage interdependencies and multiple tasks.*
Individuals' main tasks do not involve interdependent effort.	Individuals' main tasks require interdependent effort.
Individuals deal with one or two specialized tasks on a daily basis.	Individuals deal with various tasks on a daily basis.

INFORMAL ORGANIZATIONAL ARRANGEMENTS

The task structure, the formal organizational arrangements, and the individuals involved in development all facilitate innovation. The informal organizational structure also plays an important role, particularly with regard to coordination and control. Informal coordination and control are needed in order to deal effectively with the novelty, complexities, and uncertainties of innovation. Here we shall consider six aspects of informal organizational arrangements.

Supportiveness, Trust, and Cooperation

These are highly valued principles. Supportiveness is defined as providing mutual help and encouragement. Trust is defined as confidence in another's action. Cooperation is defined as working together. Collectively these principles reinforce one another and support the close collaboration that innovation requires. For example, when people trust each other they are more likely to be supportive and cooperative.

When a behavioural expectation is expressed by the majority of process participants and is not contradicted by others, it is considered to be shared. When the described behaviour exemplifies supportiveness, trust, and cooperation, these principles are judged to be highly valued. For example, when informants indicated that helping each other out is a shared expectation, they were giving an example of supportiveness.

When the actions of members of more than one organization were rooted in these principles, and when informants provided at least one example of giving support to or receiving support from other community-based organizations, then supportiveness, trust, and cooperation were considered to be highly valued principles of the community's development process.

Competition, mistrust, and independence are highly valued principles.	↔	*Supportiveness, trust, and cooperation are highly valued principles.*
Behavioural expectations reflect independence, egocentrism, competition.		Behavioural expectations reflect supportiveness, trust, and cooperation.
No support is provided to or received from other community-based organizations.		Some support is provided to or received from other community-based organizations.

Collective Identity

Collective identity refers to the individual preference for group activity and involvement.

At the community level, the development process is seen as having instilled a strong sense of collective identity if this form of identity exists in the majority of organizations.

Involvement and Participation

The levels of involvement and participation in an organization's operating activities is assessed by determining the average number of people involved in those activities. When this number is less than three, the level of involvement and participation is considered low; when more than three, it is considered high.

At the community level of analysis, when the majority of organizations have generated high levels of involvement and participation, the development process is considered to show similar attributes.

Low levels of involvement and participation	⟷	*High levels of involvement and participation*
Fewer than three participants involved in operating activities		Three or more participants involved in operating activities

Goals, Time Scales, and Outcomes

Goals represent broadly understood desired future ends. Objectives differ from goals in that they specify measurable outcomes of a shorter duration (Bartol and Martin 1991, 162; Yukl 1990, 130). A high level of agreement on goals, objectives, time scales, and outcomes is defined as a considerable degree of consensus among participants concerning the results expected (ends), the specific ways those results will be achieved (means), and when they will be accomplished.

The development process was considered to have nurtured a common view of the community's goals, as well as how and when they were to be achieved, if the majority of informants showed an awareness of the development activities of at least two other organizations and identified how the various organizations were collectively helping to solve the community's main problem.

Discord regarding goals, objectives, time scales, and outcomes	⟷	*Shared view of goals, objectives, time scales, and outcomes*
Lack of awareness of other organizations' activities and contributions to the community's goal achievement		Awareness of ongoing organizational activities and recognition of how each group is helping to solve the community's problem

Formal and Informal Business and Social Relationships

A high degree of overlapping formal and informal business and social relationships exists when internal and external personal, social, and professional relationships are intermingled in accomplishing a task.

The extent to which these relationships overlap is determined by analysing the sources of information and other resources reported by respondents. If the majority of people in an organization report formal and informal business and social relationships with these sources, then overlapping relationships are judged to exist. At the community level such relationships are considered to exist if they characterize the relationships in the majority of organizations.

Normative Integration

Normative integration refers to the extent to which entrepreneurial behavioural expectations are shared by people who work together. The greater the number of participants who report certain entrepreneurial behavioural norms, the higher the level of normative integration, which in turn implies more entrepreneurship in the organization.

Normative integration at the community level is assessed by determining the extent to which organizations share the same set of behavioural expectations. Normative integration at the organizational level is measured by conducting a content analysis of behavioural expectations and determining the number of norms that exist and extent to which they are shared.

Notes

CHAPTER TWO

1 Blakeley (1989, 127) postulates a similar argument of dependency on federal assistance by local governments in the United States.
2 For example, a particular model may be referred to by different names. Nelson (1993) and Garofoli (1992) refer to Friedmann and Weaver's model as "agropolitan development," while Pecqueur and Silva (1992) and Coffey and Polese (1985) call it "territorial development." Moreover, the descriptions of a particular model may vary substantially. Nelson (1993, 48) claims that territorial approaches do not consider the interactive effect of economic and social conditions on development; Pecqueur and Silva (1992) claim they do. Finally, while some regard a term as a model, others refer to it as a paradigm. For example, Johannisson (1990, 61) refers to a territorial paradigm, while Nelson (1993, 47) refers to territorial development theory and sets it in a growth centre context. Within theoretical frameworks, many integral concepts – such as partnerships, innovation, and entrepreneurship – are rarely defined. In the absence of clear definitions of the myriad terms, it is difficult to discern whether the theoretical frameworks could be useful for understanding development at the local level.
3 For example, Long Cycle Theory relates development to "long waves" in economic growth (Kondratiev 1935; Schumpeter 1939; Bennett and McCoshan 1993, 14), which emanate from innovations and entreprenership. Some scholars see restructuring as an attempt to increase profitability within the downturn of an economic cycle. A cycle begins when an

innovation is adopted by entrepreneurial firms. As the innovation becomes more widely adopted, economic development occurs. The end of a cycle is marked by the maturation of the adopting firms, obsolescence of the technology, and a decline in the economy (Melkers, Bugler et al. 1993, 233). Generally, this theory limits explanation to economic factors. An innovation (e.g., steel-making) is developed until it no longer significantly influences economic development, and another innovation is required to stimulate the economy. While this theory has widespread use in explaining the economic performance of countries, it has also been used to explain the economic growth achieved by certain regions through the synergistic clustering of innovative firms.

4 Other models of local development, such as Piore and Sabel's (1984) flexible specialization model or Pecqueur and Silva's (1992) models of diffuse industrialization, do consider a broad range of factors at the local level, but focus on a single local development trajectory. Their utility in broadly explaining endogenous development experiences is therefore limited.

5 The terms "spatial development model" and "territorial model" are used interchangeably in the literature.

CHAPTER THREE

1 In the early 1990s the name changed from unemployment insurance (UI) benefits to employment insurance (EI) benefits.

CHAPTER FOUR

1 Within the literature, the terms "local economic development," "bottom-up development," "grassroots development," "endogenous development," and "community development" are all used interchangeably with Community Economic Development in indicating a process in which the impetus for development is derived from the community (Fontan 1993, 3; Polese 1993, 5; O'Neill 1990, 9).

2 The terms "social exclusion" and "marginalization" are used synonymously within the social development perspective.

3 Beliefs are basic assumptions about the world and how it works which may or may not be true. For example, a person who believes that he or she is master of his or her own destiny is likely to take responsibility for improving an unfavourable situation. Values are also basic assumptions, but ones in which an "ought to" is implicit: for example, tasks should be done to the best of one's ability. Norms are socially created and sanctioned behavioural expectations (Kerr and Slocum 1987, 99) reflecting common views about "the way things are done around here"; they

facilitate the interpretation and evaluation of events, based as they are on a set of shared meanings that make it possible for people to interpret and act upon their environment: an example would be doing things on an informal basis. Attitudes are certain regularities of an individual's feelings, thoughts, and/or predispositions with respect to some aspect of his or her environment having an affective, cognitive, and/or behavioural component (Lauer and Handel 1977, 48). Although these patterns are said to arise from the human need for uniformity and consistency, they are not static.

CHAPTER FIVE

1 The population ecology perspective is derived from biological theory dealing with populations and how they evolve. Species and animal populations evolve through mutual interaction with and adaptation to their environment; this perspective sees organizations evolving in a similar fashion. The survival of an industry (or "population") depends on how well the firms within the industry adapt to and fit the environment. The focus is on the collective effects generated by competition within an industry, rather than on individual organizations.
2 Organizational assessment models focus on explaining effectiveness and are concerned with the task performance capabilities of an organization and the system's effect on behaviour.
3 See, for example, Weik (1979), Cameron and Whetten (1983), Goodman et al. (1983), and Seashore (1983) for a discussion of these criticisms.
4 Among the conceptual schemes developed from a systems perspective, perhaps the most widely recognized is that of Van de Ven and Ferry (1980). Not only does it integrate the systems, goal, and strategic constituencies perspectives, but empirical testing has provided substantial support for its main theories. However, it is oriented toward predicting and explaining the conditions under which the environment and particular design patterns (at the organizational, unit, and job levels) result in higher performance. Similarly, Lawrence and Lorsch (in Hausser 1980, 148–50) deal with effectiveness in terms of environmental transactions, while Pugh and Pheysey (1972) explain behavioural outcomes primarily in light of the effects of structure. All these models therefore lack the process emphasis required for dealing adequately with the matter at hand. Indeed, even among frameworks classified as process models, the emphasis is not always appropriate. For example, Hackman-Morris (in Hausser 1980, 143–5) focuses on explaining the individual-level, group-level, and environmental-level influences on group performance, while leaving the model's central element – the group interaction process – unspecified. The one exception is Nadler and Tushman's (1980, 261–78;

1983, 112–24; 1991, 18–34) Congruence Model of Organizational Assessment, discussed extensively in what follows.

5 "Enterprise" is a term used to denote entrepreneurial behaviour.

6 A strong culture does not preclude subcultures.

CHAPTER SIX

1 An interpretive (Hughes 1993) approach deals with meaning, as opposed to cause. It assumes that human action is not as predictable or as deterministic in its path as action within natural science. The relationship between meaning and action is mutually informing: people attach different meanings to things and act on the basis of those meanings. The social world is therefore created in and through the meanings that human beings use to make sense of the world around them. When actions are reciprocally oriented toward the actions of others, people are seen to interpret and give meaning to both their own and others' behaviour (Hughes 1993, 93–5). In viewing social interaction in relation to the meanings people give to their actions and environment, it is necessary to refer to these meanings when conducting social analysis. Fundamentally, behaviour is viewed as a manifestation of meanings, not as the result of a deterministic cause-and-effect relationship.

2 While case study research and qualitative research are treated synonymously by some (Rist 1984, 160), others (Hakim 1994, 32; Yin 1994, xiv) argue that they are distinct but overlapping research methods. Given this context, the term "qualitative research" is used, generally, to denote methods such as ethnography and grounded theory, where theory is not specified prior to data collection. Case study research is differentiated by the fact that theory development is part of the design phase of research (Yin 1994, 27).

3 These methods include interviews, analysis of documentation and records, surveys, participant observation, and non-participant observation. Triangulation is therefore an inherent characteristic.

4 In determining effectiveness of outputs, those consulted were asked to use the following criteria in identifying one community that was successful in stimulating economic activity and one that was not: an economic base rooted in the groundfish industry, geographic location outside the urban fringe, active community-based efforts in dealing with the economic crisis, similarity of endogenous resources for use in development activity, and differing levels of economic activity generated. In light of the extensive province-wide economic development knowledge accessed for this assessment, the consensus of opinion was considered a valid basis for selection.

5 Research using both subjective and objective measures of concepts lacks convergent validity, as these measures typically produce inconsistent results (Van de Ven and Ferry 1980, 59). Each type of measure is based on differing interpretations of the concepts.

6 Reliability concerns the consistency of results, while validity has to do with whether the research measures what it is supposed to be measuring. Construct validity involves establishing correct operational measures for the concepts being studied. Internal validity (for explanatory studies only) involves showing that certain conditions lead to other conditions. External validity involves establishing the domain to which a study's findings can be generalized (Yin 1994, 33).

7 To maintain a chain of evidence, verbatim responses were compiled by organization to create a case study database. For organizations with employees, two files were created: one for employee responses and one for board responses. It is on the basis of this evidence that conclusions were drawn about the process at the community level of analysis.

8 The definitions of the concepts determined whether evaluative or descriptive measures would be used.

9 The aggregation problem relates to making inferences about a group or an organization on the basis of the responses obtained from individual members.

10 Formal interviews were transcribed after each session, to identify and follow up on any deficiencies in the evidence.

11 While a first interview was not conducted with board members, they were provided with an overview of the research in the written request to attend a board meeting.

12 One significant constraint was encountered in using this approach. During the course of the preliminary investigation, the informal interview data indicated that the development process adopted in Eastern Guysborough County had undergone some significant changes during the year, and in fact was still undergoing them. Moreover, the evidence suggested that the process changes were in the direction of the entrepreneurial process elements proposed in the research framework. This finding created a major dilemma. Because a twelve-month time frame had been established for the measurement instruments to be used, it appeared likely that the expected process differences would not be found.

Nevertheless, I decided that the benefits of proceeding with the communities originally identified outweighed the risk of not finding compelling evidence to justify the theoretical framework. There were no guarantees that the same situation would not arise if another community could be found to fulfill the requirements for theoretical sampling. Indeed, a process is not static; all things being equal, people will attempt to positively influence situations. The pre-selection process indicated that other communities facing similar circumstances had significant differences in inputs that would affect the process, in terms of, for example, geographic isolation, distance from growth areas, and so on. Because the main emphasis of the research was on process, I decided that the insights gained from examining the process adopted in two single-industry communities facing a similar economic crisis could be valuable to other communities struggling to deal with adverse circumstances. Indeed, one of the problems with Community Economic Development is that the knowledge base is very limited. In particular, little has been written about practical experiences, and those accounts that do exist tend to be descriptions of specific projects and fail to capture the holistic essence of life-world CED experiences.

CHAPTER SEVEN

1 Detailed analysis of each of the organizations studied underpins the community level assessment. It is necessary (Bryman 1993, 63) to an understanding of the process at the community level.
2 This typology is detailed in the data interpretation guidelines for the community-level analysis in the Appendix.
3 The Community Development Fund (CDF) was dissolved in 1995 and its assets assumed by the BDC.
4 Administrative entrepreneurship refers to efforts aimed at changes in structure and in administrative processes. These efforts are essentially directed toward internal management and are indirectly related to the basic work activities (Ibarra 1993, 471).
5 Strategic entrepreneurship refers the adoption of a new approach in the basic work activities in efforts to address the community's main problem.
6 Although Telile was incorporated as a non-profit company in December 1994, 1995 is considered its first year of operation.

APPENDIX

1 Given its incremental nature, the process undertaken by the community can only be understood holistically by adopting a multi-level approach to analysis. The other levels of analysis used are not dealt with here.

References

Aldrich, H. 1990. "Using an ecological perspective to study organizational founding rates." *Entrepreneurship Theory and Practice* 14 (3): 7–24.

Aldrich, H. and C. Zimmer. 1986. "Entrepreneurship through social networks." In *The Art and Science of Entrepreneurship*. Edited by D. L. Sexton and R. W. Smilor. Cambridge, MA: Ballinger Publishing Company.

Amdam, J. 1992. "Local planning and mobilization: Experiences from the Norwegian fringe." In *Development Issues and Strategies in the New Europe*. Edited by Markku Tykkylainen. Aldershot: Avebury.

Anderson, F.J. 1988. *Regional Economic Analysis: A Canadian Perspective*. Toronto: Harcourt Brace Jovanovich.

Anderson, V. 1991. *Alternative Economic Indicators*. London: Routledge.

Anton, T. 1989. "Exploring the politics of state economic development policy." *Economic Development Quarterly* 3: 339–46.

Armstrong, H. and J. Taylor. 1985. *Regional Economics and Policy*. Oxford: Philip Allan.

Astley, W.G. and A.H. Van de Ven. 1983. "Central perspectives and debates in organization theory." *Administrative Science Quarterly* 28: 245–74.

Atlantic Canada Opportunities Agency. 1991. *The State of Small Business and Entrepreneurship in Atlantic Canada: First Annual Report on Small Business*. Corporate Policy, Planning and Programs Branch, Atlantic Canada Opportunities Agency.

Atlantic Canada Opportunities Agency. 1992. *The State of Small Business and Entrepreneurship in Atlantic Canada – 1992*. Corporate Policy, Planning and Programs Branch, Atlantic Canada Opportunities Agency.

Atlantic Provinces Economic Council. 1994. *Building on Strengths: Community Economic Development in the Atlantic Provinces.* Summary of conference proceedings, 8–10 March 1994, Wolfville, NS.

Bandura, A. 1986. *Social Foundations of Thought and Action: A Social Cognitive Theory.* Englewood Cliffs, NJ: Prentice-Hall.

Bannock, G. and A. Peacock. 1989. *Governments and Small Business.* London: Paul Chapman Publishing Ltd.

Bartol, K.M. and D.C. Martin. 1991. *Management.* New York: McGraw-Hill.

Bartunek, J.M. 1983. "The stages of organizational creation." Presentation at the Academy of Management Meeting, Dallas, TX.

Beer, M. 1992. "Leading change." In *Managing People and Organizations.* Edited by John J. Gabarro. Boston: Harvard Business School Publications.

Bennett, R.J. and A. McCoshan. 1993. *Enterprise and Human Resource Development.* London: Paul Chapman Publishing Ltd.

Betton, J. and G.G. Dess. 1985. "The application of population ecology models to the study of organizations." *Academy of Management Review* 10:750–7.

Bingham, R.D. and R. Mier. 1993. *Theories of Local Economic Development.* Newbury Park: Sage Publications.

Birch, D.L. 1979. *The Job Generation Process.* Cambridge, MA: MIT Press.

– 1987. *Job Creation in America.* New York: The Free Press.

Blakely, Edward J. 1989. *Planning Local Economic Development: Theory & Practice.* Newbury Park: Sage Publications.

Bolton, R. 1992. "'Place prosperity vs. people prosperity" revisited: An old issue with a new angle." *Urban Studies* 29(2) 185–203.

Borts, G.H. and J.L. Stein. 1964. *Economic Growth in A Free Market.* New York: Columbia University Press.

Bovaird, T. 1992. "Local Economic Development and the city." *Urban Studies* 29(3/4): 343–68.

Brethour, G. 1994. "Lessons learned & future research: CED & the National Welfare Grants Program." *Making Waves* 5(4): 33–5.

Brockhaus, R.H. 1987. "Entrepreneurial folklore." *Journal of Small Business Management*, July: 1–6.

– and P.S. Horwitz. 1986. "The psychology of the entrepreneur." In *The Art and Science of Entrepreneurship.* Edited by D. L. Sexton and Raymond W. Smilor. Cambridge, MA: Ballinger Publishing Company.

Brodhead, D. 1993. "CED practice in Canada: A personal view." A paper presented to the Research and Policy Symposium on Community Economic Development, Kananaskis, AB.

Bruno, A. and T. Tyebjee. 1982. "The environment for entrepreneurship." In *Encyclopedia of Entrepreneurship.* Edited by Calvin A. Kent, Donald L. Sexton and Karl H. Vesper. Englewood Cliffs, NJ: Prentice-Hall.

Bryman, A. 1993. *Quantity and Quality in Social Research.* London: Routledge.

Burke, C.D. and D.J. Ireland. 1976. *An Urban Economic Strategy for the Atlantic Region*. Ottawa: Ministry of State for Urban Affairs.

Burns, T. and G.M. Stalker. 1961. *The Management of Innovation*. London: Tavistock.

Burrows, R. 1991. "Deciphering the enterprise culture." In *Entrepreneurship, Petty Capitalism and the Restructuring of Britain*. Edited by Roger Burrows. London: Routledge.

Bygrave, W.D. 1989. "The entrepreneurship paradigm (I): A philosophical look at its research methodologies." *Entrepreneurship Theory and Practice* 14(2):7–25.

– and C.W. Hofer. 1991. "Theorizing about entrepreneurship." *Entrepreneurship Theory and Practice* 16(2) (Winter): 13–22.

Cameron, K.S. and D.A. Whetten. 1983. *Organizational Effectiveness: A Comparison of Multiple Models*. New York: Academic Press.

Canadian Labour Market and Productivity Centre. 1990. *A Profile of the Labour Force in Atlantic Canada*. N.p., n.d.

Cannon, T. 1991. *Enterprise: Creation, Development and Growth*. Oxford: Butterworth-Heinemann Ltd.

Caporaso, J.A. and B. Zare. 1981. "An interpretation and evaluation of dependency theory." In *From Dependency to Development: Strategies to Overcome Underdevelopment and Inequality*. Edited by Heraldo Munoz. Boulder, CO: Westview Press.

Cappellin, R. 1983. "Productivity growth and technological change." *Giornale degli Economisti ed Annali di Economia* 42.

– 1992. "Theories of local endogenous development and international cooperation." In *Development Issues and Strategies in the New Europe*. Edited by Markku Tykkylainen. Aldershot: Avebury.

– and W. Molle. 1988. "The co-ordination problem in theory and policy." In *Regional Impact of Community Policies in Europe*. Edited by Willem Molle and Riccardo Cappellin. Aldershot: Avebury.

Christenson, J.A. and J.W. Robinson. 1989. *Community Development in Perspective*. Ames: Iowa State University Press.

Clark, C. 1993. "Urban regeneration partnerships: An analysis of the knowledge, skills and attitudes needed by the managers of partnerships." Research conducted by Civic Trust Regeneration Unit to inform a new training and development course for partnership managers. N.p., n.d.

Coffey, W.J. 1991. "Comprehensive bases for locally induced development." In *Alternative Perspectives on Development Prospects for Rural Areas*. Edited by D. Otto and S. Deller. Portland, OR: Western Rural Development Center.

– and M. Polese. 1985. "Local development: Conceptual basis and policy implications." *Regional Studies* 19(2): 85–93.

–, W.S. Macdonald and A.S. Harvey. 1983. "Intra-regional disparities in Canada's Maritime Provinces." In *Regional Developments in the Peripheries of Canada and Europe*. Edited by Alfred Hecht. Manitoba Geographical Studies. Winnipeg: University of Manitoba.

Coleman, J.S. 1993. "The rational reconstruction of society." *American Sociological Review* 58: 1–15.

Cooper, A.C. and F.J. Gascon. 1992. "Entrepreneurs, processes of founding, and new-firm performance." In *The State of the Art of Entrepreneurship*. Edited by D. Sexton and J. Kasarda. Boston: PWS-Kent Publishers.

Coppack, P.M. 1990. "The urban field, amenity environments and local community development: Some ideas on the economic survival of small communities in the city's countryside." In *Entrepreneurial and Sustainable Communities: Proceedings of a Conference Held in St. Andrews-by-the-Sea, N.B., June 1988*. Edited by Floyd W. Dykeman. Rural and Small Town Research and Studies Programme.

–, K.B. Beesley and C. Mitchell. 1990. "Rural Attractions and Rural Development: Elora, Ontario Case Study." In *Entrepreneurial and Sustainable Communities: Proceedings of a Conference Held in St. Andrews-by-the-Sea, N.B., June 1988*. Edited by Floyd W. Dykeman. Rural and Small Town Research and Studies Programme.

Courchene, T.J. 1978. "Avenues of adjustment: The transfer system and regional disparities." In *Canadian Confederation at the Crossroads: The Search for a Federal-Provincial Balance*. Vancouver: Fraser Institute.

– 1980. "Energy resources: Consequences for the rest of Canada." *Canadian Public Policy* 6: 192–204.

– 1984. *Equalization Payments: Past, Present and Future*. Toronto: Ontario Economic Council.

Curran, J. and R. Blackburn. 1994. *Small Firms and Local Economic Networks: The Death of the Local Economy?* Newcastle upon Tyne: Athenaeum Press.

–, R. Jarvis, R.A. Blackburn et al. 1993. "Networks and small firms: Constructs, methodological strategies and some findings." *International Small Business Journal* 11(2) January–March: 13–25.

Denison, D.R. 1990. *Corporate Culture and Organizational Effectiveness*. Chichester: John Wiley & Sons.

Douglas, D. 1989. "Community Economic Development in rural Canada: a critical review." *Plan Canada* 29(2): 28–46.

Dykeman, F.W. 1990. "Developing an Understanding of Entrepreneurial and Sustainable Rural Communities." In *Entrepreneurial and Sustainable Communities: Proceedings of a Conference Held in St. Andrews-by-the-Sea, N.B., June 1988*. Edited by Floyd W. Dykeman. Rural and Small Town Research and Studies Programme.

Eccles, R.G. and N. Nohria. 1992. *Beyond the Hype: Rediscovering the Essence of Management*. Boston: Harvard Business School Press.

Economic Council of Canada. 1990. *From the Bottom Up: The Community Economic-Development Approach.* A Statement by the Economic Council of Canada, Ottawa: Canadian Government Publishing Centre.

Feller, I. 1988. "Evaluating State Advanced Technology Programs." *Evaluation Review* 12: 232–52.

Finley, L. 1990. *Entrepreneurial Strategies.* Boston: PWS-Kent Publishing Company.

Flora, J.L., J.Sharp, C. Flora and B. Newlon. 1997. "Entrepreneurial social infrastructure and locally initiated economic development in the nonmetropolitan United States." *Sociological Quarterly* 38: 623–45.

Foley, P. 1992. "Local economic policy and job creation: A review of evaluation studies." *Urban Studies* 29: 557–98.

Fontan, J.-M., ed. 1993. *A Critical Review of Canadian, American, & European Community Economic Development Literature.* Vernon, BC: CCE/Westcoast Publications.

Fothergill, S. and G. Gudgin. 1979. *The Job Generation Process in Britain.* Centre for Environmental Studies.

– 1982. *Unequal Growth: Urban and Regional Employment Change in the UK.* London: Heinemann.

Frank, A.G. 1969. *Capitalism and Underdevelopment in Latin America.* Rev. and enl. ed. New York: Monthly Review Press, Modern Reader Paperbacks.

Friedmann, J. and C. Weaver. 1979. *Territory and Function: The Evolution of Regional Planning.* London: Edward Arnold.

Fry, F.L. 1993. *Entrepreneurship: A Planning Approach.* Minneapolis/St Paul: West Publishing Company.

Galtung, J. 1981. "The politics of self-reliance." In *From Dependency to Development: Strategies to Overcome Underdevelopment and Inequality.* Edited by Heraldo Munoz. Boulder, CO: Westview Press.

Garofoli, G. 1992a. "New firm formation and local development: the Italian experience." *Entrepreneurship and Regional Development* 4: 101–25.

– 1992b. "Endogenous development and Southern Europe: An introduction." In *Endogenous Development and Southern Europe.* Edited by Gioacchino Garofoli. Aldershot: Avebury.

– 1992c. "Industrial Districts: Structure and transformation." In *Endogenous Development and Southern Europe.* Edited by Gioacchino Garofoli. Aldershot: Avebury.

Gartner, W.B. 1985. "A Framework for describing the phenomenon of new venture creation." *Academy of Management Review* 10(4): 690–706.

– 1989. "What do we talk about when we talk about entrepreneurship?" *Journal of Business Venturing* 5(1): 15–29.

Gerace, J. 1990. "Integrated Rural Development in a Principally Urban State." In *Entrepreneurial and Sustainable Communities: Proceedings of a Conference*

Held in St. Andrews-by-the-Sea, N.B., June 1988. Edited by Floyd W. Dykeman. Rural and Small Town Research and Studies Programme.

Gerstein, D.R. 1987. "To unpack micro and macro: Link small with large and part with whole." In *The Micro-Macro Link.* Edited by Jeffrey C. Alexander et al. Berkley: University of California Press.

Ghai, D. 1990. "Participatory development: Some perspectives from grassroots experience." In *Trade, Planning and Rural Development.* Edited by Azizur Rahman Khan and Rehman Sobhan. Houndmills: MacMillan Press.

Gibb, A.A. 1987. "Enterprise culture – its meaning and implications for education and training." *Journal of European Industrial Training* 11: 1–28.

– 1988. "Education for enterprise: Training for small business initiation – some contrasts." *Journal of Small Business & Entrepreneurship* 4(3).

– 1993. "The enterprise culture and education: Understanding enterprise education and its links with small business, entrepreneurship and wider educational goals." *International Small Business Journal* 11(3): 13–34.

Glaser, B.G. and A.L. Strauss. 1967. *The Discovery of Grounded Theory.* Chicago: Aldine.

Glasson, J. 1992. "The fall and rise of regional planning in the economically advanced nations." *Urban Studies* 29: 505–31.

Goldstein, H.A. and M.I. Luger. 1993. "Theory and practice in high-tech economic development." In *Theories of Local Economic Development: Perspectives From Across the Disciplines.* Edited by Richard D. Bingham and Robert Mier. Newbury Park: Sage.

Gordon, J.R. 1991. *A Diagnostic Approach to Organizational Behavior.* Boston: Allyn and Bacon.

Gould, A. and D. Keeble. 1984. "New firms and rural industrialization in East Anglia." *Regional Studies* 18.

Government of Canada, Regional Industrial Expansion. 1985. *Consultation Paper on Small Business.* N.p., n.d.

Government of Newfoundland and Labrador. 1992. *Public Consultation Process on the Strategic Economic Plan: Report to the Public.* N.p., n.d.

Guysborough County Community Development Fund. 1994. "Guysborough County Community Development Fund Sub-Committee 4th Annual Submission." Submitted to Employment and Immigration Canada, (February 5).

Hakim, C. 1994. *Research Design: Strategies and Choices in the Design of Social Research.* London: Routledge.

Hansen, N. 1989. "Poles of development." In *Economic Development.* Edited by John Eatwell, Murray Milgate and Peter Newman. London: The MacMillan Press Limited.

Hausser, D.L. 1980. "Comparison of different models for organizational analysis." In *Organizational Assessment: Perspectives on the Measurement of Organizational Behavior and the Quality of Work Life.* Edited by Edward

E. Lawler, David A. Nadler and Cortlandt Cammann. Chichester: John Wiley & Sons.

Holupka, C.S. and A.B. Shlay. 1993. "Political economy and urban development." In *Theories of Local Economic Development: Perspectives From Across the Disciplines*. Edited by Richard D. Bingham and Robert Mier. Newbury Park: Sage.

Honig, B. 1998. "Who gets the goodies? An examination of microenterprise credit in Jamaica." *Entrepreneurship and Regional Development* 10: 313–34.

Hornaday, J.A. 1982. "Research about living entrepreneurs. In *Encyclopedia of Entrepreneurship*. Edited by C.A. Kent, D. L. Sexton and K.H. Vesper. Englewood Cliffs, NJ: Prentice Hall.

Howland, M. 1993. "Applying theory to practice in rural economies." In *Theories of Local Economic Development: Perspectives From Across the Disciplines*. Edited by Richard D. Bingham and Robert Mier. Newbury Park: Sage.

Hughes, J. 1993. *The Philosophy of Social Research*. 2nd ed. London: Longman.

Huse, E.F. and T.G. Cummings. 1985. *Organization Development and Change*. 3rd ed. Minneapolis/St Paul: West Publishing Company.

Huxham, C. and C. Barr. 1993. "Collaborative advantage in community organizations." Paper prepared for the Annual Conference of the British Academy of Management in Milton Keynes, 20–22 September.

Ibarra, H. 1993. Network centrality, power, and innovation involvement: determinants of technical and administrative roles." *Academy of Management Journal* 36(3): 471–501.

Jacobs, J. 1961. *The Death and Life of Great American Cities*. New York: Random House.

Jacquier, C. and P. Mendés-France. 1992. "Une politique européenne de revitalisation des zones urbaines en difficulté." In *A Critical Review of Canadian, American, & European Community Economic Development Literature*. Edited by Jean-Marc Fontan (1993). Vernon, BC: CCE/Westcoast Publications.

Johannisson, B. 1990. "The Nordic perspective: self-reliant local development in four Scandinavian countries." In *Global Challenge and Local Response: Local Initiatives for Economic Regeneration in Contemporary Europe*. Edited by Walter Stohr. London: Mansell Publishing.

Johnson, D.W. and F.P. Johnson. 1991. *Joining Together*. 4th ed. Englewood Cliffs, NJ: Prentice Hall.

Jones, B.G. and P.D. Clark. 1976. "Psychological factors in regional economic development." In *Space, Location and Regional Development*. Edited by M. Chaterjee. London: Pion.

Joyal, A. 1993. "Canada's commitment to community development." LEDA *Magazine* no. 9: 12–15.

Kanter, R.M. 1983. *The Change Masters: Innovation for Productivity in the American Corporation*. New York: Simon and Schuster.

– 1992. "The new managerial work." In *Managing People and Organizations*. Edited by John J. Gabarro. Boston: Harvard Business School Publications.

Kao, J.A. 1991. *The Entrepreneurial Organization*. Englewood Cliffs, NJ: Prentice Hall.

Kao, R.W. 1989. *Entrepreneurship and Enterprise Development*. Toronto: Holt, Rinehart and Winston of Canada, Limited.

Keating, M. 1989. "Local government and economic development in Western Europe." *Entrepreneurship and Regional Development* 1: 301–12.

Kerr, J. and J.W. Slocum. 1987. "Managing corporate culture through reward systems." *Academy of Management Executive* 1(2): 99–108.

Kerr, S. 1991. "On the Folly of Rewarding A, While Hoping for B." In *Organizational Behavior*. Edited by Joe Kelly, J. Bruce Prince and Blake Ashforth. Scarborough, ON: Prentice-Hall Canada Inc.

Ketilson, L.H., M. Fulton, B. Fairbairn and J. Bold. 1992. "Climate for co-operative community development." Report to the Federal/Provincial Task Force on the Role of Co-operatives and Government in Community Development. Saskatchewan: Centre for the Study of Co-operatives, University of Saskatchewan.

Kilby, P. 1971. *Entrepreneurship and Economic Development*. New York: The Free Press.

Kluckhohn, F.R. and F.L. Strodtbeck. 1961. *Variations in Value Orientations*. Evanston, IL: Row Peterson.

Kockel, U. 1992. "Provisory economy and regional development: Towards a conceptual integration of informal activities." In *Development Issues and Strategies in the New Europe*. Edited by Markku Tykkylainen. Aldershot: Avebury.

Kondratiev, N.D. 1935. "The long waves in economic life." *Review of Economic Statistics* 17: 149–58.

Korten, D.C. 1990. *Getting to the 21st Century*. West Hartford, CT: Kumarian Press, Inc.

Kotter, J.P. 1992. "What Leaders Really Do." In *Managing People and Organizations*. Edited by John J. Gabarro. Boston: Harvard Business School Publications.

Kunkel, J.H. 1971. "Values and behaviour in economic development." In *Entrepreneurship and Economic Development*. Edited by Peter Kilby. London: Collier-MacMillan Ltd.

Kyle, J.D., R. Blais, R. Blatt and A.J. Szonyi. 1991. "The culture of the entrepreneur: fact or fiction." *Journal of Small Business and Entrepreneurship* 3–14.

Lamontagne, F. 1993. "Development indicators and development planning: A case study." A paper presented to the Research and Policy Symposium on Community Economic Development, Kananaskis, AB.

Latella, F. 1992. "Environment and development in the backward regions of Southern Europe." In *Endogenous Development and Southern Europe.* Edited by Gioacchino Garofoli. Aldershot: Avebury.

Lauer, R.H. and W.H. Handel. 1977. *Social Psychology: The Theory and Application of Symbolic Interactionism.* Boston: Houghton Mifflin Company.

Lawler, E.E., D.A. Nadler and C. Cammann. 1980. *Organizational Assessment: Perspectives on the Measurement of Organizational Behavior and the Quality of Work Life.* Chichester: John Wiley & Sons.

Lewis, M. 1993. "The scope and characteristics of CED in Canada." A paper presented to the Research and Policy Symposium on Community Economic Development, Kananaskis, AB.

Lorsch, J.W. 1992. "Organization design." In *Managing People and Organizations.* Edited by John J. Gabarro. Boston: Harvard Business School Publications.

Lotz, J. 1991. "Community economic development – an overview." Prepared for the Nova Scotia Department of Industry Trade and Technology.

Low, M.B. and I.C. MacMillan. 1988. "Entrepreneurship: Past research and future challenges." *Journal of Management* 14(2): 139–62.

Luther, J. 1990. "Participatory design vision and choice in small town planning." In *Entrepreneurial and Sustainable Communities: Proceedings of a Conference Held in St. Andrews-by-the-Sea, N.B., June 1988.* Edited by Floyd W. Dykeman. Rural and Small Town Research and Studies Programme.

Macdonald, S.W. 1979. "Economic dualism in the maritime provinces." Selected Papers Eighth Annual Conference of the Atlantic Canada Economics Association.

– 1988. "A regional approach to an economic development strategy for Nova Scotia." Paper presented to the Seventeenth Annual Meeting of the Atlantic Canada Economics Association, Acadia University, Wolfville, NS, 20–22 October, Halifax: Henson College, Dalhousie University.

Macey, R. 1982. "Job generation in British manufacturing industry: employment change by size of establishment and by region." Department of Industry Regional Research Series No. 4, London: HMSO.

MacLeod, G. 1986. *New Age Business, Community Corporations that Work.* Ottawa: Canadian Council on Social Development.

MacNeil, T. and R. Williams. 1994. "Evaluation framework for Community Economic Development." A report prepared for National Welfare Grants.

Mason, C. 1991. "Spatial variations in enterprise: the geography of new firm formation." In *Deciphering the Enterprise Culture.* Edited by Roger Burrows. London: Routledge.

– and R.T. Harrison. 1990. "Small firms – phoenix from the ashes?" In *Challenge and Change in Western Europe*. Edited by D.A. Pinder. London: Belhaven Press.

Matthews, R. 1983. *The Creation of Regional Dependency*. Toronto: University of Toronto Press.

McCaskey, M.B. 1992. "A framework for analyzing work groups." In *Managing People and Organizations*. Edited by John J. Gabarro. Boston: Harvard Business School Publications.

McClelland, D.C. 1961. *The Achieving Society*. Princeton: D. Van Nostrand.

McCormick, L. et al. 1987. "Community Economic Development strategies, a manual for local action." Chicago: UIC Center for Urban Economic Development, University of Illinois.

McMullan, W. E. and W. A. Long. 1990. *Developing New Ventures: The Entrepreneurial Option*. San Diego: Harcourt Brace Jovanovich.

Melkers, J., D. Bulger and B. Bozeman. 1993. "Technology transfer and economic development." In *Theories of Local Economic Development: Perspectives From Across the Disciplines*. Edited by Richard D. Bingham and Robert Mier. Newbury Park: Sage.

Mifflen, F.J. 1977. "The Antigonish Movement: A summary analysis of its development, principles and goals." *Canadian Journal of Public and Cooperative Economy* 10(1 & 2): 77–96.

Miles, M.B. and M.A. Huberman. 1994. *Qualitative Data Analysis*. 2nd ed. London: Sage.

Miles, R.E. and C.C. Snow. 1986. "Organizations: New concepts for new forms." *California Management Review* 28: 62–73.

– 1991. "Network organizations: New concepts for new forms." In *A Diagnostic Approach to Organizational Behavior*. Edited by Judith Gordon. Boston: Allyn and Bacon.

Molle, W. and R. Cappellin. 1988. *Regional Impact of Community Policies in Europe*. Aldershot: Gower-Avebury.

Murrell, D. and A. Rector. 1987. "Dualism in the Maritime Provinces: 1961–1981 – a social indicator approach." Paper presented to the Sixteenth Annual Meeting of the Atlantic Canada Economic Association, University College of Cape Breton, Sydney, NS.

Myrdal, G. 1957. *Rich Lands and Poor*. New York: Harper & Row.

Nadler, D.A. 1980. "Role of models in organizational assessment." In *Organizational Assessment: Perspectives on the Measurement of Organizational Behavior and the Quality of Work Life*. Edited by Edward E. Lawler, David A. Nadler and Cortlandt Cammann. Chichester: John Wiley & Sons.

– and M.L. Tushman. 1980. "A congruence model for organizational assessment." In *Organizational Assessment: Perspectives on the Measurement of Organizational Behavior and the Quality of Work Life*. Edited by Edward

E. Lawler, David A. Nadler and Cortlandt Cammann. Chichester: John Wiley & Sons.
– 1983. "A general diagnostic model for organizational behavior: Applying a congruence perspective." In *Perspectives on Behavior in Organizations.* Edited by J. Richard Hackman, Edward E. Lawler and Lyman W. Porter. New York: McGraw-Hill.
– 1986. *Strategic Organization Design.* Homewood, IL: Scott Foresman.
– 1991. "Organizing for innovation." In *Organizational Behavior.* Edited by Joe Kelly, J. Bruce Prince and Blake Ashforth. Scarborough, ON: Prentice-Hall Canada Inc.
National Council for Urban Economic Development. 1993. "Forces in the new economy: Implications for local economic development." Report of a Forum conducted 26 September 1992, co-sponsored by National Council for Urban Economic Development and Economic Development Administration, US Department of Commerce, Washington.
National Welfare Grants. 1991. *A social development framework for National Welfare Grants.* N.p., n.d.
Neamtan, N. 1989. "Discours de Nancy Neamtan." In *Le Local en Action.* Edited by IFDEC et ANDLP. Paris: Editions de l'Epargne.
Nelson, A.C. 1993. "Theories of regional development." In *Theories of Local Economic Development: Perspectives From Across the Disciplines.* Edited by Richard D. Bingham and Robert Mier. Newbury Park: Sage Publications.
New Economy Development Group Inc. 1992. "Defining a mid-term plan of action and research agenda on Community Economic Development." Prepared for National Welfare Grants, Health and Welfare Canada, Ottawa.
Ninacs, B. 1993. "Synthesizing the research results: Where is the common ground?" *Making Waves* 4(4): 18–20.
Nova Scotia Department of Economic Development. 1993. "A discussion paper on Community Economic Development." Planning and Policy Division.
O Cinneide, M. 1992. "Approaches to the development of peripheral rural areas: Some lessons from the Irish experience." In *Development Issues and Strategies in the New Europe.* Edited by Markku Tykkylainen. Aldershot: Avebury.
O'Neill, T. 1993. "Regional, local, and community-based economic development." A paper presented to the Research and Policy Symposium on Community Economic Development, Kananaskis, AB.
O'Neill, T. 1990. "Draft report on a policy statement for a Community Economic Development strategy in Nova Scotia." Submitted to the Nova Scotia Department of Small Business Development.
– C.R. Bryant and J. Odenthal. 1993. "Fostering the entrepreneurial community: A comparison of CED initiatives in Atlantic Canada and Eastern Ontario." *Making Waves* 4(4): 16–17.

O'Reilly, C. 1991. "Corporations, culture, and commitment: Motivation and social control in organizations." *Organizational Behavior: Readings, Cases and Exercises*. Scarborough, ON: Prentice-Hall Canada Inc.

Organization for Economic Co-operation and Development. 1993. *Territorial Development and Structural Change: A New Perspective on Adjustment and Reform*. Paris: OECD.

Pecqueur, B. 1989. *Le développement local: mode ou modèle?* Paris: Syros, Alternatives.

– and M.R. Silva. 1992. "Territory and economic development: The example of diffuse industrialization." In *Endogenous Development and Southern Europe*. Edited by Gioacchino Garofoli. Aldershot: Avebury.

Pellegria, J.-P. 1989. "Local initiatives for enterprise." OECD *Observer* no. 158 (Jun/Jul): 8–11.

Perry, S.E. 1987. *Communities On The Way: Rebuilding Local Economies in the United States and Canada*. Albany: State University of New York Press.

Piore, M. and C. Sabel. 1984. *The Second Industrial Divide*. New York: Basic Books.

Polese, M. 1993. "Community Economic Development revisited: Are the preconditions for success different from those of conventional business ventures?" A paper presented to the Research and Policy Symposium on Community Economic Development, Kananaskis, AB.

Porter, M. 1991. "Canada at the crossroads: The reality of a new competitive environment." Study prepared for the Business Council on National Issues and the Government of Canada.

Pugh, D.S. and D.C. Pheysey. 1973. "A comparative administration model." In *Modern Organizational Theory: Contextual, Environmental, and Sociocultural Variables*. Edited by Anant R. Negandhi. Kent, OH: Kent State University Press.

Putnam, R.D. 1993. "The prosperous community: Social capital and public life." *American Prospect* 13: 35–42.

– 1995. "Tuning in, tuning out? The strange disappearance of social capital in America." *Political Science and Politics* 24(4): 664–83.

Reich, R.B. 1992. "Entrepreneurship reconsidered: The team as hero." In *The Entrepreneurial Venture*. Edited by William A. Sahlman and Howard H. Stevenson. Boston: Harvard Business School Publications.

Reynolds, P.D. 1991. "Sociology and entrepreneurship: Concepts and contributions." *Entrepreneurship Theory and Practice* 16(2): 47–70.

Ring, P.S. and A.H. Van de Ven. 1994. "Developmental processes of cooperative interorganizational relationships." *Academy of Management Review* 19(1): 90–118.

Rist, R.C. 1984. "On the application of qualitative research to the policy process: An emergent link." In *Social Crisis and Educational Research*. Edited by L. Barton and S. Walker. London: Croom Helm.

Ritsila, J.J. 1999. "Regional differences in environments for enterprises." *Entrepreneurship and Regional Development* 11: 187–202.

Robertson, J. 1987. "Work, money and the local economy: some directions for the future." In *Local Initiatives: Alternative Path for Development.* Edited by A. S. Sutton. Maastricht: Presses Interuniversitaires Européennes.

Rose, G. 1982. *Deciphering Sociological Research.* London: MacMillan.

Rostow, W.W. 1991. *The Stages of Economic Growth: A Non-Communist Manifesto.* 3rd ed. Cambridge: Cambridge University Press.

Sathe, V. 1989. "Implications of corporate culture: A manager's guide to action." In *Developing Managerial Skills in Organizational Behavior: Exercises, Cases and Readings.* Edited by Lisa A. Mainiero and Cheryl L. Tromley. Englewood Cliffs, NJ: Prentice-Hall, Inc.

Savoie, D.J. 1986. *Regional Economic Development: Canada's search for solutions.* Toronto: University of Toronto Press.

– 1992. *Regional Economic Development: Canada's search for solutions.* 2nd ed. Toronto: University of Toronto Press.

Schein, E.H. 1991. "Coming to a new awareness of organizational culture." In *Organizational Behavior.* Edited by Joe Kelly, J. Bruce Prince and Blake Ashforth. Scarborough, ON: Prentice-Hall Canada Inc.

Schumpeter, J.A. 1934. *The Theory of Economic Development.* Cambridge: Harvard University Press.

– 1939. *Business Cycles: A Theoretical, Historical, and Statistical Analysis of the Capitalist Process.* London: McGraw-Hill.

Seashore, S.E. 1983. "A framework for an integrated model of organizational effectiveness." In *Organizational Effectiveness: A Comparison of Multiple Models.* Edited by Kim S. Cameron and David A. Whetten. New York: Academic Press.

Senge, P. 1990. *The Fifth Discipline.* New York: Doubleday.

Sexton, D.L. and N.B. Bowman-Upton. 1991. *Entrepreneurship: Creativity and Growth.* New York: MacMillan Publishing Company.

Shapiro, B.P. 1992. "Functional integration: Getting all the troops to work together." In *Managing People and Organizations.* Edited by John J. Gabarro. Boston: Harvard Business School Publications.

Sharp, E.B. and M.G. Bath. 1993. "Citizenship and economic development." In *Theories of Local Economic Development: Perspectives From Across the Disciplines.* Edited by Richard D. Bingham and Robert Mier. Newbury Park: Sage Publications.

Sitwell, O.F.G. and N.R.M. Seifried. 1984. *The Regional Structure of the Canadian Economy.* Toronto: Methuen.

Springate, D. 1973. *Regional Incentives and Private Investment.* Montreal: C.D. Howe Institute.

Stata, R. 1989. "Organizational learning – the key to management innovation." *Sloan Management Review* (Spring): 63–74.

Statistics Canada. 1994. *Profile of census divisions and subdivisions in Nova Scotia, Part B*. Ottawa: Industry, Science and Technology Canada, 1991 Census of Canada, Catalogue number 95–313.

Stevenson, H.H. and D.E. Gumpert. 1992. "The heart of entrepreneurship." In *The Entrepreneurial Venture*. Edited by William A. Sahlman and Howard H. Stevenson. Boston: Harvard Business School Publications.

Stevenson, L. 1996. *The Implementation of an Entrepreneurship Development Strategy in Canada: The Case of the Atlantic Region*. Paris: OECD.

Stöhr, W.B. 1990. *Global Challenge and Local Response: Local Initiatives for Economic Regeneration in Contemporary Europe*. London: Mansell Publishing.

– 1992. "Local initiative networks as an instrument for the development of peripheral areas." In *Development Issues and Strategies in the New Europe*. Edited by Markku Tykkylainen. Aldershot: Avebury.

– and F. Taylor. 1981. *Development From Above or Below?* Chichester: John Wiley and Sons.

Sudman, S. 1976. *Applied Sampling*. London: Academic Press.

Swack, M. and D. Mason. 1993. "Community Economic Development: An overview of the U.S. experience." Paper presented to the Research and Policy Symposium on Community Economic Development, Kananaskis, AB.

Tichy, N.M. and H.A. Hornstein. 1980. "Collaborative organization model building." In *Organizational Assessment: Perspectives on the Measurement of Organizational Behavior and the Quality of Work Life*. Edited by Edward E. Lawler, David A. Nadler and Cortlandt Cammann. Chichester: John Wiley & Sons.

Timmons, J.A., L.E. Smollen and A.L.M. Dingee, Jr. 1985. *New Venture Creation: A Guide to Entrepreneurship*. 2nd ed. Homewood, IL: Irwin.

Troughton, M.J. 1990. "Decline to development: Towards a framework for sustainable rural development." In *Entrepreneurial and Sustainable Communities: Proceedings of a Conference Held in St. Andrews-by-the-Sea, N.B., June 1988*. Edited by Floyd W. Dykeman. Rural and Small Town Research and Studies Programme.

Tushman, M. and D. Nadler. 1986. "Organizing for innovation." *California Management Review* 28(3): 74–92.

Ulrich, D. and J.B. Barney. 1984. "Perspectives in organizations: Resource dependence, efficiency, and population." *Academy of Management Review* 9: 471–81.

UN World Commission on Environment & Development. 1987. *Our Common Future*. Oxford and New York: Oxford University Press.

Van de Ven, A.H. 1986. "Central problems in the management of innovation." *Management Science* 32: 590–607.

– 1993. "The development of an infrastructure for entrepreneurship." *Journal of Business Venturing* 8: 211–30.

– and D.L. Ferry. 1980. *Measuring and Assessing Organizations.* Chichester: John Wiley & Sons.

van Rees, Wim et al. 1991. *A Survey of Contemporary Community Development in Europe.* The Hague: Opbouwteksten.

Vazquez-Barquero, A. 1992a. Local development and flexible accumulation: Learning from history and policy. In *Endogenous Development and Southern Europe.* Edited by Gioacchino Garofoli. Aldershot: Avebury.

– 1992b. "Local development and the regional state in Spain." In *Endogenous Development and Southern Europe.* Edited by Gioacchino Garofoli. Aldershot: Avebury.

– 1992c. "Local development initiatives under incipient regional autonomy: The Spanish experience in the eighties." In *Endogenous Development and Southern Europe.* Edited by Gioacchino Garofoli. Aldershot: Avebury.

– 1992d. "Local development and flexibility in accumulation and regulation of capital." *Entrepreneurship & Regional Development* 4: 381–95.

Vecchio, R.P. 1991. *Organizational Behaviour.* Chicago: The Dryden Press.

Verba, S. and N. Nie. 1972. *Participation in America.* New York: Harper and Row.

Verge, H. 1992. "Draft Notes for Discussion – A Provincial Policy for Facilitating Community Development." N.p., n.d.

Vesper, K.H. 1990. *New Venture Strategies.* Englewood Cliffs, NJ: Prentice-Hall Inc.

Voluntary Planning. 1991. *Creating Our Own Future: A Nova Scotia Economic Development Strategy.* November 1991. Halifax, NS: Voluntary Planning.

Walton, R.E. 1992. "From control to commitment in the workplace." In *Managing People and Organizations.* Edited by John J. Gabarro. Boston: Harvard Business School Publications.

Wanous, J.P. and A. Zwany. 1977. "A cross-sectional test of need hierarchy theory." *Organizational Behavior and Human Performance* 18: 78–97.

Weaver, C. 1984. *Regional Development and the Local Community: Planning, Politics and Social Context.* Chichester: John Wiley and Sons.

Weber, M. 1947. *The Theory of Social and Economic Organization.* Translated by A.M. Henderson and Talcott Parsons. New York: The Free Press.

– 1969. *The Theory of Social and Economic Organisation.* Edited by Talcott Parsons. New York: The Free Press.

Webster, A. 1990. *Introduction to the Sociology of Development.* 2nd ed. Houndmills: MacMillan Education Ltd.

Webster's Encyclopedic Dictionary: Canadian Edition. 1988. New York: Lexicon Publications, Inc.

Weick, K.E. 1979. *The Social Psychology of Organizing.* 2nd ed. Reading, MA: Addison-Wesley.

Wellhofer, E.S. 1989. "Core and periphery: Territorial dimensions in politics." *Urban Studies* 26: 340–55.

Wellman, B. and S.D. Berkowitz. 1991. "Introduction: Studying social structures." In *Social Structures*. Edited by B. Wellman and S. D. Berkowitz. Cambridge: Cambridge University Press.

–, P.J. Carrington and A. Hall. 1991. "Networks as personal communities." In *Social Structures*. Edited by B. Wellman and S.D. Berkowitz. Cambridge: Cambridge University Press.

Wever, E. 1985. "New firm formation and regional policy in the Netherlands." *Tijdschrift voor Economishe en Sociale Geografie*. Vol. 67.

Wiewel, W., M. Teitz and R. Giloth. 1993. "The economic development of neighborhoods and localities." In *Theories of Local Economic Development: Perspectives From Across the Disciplines*. Edited by Richard D. Bingham and Robert Mier. Newbury Park: Sage Publications.

Woods, P. 1986. *Inside Schools: Ethnography in Educational Research*. London: Routledge & Kegan Paul.

Woodward, R. 1974. "The capital bias of DREE incentives." *Canadian Journal of Economics* 7: 161–73.

Yin, R.K. 1994. *Case Study Research: Design and Methods*. 2nd ed. London: Sage.

Zaleznik, A. 1992. "Managers and leaders: Are they different?" In *Managing People and Organizations*. Edited by John J. Gabarro. Boston: Harvard Business School Publications.

Zaltman, G., R. Duncan and J. Holbek. 1973. "Innovations and organizations." In *Endogenous Development and Southern Europe*. Edited by Gioacchino Garofoli. Aldershot: Avebury.

Index